Pascal Primer

by
David Fox
&
Mitchell Waite

Howard W. Sams & Co., Inc.
4300 WEST 62ND ST. INDIANAPOLIS, INDIANA 46268 USA

International Standard Book Number: 0-672-21793-7
Library of Congress Catalog Card Number: 85-53275

Printed in the United States of America.

Preface

If you are learning programming, Pascal is a powerful language you should know about. This book was designed for people who have dabbled in the popular language BASIC and wish to learn the exciting capabilities of Pascal. Today most experts agree that Pascal is on its way to becoming the standard high level language of the entire computer industry. In fact, the United States Department of Defense has adopted a language which is a Pascal descendant (Ada) as the official standard computer language for this country's future computer program development. The reason for Pascal's wildfire acceptance is simple: it is one of the least ambiguous programming languages you can find. Pascal contains the very best of several well known languages, like BASIC, FORTRAN, and COBOL. But the cornerstone of Pascal's permanent future probably lies in the fact that, unlike any of its predecessors, it is "self-documenting." It is made up of English-like sentences that are arranged so that you can practically read a finished program like a novel or a cookbook. Pascal is a *structured* language, which means it requires the programmer to define the nature, type, and range of items in an exacting and precise way. This is beneficial because you must think about the problem you wish to solve before sitting down to create a program. It also means that your program is more likely to run the first time and have fewer bugs to identify and unravel.

It is becoming obvious that Pascal is an ideal first language for programmers. This is especially true if one plans to make a professional career of programming. Students who learn Pascal as their first computer language have a relatively easy time learning other languages. Pascal programmers have a much better chance of developing good habits and learning the essential skills of problem definition and solution structuring. On the other hand, people who take on BASIC as their first language may have an easier time of it initially but not in the long run. BASIC programmers tend to develop bad programming habits which must be "unlearned" in order to master a structured language like Pascal.

Learning the structure may be difficult, but it's well worth the effort since the very nature of this structure is what makes Pascal unique and extremely versatile. You see, a Pascal program is developed in modules, which can be easily serviced, modified, and, most importantly, understood by other programmers at some future date. Thus, a Pascal program is more reliable and more responsive to changing needs than an equivalent BASIC or FORTRAN program. If speed is crucial to your application, then you will definitely want to examine Pascal. Because it is *compiled*, it is from 7 to 10 times faster than BASIC (on the same computer) and 50% faster than FORTRAN. In many cases Pascal will be only 1 to 5 times slower than pure machine code!

There are several variations of Pascal on the market today, and most are very close to the original standard. The version of Pascal described in this book is University of California at San Diego Pascal™* (or just UCSD). Although this book is written for *any version* of UCSD Pascal, special notes are given for Apple Computer®** owners.

If you are one of the many people who have a personal computer running with BASIC, then there is probably a version of Pascal available for it now (or one in the making). And because of its overwhelming power, installing Pascal in your computer will transform it into an entirely different machine with new features and capabilities. For example, the Pascal Editor used on the Apple for creating source programs can also double as a word processor for writing justified letters and manuscripts! Today you can purchase a Pascal language for under $200 on a floppy disk. A complete computer system for running Pascal, with disk drive, 64K bytes of RAM memory, and color graphics is under $2600. For those on a budget who may wish to just get their feet wet, many computer learning centers have popped up across the country. These offer low cost rental time on computers for under $3.00 per hour. Computer stores and demo rooms also can give you a demonstration of Pascal. Most universities and many colleges and high schools offer courses on Pascal.

Using examples that are easy, fun, and useful, this book is the first to offer the subject of Pascal in a down to earth fashion that can be learned quickly, even if you only know a little about programming. We have attempted to present Pascal in a uniquely friendly and humorous way, rather than the overly stuffy and heavily symbolic manner abounding in other Pascal texts. One of the authors of this book is the originator of the first public-access microcomputer learning center on the planet. The other is an author of the popular Sams Primer book line.

This book is committed to the mastery of Pascal without tears.

DAVID FOX
MITCHELL WAITE

---

* UCSD Pascal is a trademark of UC Regents, San Diego campus.
** Apple is a registered trademark of Apple Computer Inc.

*This book is dedicated to Jessica Fox
and all other children of the future.*

Acknowledgments

It started with a dream and ended in an envelope with first class postage. In between went hundreds of hours of research, programming and study, 1,000,000 key-strokes, several long debates, and many good laughs. The authors would like to express their thanks and deep appreciation to the people who participated in molding this book into its final form:

Annie Fox for her extreme patience, methodical proofing of the manuscript, and her personal contact with Uncle Pascal.

Randee Fox for her precious illustrations which adorn the book.

John Scribblemonger (alias Scot Kamins) for his unabashed, perceptive, and totally disarming (sensitive) review.

We would also like to thank Jim Merritt, Philip Lieberman, Corey Kosak and Chris Wells for reviewing the manuscript for technical accuracy, and Jim Ayers, Edwin and Eric Braun, and Ken Klein for their constructive feedback.

Our appreciation goes to MicroPro® for giving us a copy of their fabulous wordprocessing package, WordStar®, which accepted our 1,000,000 keystrokes without losing one, Comprint for their 80 column printer which generated the program listings, and Computerland of Marin for the loan of M&R Enterprise's Sup'R'Terminal 80 character board which allowed us to enter our programs in UPPER and lower case. We'd also like to thank Apple Computer Inc.® for their responsiveness and support.

Finally, we humbly thank Kenneth Bowles for bringing Pascal to the U.S.A., and Niklaus Wirth for creating it in the first place . . . the world of programming will never be the same!

DAVID FOX
MITCH WAITE

Contents

— CASE and BOOLEANs — The Metric Conversion Program Once Again
— Quiz

on the left is Uncle Blaise Pascal and his elves, on the right is the Sheriff of Buggingham and his little buggers, and above is the Priestess of Programming.

R.Fox

Introduction: An Overview of Pascal

Who This Book Is For

This book is written for people with some experience in the BASIC programming language—however, you *don't* need to be an expert in it. We have gone to some lengths to compare Pascal features with their equivalent features in BASIC when we thought it would be helpful. In case you have never learned BASIC (or any other computer language, for that matter) *don't worry*, this book will still prove invaluable in learning how to use the amazing power of Pascal.

What This Book Is Really About

Pascal is a remarkable computer language with the features and capabilities that you find only among the most exotic and expensive languages. Being so sophisticated, it may come as no surprise that there are several components to the actual Pascal system you use on a microcomputer. Although we will briefly explain these parts later in this chapter, we want to point out that this book is mainly about using Pascal to write powerful programs. This book is *not* about the Pascal compiler which converts your typed-in program to a set of efficient "boiled down" instructions that run fast and furiously on your microcomputer. This book is also *not* about the two tools that help you write your Pascal program: the Editor and the Filer. The Editor, for creating the typed-in program, and the Filer, a program that allows you to move

Pascal program files around. The Compiler, the Editor, and the Filer are not standardized, and may never be, so we'll leave their explanation to the manufacturers' manuals. What is standardized, however, are Pascal's statements, facilities, and keywords.

Predictably, the computer world being as it is, there currently exist disputes among manufacturers regarding the "standards" for Pascal statements. We looked around at several versions of Pascal available for microcomputers and found that the UCSD version is the most widely used. This is the version we used while writing this book.

UCSD Pascal was developed over an eight-year period (and a $2 million investment) at the University of California at San Diego. It is now marketed commercially by several software houses (see references at the end of this chapter for a partial listing of them). We used an Apple II computer to develop the UCSD Pascal programs in this book, but *regardless of the computer and the Pascal which you have access to,* you will find this book applicable to your version. Use this book as an adjunct to the reference manuals supplied with your Pascal. The idea is to refer to your manual when we point out something about Pascal that is nonstandard. We'll tell you when this comes up. This book can be used in a beginning Pascal class, along with a student workbook prepared by the instructor to fit the specific computer Pascal is run on. Or this book can be read through on quiet evenings, like a novel.

SKIP THIS CHAPTER

Beginning a book on a computer language as powerful as Pascal could be an awesome experience. Since a primary purpose of Pascal is for teaching computer science, you would think it would be complicated, right? Well, we are about to shatter that expectation. We are sorry to disappoint you, but this book is not intimidating, frightening, or even mildly overwhelming. There are no strange and confusing roadblocks, boring technicalities, or pedantic passages. **In fact, the real good news is that you can skip this entire** chapter and begin your reading with Chapter 2! That's because this chapter is simply a gentle introduction to Pascal . . . what it is, where it came from, why it's so special, how it's internally organized, and how it's used by a programmer. The rest of this chapter gives a brief history of Pascal's evolution and ends with a biography of Blaise Pascal, the man for whom this language was named. If you're the kind of person who hates to read Prefaces or Tables of Contents to discover how a book is organized, we have more good news. The next section explains the book's structure and how to best use it to learn Pascal. It would probably be a good idea to read it; then you may skip to Chapter 2 if you like.

HOW THIS BOOK IS ORGANIZED

This book is organized into 10 chapters. Each one, except the first, has a group of true/false and multiple-choice questions which allow you to test your understanding of the major concepts. The answers to the questions are given in Appendix H. Unlike most books on Pascal, this one doesn't try to stuff everything there is to know about Pascal between its covers. Rather this book explains the most often used and easy to understand features of the language.

Chapter 1 is an overview of Pascal and will bring you up to date on what it is, what makes it so popular and how its various components work together. We compare Pascal to BASIC, tell you the difference between a compiler and an interpreter, and what "P-code" is all about.

The chapter ends with a history that traces the path from Pascal's birth to its commercial acceptance today on microcomputers. And the grande finale is a biography of old Blaise Pascal himself.

Chapter 2 explains a Pascal program's structure, the **WRITE** and **WRITELN** statements, and the **GOTOXY** cursor control statement. You write your first program here.

Chapter 3 is about Pascal variables and inputting information with **READ** and **READLN**. You learn about normal variables, like those in BASIC (**INTEGER, STRING, CHAR,** and **REAL**) and some special ones (**LONG INTEGER** and **BOOLEAN**).

Chapter 4 introduces one of Pascal's most heralded and powerful features, **PROCEDURE**s, and shows how they make life really easy for the programmer.

Chapters 5 and 6 present our first excursions into program control. You learn about Pascal's BASIC-like decision making statements: **FOR** loops, **IF-THEN** and **IF-THEN-ELSE**. Chapter 5 presents a useful Loan Payment program and formatted output control. Chapter 6 presents a Metric Conversion program to illustrate control and the use of Boolean true/false type variables.

Chapter 7 expands upon the previous chapter, showing off some of Pascal's decision making statements, not available in most BASICs: **WHILE, REPEAT-UNTIL** and **CASE**. Our Metric Conversion program is enhanced to make use of these features.

Chapter 8 takes us further into the details of procedures, such as parameter passing. It also explores "numeric functions," such as **ABS, TRUNC, SIN, COS, LOG,** etc.

Chapter 9 is about **STRING**s, **STRING** functions, and **LONG INTEGER**s. It covers the way UCSD Pascal handles **STRING**s with its powerful built-in string manipulation tools and shows how to use **STRING**s and **LONG INTEGER**s together to make the Loan Payment program "bullet proof."

Chapter 10 presents Pascal arrays and the subtle concept of sets. Variable "types" are also presented and you get a taste of how to create custom variables, not found in any other language.

Also, included in the Appendices is additional information about Pascal: advantages and disadvantages of Pascal; other components of a Pascal system; the secrets of interfacing assembly language routines to Pascal (which you definitely don't have to know about to use Pascal); answers to the quizzes; and other useful tidbits.

WHAT IS NOT INCLUDED

There are a number of Pascal features we chose to exclude from this book. Information about them is available in advanced Pascal books. This is a *beginning* book, and we want to thoroughly cover introductory concepts and not try to overwhelm you with *all* of Pascal's wonderful features. Not included are:

1. Use of the **GOTO** statement.
2. **RECORD TYPES** and the **WITH** statement.
3. **FILE TYPES (CLOSE, EOF, RESET, REWRITE, GET, PUT, SEEK)**
4. **PACKED ARRAY**s **(SCAN, MOVELEFT, MOVERIGHT, FILLCHAR)**
5. **POINTER TYPES (NEW, DISPOSE)**
6. Use of recursion.
7. **SEGMENT PROCEDURES**
8. **EOLN**
9. **BLOCKREAD, BLOCKWRITE**
10. Graphics

Begin Your Journey. Now that you know how we shaped the book, you can start your journey. We make one prediction (or Uncle Pascal makes it): After you learn to use Pascal, your relationship to computers and how you create programs will totally change. We invite you to take the plunge.

WHAT IS PASCAL?

Pascal is a programming language on its way to becoming *the* language of the future. Pascal was created mainly by one man, Niklaus Wirth, a professor in Zurich, Switzerland, as an answer to a growing crisis in the computer community—runaway software costs—and also as an ideal language for teaching students good programming skills. Pascal's magic is partly in its *unambiguous* nature . . . a program written in Pascal reads (almost) like an English language description of a problem's solution.

Pascal is a *structured* computer language, one which allows the instructions of the program to be grouped into orderly "sections" that are "self-explanatory." A structured language, as contrasted with an unstructured language, has a clear beginning, a clear ending, and a series of bite-sized modules that are easy to digest. There is no question as to which parts of the program do what. We can use a house as an analogy: a house built without a foundation or any plans (unstructured) is more likely to fall apart in the event of an earthquake than a house which was built "to code." Remodeling a house with a set of plans is much easier than if you have to guess how it was put together. For example, if you want to knock out a wall to expand your bedroom, it would be nice to know whether any electrical wires are in the way. Having plans to follow always makes things easier.

The *modularization* which a structured language allows lets you build definitions (called **PROCEDURE**s and **FUNCTION**s) which can then be used in other definitions. These "customized modules" can be used again and again in later programs. However, the most important aspect of a structured language, like Pascal, is that programs written in it can be so clear, concise, and self-documenting that even someone other than the original programmer can understand what the program is supposed to do! Contrast this to programming languages which *hinder* the creation of self-documenting code (e.g., most versions of BASIC). Trying to comprehend an unstructured program is often like going on a wild goose chase—one part of the program sends you to another part which sends you to another part which sends you . . . . And when you get to a part, there very often isn't any clue as to what is supposed to transpire there! Variable names in BASIC (see Chapter 3) are usually too short to convey any meaning, there aren't enough comments throughout the program, and the program *looks* like one huge undecipherable block with a bunch of line numbers of up to six digits on one side. *Weeks* or *months* may be spent before one can fully comprehend the program's purpose! In fact, some programs may never be decipherable. (However, writing a program in Pascal doesn't in any way guarantee that the program will be readable.)

THE CRISIS THAT GAVE BIRTH TO PASCAL

In the mid 1960's, the cost of computer programs became a huge problem for companies which did a lot of data processing. Not only were the costs to produce a program being misjudged, but the schedules created to predict when a program was to be finished were the objects of cynical jokes, such as "We are just about ready to produce the schedule for how long it will be before we can produce the schedule" or "We need it by yesterday." Program schedules were frequently a thorn in the side of company managers . . . it was difficult to get the programmer to make meaningful estimates as to how long a problem takes to program in a particular language, and how easily the language of choice can be used to solve the problem. Program schedule timing became less and less reliable. Corporations were at a critical junction. Such problems stemmed from:

- poor management of programming projects
- undisciplined program code
- inadequate documentation
- low programmer productivity

Pascal came as a well-timed solution to all these problems. The instructions which make up Pascal are "disciplined" which means that Pascal is a "block structured" language . . . it is organized into blocklike *modules* that make it easier to design and develop a program. Pascal forces the programmer to be concise and exact. The blocklike modules are read like the paragraphs of a book —*each should contain just enough information for one to understand its purpose.*

THE RAT'S NEST ANALOGY TO PASCAL

One way to quickly appreciate Pascal is through a simple analogy to electronic hardware. Previous to Pascal, programs looked like the "rat's nest" of wires that one found in early television sets and radios. These programs consisted of strange symbols and unintelligible codes that only an extremely patient soul could interpret. A Pascal program, however, is more like the present day television sets that are built with plug-in printed circuit boards. When something goes wrong, the bad board (the bad module) can be quickly isolated and replaced or modified to work correctly. Which would *you* rather fix? Because of its modu-

lar nature (and a few other nice features which we'll cover later on), Pascal is a highly transportable language. By transportable, we mean that (hopefully) any Pascal program can run on any computer. In theory, a Pascal program written for a giant IBM 370 computer will also run on an inexpensive Radio Shack TRS-80®*. This is not possible with a loosely defined language like BASIC (and unfortunately, it is not *always* possible in Pascal).

The modular nature of Pascal is either a blessing or a curse, depending on whom you ask. It is a blessing in that the program modules can be "revised" or "updated" with relative ease, and realistic estimates can be made for development time schedules. Reliability increases when Pascal is used (yes, a program has degrees of reliability)

—less "bugs" are likely to find their way into a Pascal program than into a BASIC program.

On the other hand, using Pascal's modules requires more attention on the part of the programmer—everything has to be specifically described, defined and listed in a predefined manner which means more typing, planning, and things to consider. But these things that don't get considered in unstructured languages are the same ones that cause all of the problems!

Look at the following program sections written in Pascal and BASIC. They both do the same thing. Without getting into what they do or how they work, we present them for comparison. Here is the Pascal example:

```
FOR TermNow := NumberOfTerms DOWNTO 1 DO
    Harmonic := Harmonic + 1/TermNow;
```

Here's the same thing in BASIC:

* TRS-80 is a registered trademark of Tandy Corporation.

```
120   FOR I = N TO 1 STEP − 1
125   LET H = H + 1/I
130   NEXT I
```

Note the use of longer and more descriptive variable names in the Pascal example as well as the use of UPPER and lower case, and the more sensible naming of keywords (**DOWNTO** instead of **STEP** −1). As you read on in this book, you'll discover more of the advantages of Pascal.

NOT A BLACK AND WHITE WORLD

We don't wish to give the impression that all versions of BASIC are poor and unstructured. But we aren't aware of any that have all of the features that Pascal has. Sure, many minicomputers (such as Hewlett-Packard's) have BASICs that have allowed formatting of program statements for years. On the microcomputer level, the CBASIC language, which runs under CP/M™* (a popular 8080 microcomputer operating system) *does* allow extremely readable programs. The lines can be indented and line numbers are *optional* rather than mandatory. And then there's Microsoft®** BASIC, which allows the use of multiple colon (:) characters to shape the indentation of a program line. But the ability to format the program statements is only the first step towards making a language into a structured language. The ability to create independent subprograms (Procedures and Functions), to protect the variables in these subprograms from the rest of the program or to make the variables accessible to certain parts of the program, and the ability to set up controlled communication between these subprograms are all features that most BASICs can't touch. (Not to

---

* CP/M is a registered trademark of Digital Research.
** Microsoft is a registered trademark of Microsoft.

mention being able to invent your very own variable types!) The main difference in all of this is that Pascal was created as a structured language, while in BASIC, structuring is *added on*.

Perhaps a word from Uncle Pascal (who is on a special retainer for the unique and pithy pronouncements he contributed to this book).

 Uncle Pascal says while some BASICs allow indented formatting and some BASICs allow structured program statements, all Pascals allow both, plus much, much more. *You can paint a shack to look like a gingerbread house, but if you bite into it, you won't get a mouthful of sweets!*

WHY IS PASCAL SPECIAL?

We have mentioned that Pascal is a well organized and easily read language whose modular nature makes its programs more reliable and easier to manage. But this is only part of the story.

Pascal's Magic Data Structures

This is something few BASIC programmers would recognize as important, at first. *User-defined data types* refer to the ability to create your own "customized variable types," in the terms of the actual problem you're trying to solve. In most BASICs, we are given 3 or 4 possible types, *and that's it*. We can let a variable be a real number, an integer number, or a string of letters*. Pascal has these same variable types in addition to allowing you the freedom to make up your own! An example: Suppose you wanted to represent the shapes SQUARE, ROUND, RECTANGULAR, OBLONG, ROD, and CONIC in your program. In BASIC you could either represent them with numbers, or in some BASICs as an array of strings. This means creating a program operation (like searching for a shape) in BASIC will involve some rather obtuse and indirect numeric statements. You wouldn't be able to look at the statement and know that A$(35) represents a ROD shape, for example. Pascal's magic allows you to create a *new* type of data (variables), called, for example, **Shape**, which can take on only the "shape values" given above. Your program statements can say things like "**IF Shape = ROD THEN RemoveFromInventory**" which clearly tells us what's going on. Contrast this with IF SHAPE$ = A$(35) THEN GOSUB 1000. Which is easier to read? Pascal allows any kind of variable you can dream up. The idea is to

bend the program to fit the problem the way you would describe it to a person, rather than restricting yourself to the narrow constructs of the language itself, as you are forced to do in BASIC.

More Than a Language

The UCSD version of Pascal is not just an isolated language; rather, it is a complete "operating system" with several individual programs. To get a better idea of what these system parts are, we will cover them now. If you're familiar with BASIC, which allows you to simply turn on the computer and start typing in your program statements, you may be in for a surprise with Pascal.

How It Works

Pascal is a *compiled* language*. A compiled language is one which first requires you to send your original "typed-in" program to the "compiler." The compiler is a very large program itself (don't fret, you never have to read it!) which converts your original Pascal statements to a "boiled-down" set of instructions for the particular computer you are using. This set of instructions is often called the "object code" for the original program. It's this object code which is executed when we "run" the program.

There are four steps in working with a compiled language like Pascal:

1. Write the original program (type it in)
2. Compile it
3. Fix the errors
4. Run it

If a computer language isn't a compiled language, it is probably an "interpretive language." Most BASICs are interpretive languages, and there are only three steps:

1. Write the program
2. Run it
3. Fix the errors

The step that's missing is the separate "boiling-down" step. Every time a program is run in an interpreter language, the actual keywords are scanned and analyzed, then each one triggers a built-in package of instructions that *does* what the keyword implies (e.g., PRINT, GOTO, INPUT, etc.). This constant scanning means that both the interpreter program and the original source statements must be carried along in memory at the same time. This takes up lots of memory space

---

* In some cases, "double-precision" real numbers.

* There are noncompiled and pseudo-compiled Pascals, but for now we'll keep it simple and ignore these.

compared to the compiler's boiled-down object code. Finally, the actual scanning and recognizing phase of the interpreter can slow the program's execution speed considerably. However, the interpreter approach is simpler for debugging and development of a program . . . and that's why many manufacturers use it.

Imagine our language type as a "door opener." There are two kinds of door openers: "interpreter openers" and "compiler openers." An interpreter opener has a rough job. He must carry a large bag of keys wherever he goes. Each time he comes to a locked door (a high level source statement) he must sift through the bag (of built-in instructions) to find the one key that unlocks the door. Traveling around in a house (the program) filled with locked doors means dragging along this cumbersome, unwieldy sack of keys (oh, my aching back!) and constantly digging and searching through it for the right key.

Now, a compiler door opener's job is a different story. He has every key he'll need for his trip through the house arranged on a convenient key ring *before* entering the front door. His plan for moving through the house has been plotted and perfected ahead of time. This means his journey through the house is a breeze . . . he simply takes the next key on the ring, inserts it in the lock, twists gently and the door swings open.

The compiler door opener doesn't have to sift through the bag (the analysis stage of the interpreter) at all. In fact, *there isn't even any bag!* Of course, there *are* drawbacks to the compiled door opener. The original arranging of keys on the ring is time consuming, both choosing the correct order as well as actually getting them on the ring (long fingernails and strong hands are needed). Unlike the interpretive opener which allows carrying around a complete bag of instructions, the compiler opener must install only the

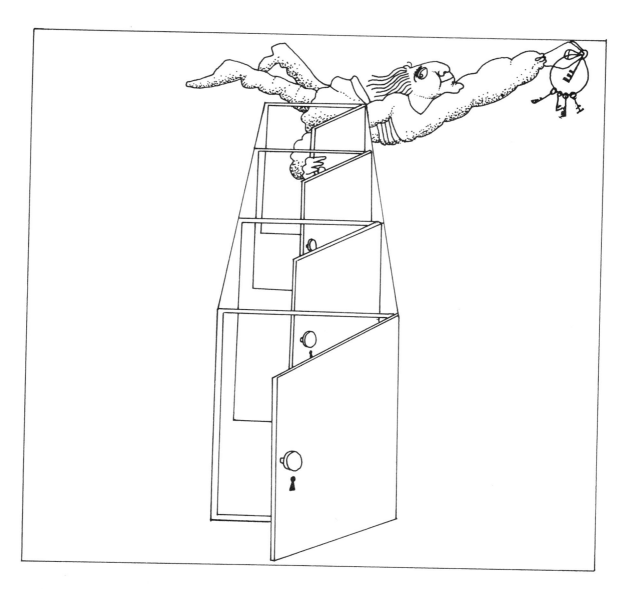

necessary keys on the ring before he can discover if the program will run. This extra step means it will take longer to get the bugs out of a compiled program (the opener would have to take apart the ring and put a new one together). But once done, the program runs much faster than the interpreter version.

Fig. 1-1A illustrates the BASIC interpretive process. Contrast this with the Pascal compiler process in Fig. 1-1B.

THE PARTS OF PASCAL

Although a Pascal Compiler is a program that can be purchased separately from several sources, to actually work with Pascal, you need at least two other programs (or facilities) on your computer: an Editor and a Filer (see Fig. 1-2). An Editor,

as you may already know from playing around with microcomputers, is used to type in your original program, (1a) in Fig. 1-3. The program is saved in the computer's memory (RAM) as it is typed in. Most Editors have facilities to make it very easy to change text, make corrections, move text around, etc. Once you have finished typing in a complete program, you use the Editor to permanently save it onto a diskette (1b). The next usual step is the actual compiling stage (2) which converts the source code statements (which are typed in and are now on the diskette) into an "object code" program (which is also stored on the diskette). You can now run (execute) this object code (3) or make a permanent copy of it on another diskette (4). When your program is finished running, the computer enters a special mode that provides you with a menu to choose which "system" program (i.e., Compiler, Editor,

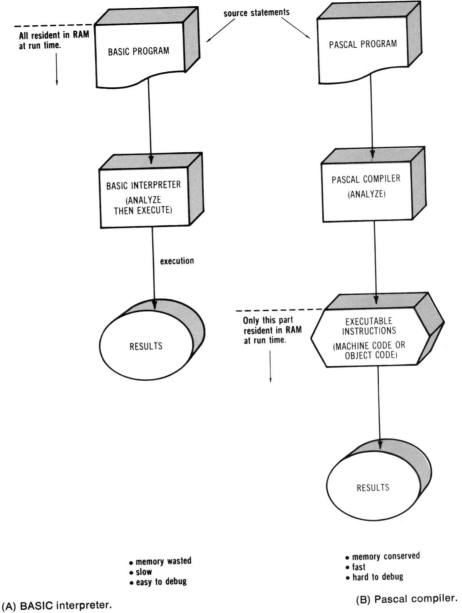

Fig. 1-1. BASIC interpreter versus Pascal compiler.

(A) BASIC interpreter.

(B) Pascal compiler.

etc.) you want to use next. To save the object code and the text file, we use a system program called the Filer (available in some popular versions of Pascal). Basically, the Filer is used to "keep track" of the files on the diskette—it's not really part of the edit-compile-run process. It can get the old text source file ready for editing, it can rename files, delete them, and so on. Now, understand that there are no Filer or Editor standards . . . so we can't really tell the whole story.

There are usually other parts, besides the Editor, Compiler, and Filer, that are used by a Pascal

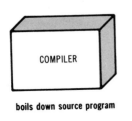

boils down source program

creates source program

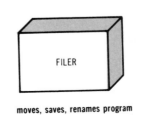

moves, saves, renames program

Fig. 1-2. Three main parts of a Pascal system.

1. Create 'source' file using Editor, save on disk as text work file. A 'work' file is a temporary development file.

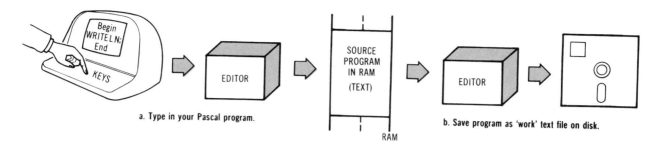

a. Type in your Pascal program.

b. Save program as 'work' text file on disk.

2. Compile source to 'boiled down' object code, save as 'code' work file on disk.

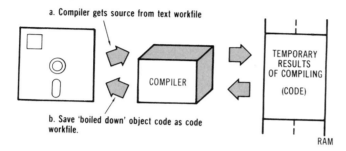

a. Compiler gets source from text workfile

b. Save 'boiled down' object code as code workfile.

3. Run (Execute) the object code program.

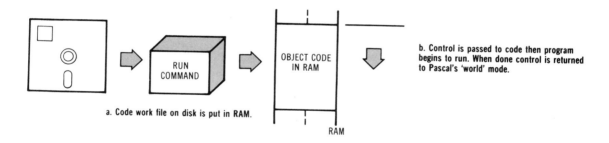

a. Code work file on disk is put in RAM.

b. Control is passed to code then program begins to run. When done control is returned to Pascal's 'world' mode.

4. Go back to step 1 and re-edit the source or save the text and code under desired file name using the Filer.

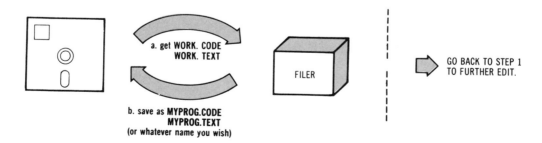

a. get WORK. CODE
WORK. TEXT

b. save as MYPROG.CODE
MYPROG.TEXT
(or whatever name you wish)

GO BACK TO STEP 1
TO FURTHER EDIT.

Fig. 1-3. Using the parts of UCSD Pascal.

programmer. However, these other parts can be ignored except by only the more sophisticated users. Appendix C contains a section on these other parts if you are curious.

This Book Is About Writing Pascal Programs

It would be tempting to describe the extremely useful features of the Pascal Compiler, Editor,

and Filer. However, since none of these programs are standardized, this wouldn't really be that helpful. We can't explain the many different Compilers, Editors, and Filers so we will only concentrate on how to write the actual Pascal program, and more specifically, using the UCSD version of Pascal, developed by Kenneth Bowles and UCSD students (and available on most microcomputers). Depending on the computer you are using with Pascal, there will be a Compiler, an Editor, and a Filer which you will have to learn about from your Pascal's operating manual before you can actually test (run) your program. Regardless of which computer you use, this book is geared to tell you primarily about how the standard Pascal language works, with sidelights when we encounter something special about Apple or UCSD Pascal. Again, this is not a book on using the entire Pascal system . . . consult your manual for such details*.

_____
*If you just buy the Compiler, you must already have an Editor and Filer.

A LITTLE HISTORY OF THE LANGUAGE

Pascal's history begins in the early 1960's with one man's dissatisfaction with the numerous computer languages in use at that time. In 1965, Professor Niklaus Wirth at the Swiss Technical Institute (ETH) in Zurich, Switzerland, presented a new language as an enhancement and replacement for ALGOL 60 (the most popular teaching-type programming language world-wide at that time, and rivaled only by FORTRAN and COBOL in the U.S.). Wirth based Pascal on ALGOL because of ALGOL's superior structuring and flexibility*. What he did was to drastically improve on its data structuring facilities. Wirth was painfully aware that the first computer language which a student is taught "profoundly influences his habits of

_____
*ALGOL was an elegant European language used for teaching and business programming throughout the world. However, because it was such an old language (developed in 1955) and for some strange political/economic reasons (IBM rejecting ALGOL, for example), ALGOL never caught on in the U.S.A. Instead, FORTRAN swept over ALGOL in the U.S.A., and then did the same in Europe.

thought and invention, and that the disorder governing these languages directly imposes itself onto the programming style of the students." In other words, one's first programming experience with any language colors your habits from then on. Wirth presented his ideas to the world but found little support from the technical community. Pressing on, Wirth presented a preliminary draft of Pascal in 1968 and in 1970. The first Pascal compiler (strangely enough) was written in FORTRAN on a CDC 6000 computer (a gigantic machine). This Pascal proved a failure and was dumped. Next, Wirth created a second Pascal compiler, this time written in Pascal*; it worked and Pascal was officially announced in 1971 by Wirth (see references 1 and 2). Of course, keep in mind there were no micros at this time, no Apples, no low cost computers, and thus Wirth's publications, appearing in the sophisticated *Acta Informatica* only became known in academic circles. Unfortunately, in the U.S., IBM had chosen FORTRAN over ALGOL and all this hoopla about Pascal was a lost cause stateside (except for an insightful semiconductor manufacturer called Texas Instruments, who began searching for a perfect language for writing control-type software).

Wirth continued to perfect the language and a more formal definition was published with C.A.R. Hoare in 1972 (3) which improved the syntax, and in 1973-1974 a revised report and user manual (4) was published. Since that time, the use of Pascal has rapidly grown in popularity and is now used in many high schools, trade schools, and in over 400 universities. Initially, Wirth handled distribution of the compiler from Zurich; but as the language expanded, several dialects began to appear in several universities.

The main push for Pascal here in the U.S. was due to Kenneth Bowles at the University of California at San Diego. Bowles recognized, quite wisely, that regardless of how wonderful Pascal (or any other language) was, the one factor needed to make Pascal popular *fast* was to make it very easy to adapt the compiler to different computers, particularly to different microcomputers. If Pascal only took a few man months to adapt to a Z80, a 6502, or an 8080, then lots of people with micros could begin using Pascal right away,

and this would quickly get Pascal's name floating around, and so on. Bowles and his students knew that writing a pure Pascal Compiler for each individual micro on the market would take years of effort. So they developed a simple solution. UCSD's Pascal would be a "pseudo-compiler" like Wirth's, instead of a true compiler. There would be a compiler that outputted "P-code" (pseudo-code, P-*machine*) instead of machine code (code/native code, N-code). This compiler would produce the same P-code regardless of the processor (machine) used (see Fig. 1-4). P-machine means the Compiler doesn't produce pure executable machine code for the microprocessor. It creates a "massaged" code called "P-code" which must be "interpreted" (analyzed). It never produces pure executable object code. By adding this interpreter we can easily modify a Pascal Compiler for any microprocessor by rewriting just this part. Thus, with a P-code Pascal you can write programs on an IBM 370 that run on a TRS-80.

P-code is a set of fast instructions that still can't be directly executed (that's why it's called pseudo-code, phoney code?). The P-code requires an interpreter (like most BASICs do) to work. The P-code interpreter analyzes each P-code instruction and triggers the right action for that instruction. But because the P-code is slightly boiled-down before hand, the P-code interpreter can work (scan) much *faster* than the BASIC interpreter. So we are still ahead of the game. Bowles realized that all micros could use the same Pascal Compiler and only a separate P-code interpreter would be required for each machine. It turns out that the interpreter is very easy to write (Bowles' goal) for any computer . . . the compiler does all the heavy work making the P-code. When you finally run the program the P-code is sent to the interpreter which has a simple job now. It's as if the P-code were a partially digested code, ready to give fast energy. Thus, we can ship P-code around, and it will work on any micro. P-code has its problems too, however. It is slower than pure object code and therefore more difficult to use in real time applications (i.e., where a computer controls an assembly line or a machine), and it doesn't support bit i/o manipulation (for control type uses). Still Bowles' UCSD Pascal was easy to adapt and a powerful Editor and Filer system had emerged, so that it wasn't long before UCSD Pascal was offered commercially. Many technical people saw the value of Pascal and realized its future and its place in their work. Pascal was seen as important as BASIC, and soon many companies were offering dialects of Pascal. (These

---

* If this seems like a "chicken before the egg" paradox, i.e., where does the first Pascal Compiler come from, the answer is that you can write a "minimal" Pascal Compiler *in Pascal*, then hand translate this to object code to create the first Pascal Compiler, then compile a bigger version of Pascal written in minimal Pascal, and so on. This is known as bootstrapping.

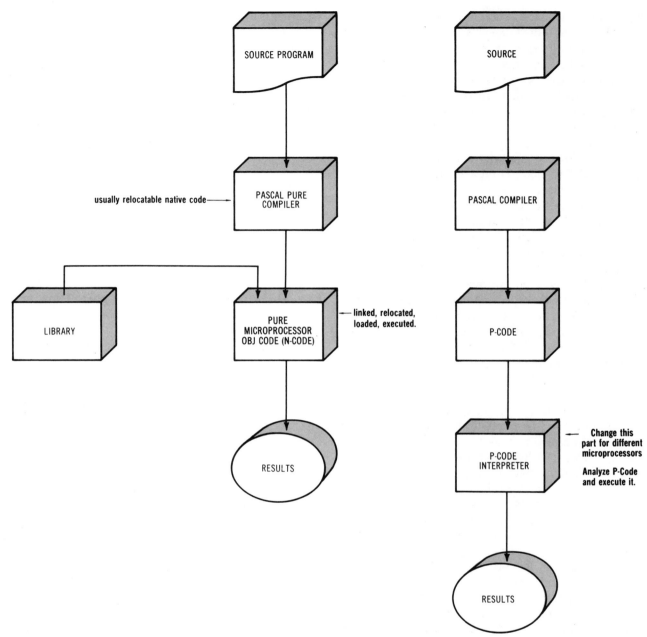

SOURCE PROGRAM

usually relocatable native code → PASCAL PURE COMPILER

LIBRARY

PURE MICROPROCESSOR OBJ CODE (N-CODE) ← linked, relocated, loaded, executed.

RESULTS

SOURCE

PASCAL COMPILER

P-CODE

P-CODE INTERPRETER ← Change this part for different microprocessors

Analyze P-Code and execute it.

RESULTS

(A) Pure compiler produces N-code (N=native).

(B) P-machine produces P-code.

Fig. 1-4. What is a P-machine?

same companies could then count on graduates from university computer science departments being able to understand their projects!)

Whereas Bowles' P-code Pascal made all microprocessors look and work more or less alike (ouch ... all that time investment in choosing the XYZ-80), versions of pure Pascal have appeared which are created for specific micros and are optimized for that processor.

Most "pure" compilers are faster running than P-code Pascals and feature extensions (like boolean bit manipulation of memory) and some omis-

sions (like lack of reals). Earlier we said there was a Pascal standard. There is, and many companies stick to it. However nothing can prevent a manufacturer or software house from calling something "Pascal," souping it up with nonstandard goodies, and advertising it as "enhanced" Pascal. The lesson here is *caveat emptor* (let the buyer beware) and understand what you give up when you choose super Pascal ZYX, for example, over a UCSD standard Pascal.

The bottom line on all these versions of Pascal is this: it doesn't really matter. Pascal will survive and catch on regardless of a specific version's mismatch to Wirth's Pascal. The looseness of the Wirth standard will lead to many dialects and extensions, just as BASIC has become popular in spite of the many versions*. One will always ask "which Pascal?" Each company will push their Pascal as the best. Programmers will undoubtedly be forced to shift gears as they approach each new Pascal dialect. Still, the situation has improved, and only better, safer, clearer programs can result from the popular use of Pascal.

A PRESENT DAY EXAMPLE: APPLE PASCAL

Apple Computer Corporation's Pascal is a version of UCSD Pascal (P-machine) which is, according to Apple's manual, "an extensively modified descendant of the P-2 pseudo machine from Zurich" (translate: it's UCSD's Pascal). To this, Apple Pascal has added its own extensions which contain libraries of special nonPascal functions such as graphics or machine i/o. In the Apple, you place the words "USES APPLEGRAPHICS;" at the beginning of your source program, and then you can use the exciting three-dimensional graphics keywords in your program. If you don't use the Apple extensions, the program should run on a TRS-80 (or any other machine) with UCSD Pascal. If you do use the extensions, only other Apples with UCSD Pascal can run the program.

The Amazing Blaise Pascal

Blaise Pascal was perhaps the first child computer-freak-home-hobbyist. He was born in France in 1623 and educated at home. When he was 12 years old he discovered the first proof to Euclid's Proposition 32, something few thinkers of today can handle. He was one of those kids that today, if given a computer and left alone, would soon be designing an improved model. At 16, Blaise presented his famous theory in projective geometry. One year later, he began developing a calculating machine for his father's tax business. Fascinated by the calculator's potential, he had a working model in two years. He went on to have over 50 such machines constructed. His calculator was the rotating drum type, which works something like an odometer of a car. His innovation was a ratchet linkage that transferred a carryover to the next drum.

When Pascal was 22, he was converted to "Jensinism," a religious order in conflict with the Roman Catholic Church at that time. The followers of Jen-

---

* Also ANSI (American National Standards Institute), IEEE (International Electronic and Electrical Engineers), and ISO (International Standards Organization) are preparing a joint final draft of the International Pascal Standard.

---

sinism claimed that the Church was wrong to mix logic and rules of reason with God's truths. For example, the Church would condemn certain concepts of science if they conflicted with the Bible or if they conflicted with the Church's power! Pascal agreed with Jensinism and said religion was a spiritual, mystical, personal experience and "reason" alone could not be our guide in the affairs of men—spiritual experience transcended reason.

At 23, Pascal got interested in vacuums, met Descartes, and published a famous treatise on vacuums*, and one on conic sections (three dimensional cones). By the time he was 28, he was once again involved in math research and at 31 had established the fundamental foundations of integral calculus and probability theory†.

His involvement in Jensinism increased, and during the same year, he had a religious/mystical experience, joined the Jesuits, and wrote a book called the *Provincial Letters*, which swayed public opinion to support the Jensinists. This book is considered to be the beginning of French classical literature.

At 35, he shocked the academic world when he challenged all mathematicians to a contest in math, then awarded himself the prize!

Pascal's health was always poor, and it was wondered if his intense studies were the cause of his ill health, or if his frailness led to his intense studies. As his health got worse, he became more mystical in his interests. In his later years, he became infamous for his magic squares—organizations of numbers arranged in rows and columns, which result in wonderfully interesting mathematical relationships. For example, when you add all the numbers in any row, the number in each corner square is produced. Pascal's special contribution was his mystic hexagram (see the end of this chapter). At 39, in the last months of his life, he created the plans for the first public transportation system—now the omnibus service in Paris.

Pascal has been called a mathematician, a physicist, and a religious thinker. Perhaps Wirth named his language after him because he identified with Pascal's individual/independent/eccentric/mystical nature (or perhaps he just liked Pascal!).

Today, many items of science are named after Pascal:

The **pascal** (Mechanics) is a unit of pressure (also called the **torr**).

Pascal's Law: (Fluid Mechanics) confined fluid transmits pressure uniformly in all directions.

Pascal's Theorem: (Math) inscribing a simple hexagon in a conic makes three pairs of opposite sides meet in collinear points.

Pascal's Triangle: (Math) [also **Pascal's Mystic Hexagram**] Also known as a binomial array; this is a

---

* Pascal's Law.
† A toothache is supposedly responsible for this discovery—to take his mind off the pain, he spent his time thinking about circles.

23

triangular array of binomial coefficients, bordered by 1's, where the sum of any two adjacent entries from a row equals the entry in the next row directly below.

REFERENCES

1. N. Wirth, *The Programming Language Pascal*, Acta Informatica, 1, 35-63, 1971.

2. N. Wirth, "The Design of a Pascal Compiler," SOFTWARE-Practice and Experience, 1, 309-333, 1971.

3. C.A.R. Hoare and N. Wirth, "An Axiomatic Definition of the Programming Language Pascal," Acta Informatica, 2, 335-355, 1973.

4. K. Jensen and N. Wirth, *Pascal User Manual and Report*, 2nd Edition, Springer-Verlag, 1978 (c)1974.

5. R. Bates and D. Johnson, "Putting Pascal to Work," Electronics, June 7, 1979, 111-121.

6. K. Doty, "A Top Down Evaluation of Pascal," Computer Design, May 1980, 167-177.

7. J. Hemenway and E. Teja, "Pascal Update," EDN, April 1980, 101-105.

8. Dr. L. Leventhal, "Using Pascal in Industrial Environments," Digital Design, May 1980, 26-30.

9. K. Bowles, *Beginner's Guide for the UCSD Pascal System*, Byte/McGraw-Hill(c) K. Bowles, 1980.

10. J. Raskin and B. Howard, Editors, *APPLE PASCAL REFERENCE MANUAL*, (c) 1979 Apple Computer Inc., 312 pgs, product #A210019.

UCSD PASCAL DISTRIBUTORS

Apple Computer, Inc., 10260 Bandley Drive, Cupertino, CA 95014 (408) 996-1010

SofTech Microsystems Inc., 9494 Black Mountain Road, San Diego, CA 92126 (714) 578-6105

FMG Corporation, 5280 Trail Lake Drive, Suite 13, Ft. Worth, Texas 76133 (817) 294-2510. Versions for TRS-80 Models I, II, and III.

North Star Computers, Inc., 1440 Fourth Street, Berkeley, CA 94710 (415) 527-6950

PCD Systems, Inc., P.O. Box 143, Penn Yan, New York 14527 (315) 536-3734. Versions for TRS-80 Model II and computers with CP/M.

chapter 2

Pascal: Beginning Concepts

Pascal has a number of commands and keywords which are used to get the computer to do something. In some cases, these Pascal commands are exactly the same as the equivalent commands in the popular computer language, BASIC (which certainly makes life easier if you already know BASIC). But in many cases, Pascal has its own specific rules of syntax to follow, many of which are very different than the syntax rules of BASIC.

This means that learning Pascal once you know BASIC is easier. It is much the same as learning to speak Cockney English after you've been brought up in America. The general language is still English (computerese), the meaning is similar, but the accent, the grammar, the slang, and the social rules are different. At first, you may find yourself mentally translating some of the slang to its American equivalent, but later it will become natural to *think* in Cockney. Also, when first learning a language, it is much easier to read or listen to the language than it is to actually write it or speak it. (Isn't it always easier to *translate* something than to *generate* it from scratch?) This is partly because you don't have to remember all of the new rules of grammar (syntax) and partly because you don't have to dredge up the new words from your memory; you just have to recall their meaning.

In this chapter we are going to take a superfast walk through the fundamental "bottom line stuff" of Pascal like the mandatory rules of program structure (**PROGRAM, BEGIN,** and **END**), the **WRITE** and **WRITELN** statements for outputting information, and the **GOTOXY** statement for "cursor control." After learning these rules, you will be prepared to delve much deeper into Pascal in the following chapters.

If you have a computer running Pascal, then this chapter would be a good place to also learn how to edit, compile, and execute your programs. Since these steps are somewhat different in each version of Pascal, we will not be going into them in this book. Please check the documentation that came with your version of Pascal—it should give a good description of editing, compilation, and execution.

The key to speaking any language fluently is *practice.* We know, you've been hearing *that* since your mother tried to get you to practice the piano or the piccolo. Unfortunately, for those of us who aren't gifted with a photographic memory and can't stand the confusion that accompanies learning something new, your mother was right. Therefore, as you read through this book, take the time to do the quizzes and suggested exercises. These have been specially prepared so you can check your understanding as you read along.

PROGRAM STRUCTURE: PROGRAM, BEGIN, END

Before we jump into the action commands of Pascal, we need to learn about the "structure" of a Pascal program. One of the greatest differences between Pascal and BASIC* is that if you don't follow the structural conventions when writing a Pascal program, it won't run (it won't even compile). BASIC, on the other hand, doesn't really have any structural conventions unless you want to include the use of line numbers or the fact that some versions of BASIC require an END statement at the end of a program.

---

* Note: we will make many comparisons between BASIC and Pascal. For a good BASIC book, see BASIC Programming Primer, Howard Sams.

There are essentially two different types of words used in a Pascal program:

Reserved words (*keywords*) — these are the words which have some special significance or meaning in Pascal. Their meaning was defined when Pascal was developed. We will indicate reserved words by writing them in **BOLDFACE UPPER CASE** letters throughout the text of this book.

Identifiers — these are the names which you as the programmer make up to "identify" the "boxes" in the computer's memory (variables) and the various sections of a Pascal program. It's important to use names which help you to remember what the purpose of the identifier is. Identifiers will be written in **Boldface Upper** and **Lower Case** letters throughout the text of this book.

When reserved words or identifiers appear in the program listings in this book, we won't use boldface, but we will still use the convention of printing reserved words in UPPER CASE and identifiers in Upper and Lower Case.

Starting the PROGRAM

The following rules are true for *all* Pascal programs:

Always start a Pascal program with:

> PROGRAM Name;
> *Note . . . you must include the semicolon.*

This statement "declares" the name of your program. The word **PROGRAM** is a reserved word (written in **BOLD FACE UPPER CASE**) and the word **Name** is an identifier (**Bold Face Upper and Lower Case**). Using a name allows you to identify the purpose of the program. Just put the name you want to use where the word **Name** is. Notice the semicolon (;) at the end of the line. These semicolons belong at the end of each statement.

Pascal Names

Here are the few simple rules to follow when naming things in Pascal:

1. Names must start with a letter of the alphabet.
2. The characters that follow the first character must be either letters or numbers.
3. Names can be as long as you like, but only the first eight letters are guaranteed to be recognized by the computer. (Some Pascal versions recognize more than the first 8 letters.)
4. Names may *contain* Pascal "reserved words" but can't *be* reserved words.

Some sample names are:

Payroll	Ramrod2	
Alphabet2Game	NewProgram	*contains reserved word* **PROGRAM**

Some versions of Pascal don't allow lower case letters in identifiers (names), while other versions allow other characters (such as _ @ or #) to be a part of legal names. Here are some *illegal* examples:

3Step	*first character is not a letter*
Re-Do	*illegal character (-)*
Launch Ship	*illegal character (space)*

If your version of Pascal *does* allow lower case letters in identifiers, they may be interpreted as UPPER CASE letters by the compiler, thus

DAYOFWEEK	and	DayOfWeek

would be interpreted as the *same name*. Check your Pascal manual.

What's in a Name?

Why even bother using names? Over and over again, we will be stressing how important it is to use names that mean something to you while writing in Pascal. Imagine what the world would be like if everything had names like XZ or A1! Boring, confusing, monotonous!? Pascal makes it very easy to use interesting, exciting, and meaningful names so why bother using a name like EX1A?

BEGINnings

The next mandatory thing you need in all your Pascal programs is the reserved word:

> BEGIN

This means that the main part of the program is about to follow. **BEGIN** does not have a semicolon after it (so much for rules*).

After **BEGIN** comes the real meat of all Pascal programs (or texturized soy protein if you're a vegetarian). We'll spend most of the rest of the book examining the marvelous things that occur after the word **BEGIN**.

---

* Actually, the rules aren't being broken as we'll see in Chapter 5 in the More On Semicolons sidebar—**BEGIN** *could* "legally" have a semicolon after it.

ENDings

And at the very end of the program comes another reserved word:

> ## END.

with a *mandatory* period (.) added for extra finality.

 Uncle Pascal says: If you don't follow my rules, like leaving out the period after the **END**, no matter how perfect your program . . . it isn't going to run. *He who pays not his electric bill eats cold spaghetti in the dark!*

Okay . . . review time. Here's how the structure of every Pascal program on earth must be:

```
PROGRAM Name;
BEGIN
    :
    :
  { body of program }
    :
    :
END.
```

Now that we have the fundamental structure down, let's put some stuffing into it.

WRITELN AND WRITE

The first thing you probably were taught when you were learning BASIC was the keyword or reserved word "PRINT." Let's learn Pascal in the same order. The Pascal equivalent is*:

> ## WRITELN

WRITELN (pronounced WRITE LINE) is used to transfer text or numbers from the program to the screen (or output device, i.e., printer). To make the computer say "Hello there, my name is Florence" you would enter into your program:

> WRITELN('Hello there, my name is Florence');

Note the parentheses "()". Whenever you want to write something on the screen, place it within the

---

* WRITELN is not really a reserved word, it is a *predeclared identifier*. Many of the Pascal commands are actually *built-in* routines which have been assigned a name (identifier). The programmer can steal these names for original routines if he/she wishes. However, the built-in routine will no longer be accessible. We will refer to these predeclared identifiers as if they were reserved keywords to keep things simple. See Chapter 8 for more on this.

parentheses after a **WRITELN**. Next notice the apostrophes, or single quotes (') inside the parentheses. These are equivalent to the double quotes (") used in BASIC. Use them to surround a *string of characters* (called a *string*) that you want the computer to print out. Finally, notice the required semicolon found at the end of the line which we're sure you won't forget.

The **LN** part of **WRITELN** tells Pascal that the entire message between the apostrophes should be output on the same line, and the cursor* should end up on the extreme left of the *next* line when done. For example:

> WRITELN('This is a Pascal message');

will output this when executed:

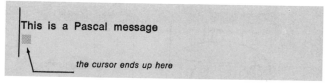

the cursor ends up here

What **WRITELN** does (after it prints out what's within the apostrophes) is called an automatic carriage return/linefeed.

The next keyword is:

> ## WRITE

which is equivalent to using a BASIC PRINT statement with a semicolon at the end. The semicolon in BASIC suppresses the automatic carriage return/linefeed at the end of the line. This means that the next line of text will be connected to the end of the last line of output. In Pascal, the **WRITE** command has the same effect—it prints out text and lets the cursor sit at the end of the line.

For example, the following lines:

> WRITE('Hello there,');
> WRITELN(' you sure look swell today!');
> *notice leading blank*

will be printed as:

> Hello there, you sure look swell today!

We put the **WRITELN** last so the next output string starts at the beginning of the next output line. The leading space, **WRITELN** ('_you...'), keeps the comma from the line before separated from 'you'. You can remember the difference be-

---

* The cursor is the little white box (or underline) which seems to write the text on the screen. If the screen were a blackboard, the cursor would be the point of the chalk.

tween **WRITELN** and **WRITE** by thinking of **WRITELN** as "*Write* a complete *line* of text" and **WRITE** as "*Write* some text and then wait . . .".

Our First Program

Now let's put together all of the above elements and create our first simple Pascal program called **WriteABit**, as shown in Listing 2-1.

Hopefully you recognized the keywords **PROGRAM, BEGIN, END, WRITELN,** and **WRITE** and noticed an absence of line numbers.* While using Pascal, you'll never have to worry about how to squeeze 3 lines of statements between lines 120 and 121 (as you might in BASIC) ! Normally you go into the Pascal "Editor" and just *insert* the new line.

Take a look at the way the program is indented between the keywords **BEGIN** and **END**. Indenting is used to make the program more "readable"

and is an essential part of good programming style. The program would run just as well without indentation, but readability would suffer, especially later on when your programs become much more complex. You'll learn as we go on how indenting lets us modularize a program into pieces we can understand.

Here's what appears on the screen when we compile and run our first program, **WriteABit**:

> Learning Pascal is not really difficult.
>
> What's really difficult is "UNLEARNING" all of the habits you acquired while using BASIC!

Make sense?

Spaced Out Pascal

Very often, indentation in BASIC isn't practical (even if it's possible to do in your particular flavor of BASIC) because the extra indented spaces take

---

* Line numbers are mandatory in most versions of BASIC where they are necessary to keep the statements in order.

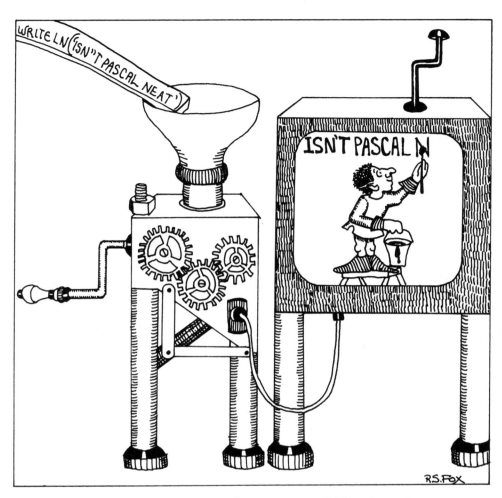

up precious memory—when every byte of memory is needed, why "waste" it on the program's appearance! (This is also the reason why most BASIC programs don't have enough REMarks or comments.) But since Pascal is a compiled language, all spaces (other than those within apostrophes) are compressed out of the final compiled code. Also, many Pascal editors (i.e., UCSD) are designed to facilitate the use of indenting—a special code is used at the beginning of each indented line to tell the editor how many spaces to indent (rather than actually saving the spaces in the text file). So when you press RETURN at the end of an indented line, the editor remembers how many spaces you were indenting and automatically indents the next line.

Here are some facts to remember about outputting in Pascal. Refer to **WriteABit** for some examples:

1. Notice that you can use **WRITELN**; by itself to create blank lines (equivalent to a PRINT in BASIC with nothing following it).
2. If you want to use an apostrophe (single quote) in a word, just put two of them together as we did in the word What's (i.e., What' 's). Since quotation marks (") have no special meaning in Pascal (as they do in

BASIC), there is no reason why they can't be included as part of a string.
3. Note our use of **WRITE**—although we could have placed all the information within the **WRITE** (in our sample program) and the following **WRITELN** on one line, we wanted to include a **WRITE** command just for example.
4. While programming in BASIC, it's all right to let a string (a series of characters surrounded by quotes—"This is a string") extend beyond one line. This is a no-no in Pascal.

Let's elaborate on this last tidbit. For example, the BASIC statement:

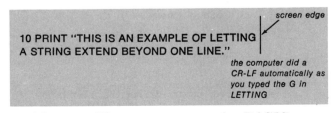

10 PRINT "THIS IS AN EXAMPLE OF LETTING A STRING EXTEND BEYOND ONE LINE."

screen edge

the computer did a CR-LF automatically as you typed the G in LETTING

would run without any errors in BASIC even

Listing 2-1.

```
PROGRAM WriteABit;

BEGIN
  WRITELN;
  WRITELN('Learning Pascal is not really difficult.' );
  WRITELN;
  WRITELN('What''s really difficult is "UNLEARNING"' );
  WRITE('all of the habits you' );
  WRITELN(' acquired while' );
  WRITELN('using BASIC!' );
END.
```

though running this on a computer with a 40 character screen width would yield:

```
THIS IS AN EXAMPLE OF LETTING A STRING E
XTEND BEYOND ONE LINE.
```

It doesn't look very good at all because the word "EXTEND" is broken in two. In BASIC, the computer will do an automatic carriage return/line feed when it reaches the end of the screen, so we don't have to worry about the computer giving us an error.

In Pascal, *however,* a string is considered to be a *single element* and it *can't* be broken up into separate lines. Doing the following in Pascal would yield a compiler error*:

```
WRITELN('This is an example of letting a
          string extend beyond one line.');
```

Therefore, in Pascal you must break such a long string into two statements:

```
WRITELN('This is not an example of letting a');
WRITELN('string extend beyond one line.');
```

It is acceptable in Pascal to place more than one "element" (i.e., multiple strings inside apostrophes) between the pair of parentheses of a **WRITELN** statement; just make sure you separate the elements with commas. If you do this, then it's fine to break up the statement into two or more lines. All of the following are legal in Pascal:

```
WRITELN('This is an example',' of separate',' elements.');
WRITELN('This is an example',
        ' of separate',' elements.');
WRITELN('This is an example',
        ' of separate',
        ' elements.');
```

_____
* A compiler error occurs during the compilation of a program when the compiler finds that a Pascal rule (syntax, misspelling of a keyword, etc.) was broken.

The output for all of the above constructs will be the same:

This is an example of separate elements.

 Uncle Pascal says: Don't let a **WRITELN** or **WRITE** string occupy two lines unless commas are used. *If you cut your eye glasses in half, they won't stay on your nose.*

Now it's your turn. Create your own program using just what you have learned so far—experiment with **WRITELN** and **WRITE**.

CURSOR CONTROL: GOTOXY

Many versions of Pascal (especially those designed for microcomputers) have a means to allow you to place the cursor at any location on the screen. This cursor placing statement is called **GOTOXY** and it is used in the form:

```
GOTOXY(Xcoord, Ycoord);
```

where **Xcoord** and **Ycoord** are the X (horizontal) and Y (vertical) coordinates which you want the cursor to move to. The range for **Xcoord** is from 0 (left side of screen) to the maximum screen width (39 for a 40 character screen, 79 for a 80 character screen). The range for **Ycoord** is from 0 (top of screen) to 23 (if your screen will display 24 lines of text). The following two statements, when used in a Pascal program, will place the cursor at the top left corner of the screen and write a message:

```
GOTOXY(0,0);
WRITELN('Top left of screen');
```

Here is how this will look on your screen:

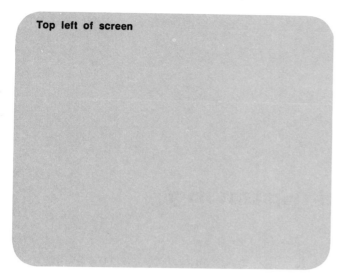

Top left of screen

The program shown in Listing 2-2 will place a number in each of the four corners of a 40 character by 24 line screen and one more number in the center.

This is how **CursorDemo** will look on your screen:

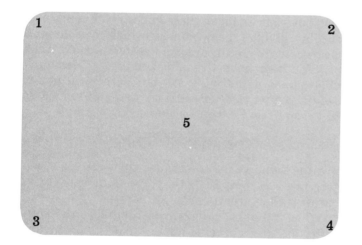

Use **GOTOXY** to make the output of your programs look pretty!

Take the following quiz before you move on to bigger and better things in Pascal in the next chapter.

QUIZ

1. Which of the following are *not* valid program names?
   A. Prog1   D. Program
   B. Check Writer   E. TOBEGIN
   C. WRITER   F. 2Step

True or False

2. The semicolon at the end of a line is used for appearances only.

3. Elements in a WRITELN statement are separated with semicolons.

4. It's a waste of memory space to indent in Pascal.

5. There are 8 errors in this program. What are they?

```
PROGRAM Starting Out
BEGIN
   WRITELN("This is an example of what not')
   WRITLEN('to do in Pascal because if you');
   WRITELN('do, your program won't compile);
END
```

6. What would the statement look like which will place the cursor on line 7 at the 12th position on your screen?

Listing 2-2.

```
PROGRAM CursorDemo;

BEGIN
   GOTOXY(0,0);
   WRITE(' 1' );
   GOTOXY(39,0);
   WRITE(' 2' );
   GOTOXY(0,23);
   WRITE(' 3' );
   GOTOXY(39,23);
   WRITE(' 4' );
   GOTOXY(19,11);
   WRITE(' 5' );
END.   (* CursorDemo *)
```

chapter **3**

Variables and Inputting

Now that you know how Pascal likes to be set up (*PROGRAM, BEGIN, END.*) and how to output to the screen (*WRITE, WRITELN,* and *GOTOXY*), you are ready for some of Pascal's deeper meanings. In this chapter, we will explore how variables are used in your programs, how strings are seen by Pascal, and finally, how we go about inputting information into the program from the human user. This may seem like a lot of material to present at once, but don't worry, we'll make it easy for you!

VARIABLES

In BASIC, you were probably taught that variables were these little memory boxes where you could store either numbers or letters. The numeric variables had funny names like W1 or TT and the letter-type variables ended with a dollar sign ($), like BU$ or Z$, so you could tell them apart from numeric type variables. In most BASICs the computer would only look at the first two characters of the variable's name (i.e., the BASIC would think that ALPHABITS and ALPO were the same variable though one is a breakfast cereal and the other you would only feed to your dog!). If you made the names any longer, you were "wasting memory" again . . . a big no-no in BASIC. And heaven help you if you used a name with a BASIC "reserved word" (a word which is reserved for the language's commands and keywords) hidden in it like TOY$ (contains TO) or MONTH (contains ON—both are reserved words in BASIC). So, invariably when you returned to a BASIC program that you hadn't looked at for a while, all those two letter variable names which had so much meaning to you at one time were now as clear as some form of ancient hieroglyphics. And how many times have you revised a program by

adding new program statements (including some new variables) only to find that a strange new bug popped up in a remote part of the program? In many cases, you probably discovered that you had unwittingly reused an important variable name and thus reassigned its contents when you shouldn't have.

In Pascal, variables are still little boxes in memory, but you can make these boxes *much* more useful by giving them names which are longer, clearer, more significant, and easier to keep track of. You also have the added ability to let variable names be as wide as your screen, although *only the first eight characters are guaranteed to be recognized by the computer*. For example:

> **BreakWater** and **BreakWatch**

are the same variable because the first eight letters are the same in both, so we still need to be careful when creating Pascal names.

When a Pascal program is compiled, the computer assigns a specific number code to each variable in the program which it uses to keep track of them. This way the longer names don't take up any extra memory than shorter ones! This means that instead of using **T** for total, or **TTAL**, or even **TOTAL**, you can use a name which is as clear as **TotalAmountPaid** (even though just the first eight letters, **TotalAmo**, are significant). Isn't that convenient! Variable names, just like program names, are *identifiers* so the rules for variable names are exactly the same as the rules for program names which we learned in Chapter 2. Here they are for you again:

1. Names must start with a letter of the alphabet.
2. The characters that follow the first character can be either letters or numbers.

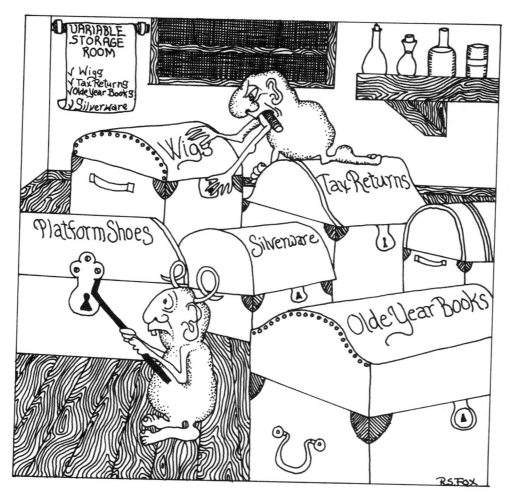

3. Names can be as long as you like, but only the first eight letters are recognized by the computer. (Some Pascal versions recognize more than the first eight letters.)

4. Names can *contain* Pascal "reserved words" but can't *be* reserved words.

Again, the letters in an identifier may be UPPER and lower case in many versions of Pascal.

For an example of Rule 4, look at the name of the previous program, *WriteABit*. There won't be any problems because the word, **WRITE** is contained *within* the name.

 Uncle Pascal says: Use fully descriptive variable names. If you are talking about Annual Interest Rates, use **AnnualInterestRate** because calling it **INTR** is likely to confuse you. *He who calls a bee a butterfly is sure to get stung!*

VARIABLE TYPES

So far we have talked about variable names, but said little about *what* the variables represented. Is

AnnualInterestRate a number? If so, what kind of a number? How big is the number? Is it a decimal number?

A variable doesn't have to contain a number. It can hold a letter, a punctuation symbol, a string of letters, a word, or an entire sentence. So a variable not only has a name, it also has a *type* which tells the computer what kind of information the variable will hold (i.e., what will be inside the boxes in memory). In dealing with variables in Pascal, just as in dealing with blood types (A, B positive, etc.), if you try mixing types, you can get into *big* trouble.

There are six types of defined variables in UCSD Pascal: **INTEGER**s, **LONG INTEGER**s, **REAL**s, **STRING**s, **CHAR**acters, and **BOOLEAN**s. Two of these, **LONG INTEGER**s and **STRING**s are not included as predefined variable types in "standard Pascal" although most of the Pascals for microcomputers do have them. For now, let's only look at **INTEGER**s and **STRING**s (we'll look at the other types later on in this chapter). First some facts about **STRING** and **INTEGER** variables.

STRING Variables

STRING variables can contain any character or characters that you can type from the keyboard or display on the screen: number, letter, punctuation . . . anything. As in **WRITELN**, if you want to use apostrophes, just type two in a row. Unless you say otherwise, **STRING**s can contain up to 80 characters (we'll talk about how to change their size in Chapter 9). Here are a few strings:

'I am a string.' 'SO AM I!'

'** I **' '$12.99'

INTEGER Variables

INTEGER variables can be any positive or negative integer number (no decimal point). In Apple Pascal, an **INTEGER** can have a value from −32768 to +32767 (some versions of Pascal have wider ranges). Here are a few legal integers:

128   −3200   8080   0

You can quickly discover what the allowable **INTEGER** range is for your version of Pascal by placing the following statement into a program:

```
WRITELN(MAXINT,'        ', − MAXINT);
```

On the Apple, the output will be:

```
32767        −32768
```

The people who created your version of Pascal placed the MAXimum INTeger value into this *constant*. All versions of Pascal have this "pre-declared constant" value.

CALCULATIONS

The following numeric operators are used in Pascal. These operators are used to perform calculations on numbers and on numeric variables. Most of these will probably be familiar to you.

+	Addition
−	Subtraction
*	Multiplication
/	Real division—will always yield a real (decimal) number
DIV	Integer division—divide the numbers and truncate (chop off) everything after the decimal point
MOD	Modulus (A **MOD** B yields the remainder after dividing A by B)

Some Rules

It *is* all right to divide one integer by another using the Real Divide (/). *However,* the result will never be an integer—it will always be a real

number (that is, there will be a decimal point in the number—see the section on Reals towards the end of this chapter). So for now, when you want to divide one integer by another, use the **DIV** operator, not the /.

Precedence in Calculations—Parentheses can be used for clarity and to indicate the order in which a calculation is to be carried out. Look at how Pascal would calculate the following examples:

$$5 + 3 * 2 = 11$$
$$(5 + 3) * 2 = 16$$

There are a few things to note here. In the first example, the computer multiplies before it adds, even though the + sign came before the * sign. In the second example, we used a left and a right parenthesis to make the addition happen *before* the multiplication. We say multiplication has *precedence* over addition and subtraction. Parentheses override these precedences of Pascal. Here are two more examples:

$$6 + 4 \text{ DIV } 2 - 1 = 7$$
$$(6 + 4) \text{ DIV } 2 - 1 = 4$$

Like multiplication, division occurs before addition or subtraction. Here is a final example:

$$4 * 4 \text{ DIV } 2 \text{ DIV } 2 = 4$$

Here the operators are * and **DIV**. These operators have "equal" precedence (+ and − also have "equal" precedence), and in this case Pascal evaluates the expression from left to right. In our example, Pascal multiplies 4 * 4, **DIV**ides by 2 to get 8 and **DIV**ides by 2 again to get 4. So, multiplication and division take precedence over addition and subtraction.

Stuffing the Variables

Here are a few examples of how we set up a variable, place data into it (initialize it), in Pascal. Notice the funny symbol := which we use:

STRINGs		INTEGERs	
Alphabits	:= 'Food'	AgeInYears	:= 14
Sex	:= 'M'	Sum4	:= 118
ZipCode	:= '94947'	Temperature	:= −60

The colon equal sign combination (:=) is used in Pascal instead of the equal sign (=) from BASIC to perform the actual assignment. This sign (:=) means "assigned," "replaced by," or "gets." In the previous example, the string value* **Food** is *as-*

---

* Calling a string of characters a "value" may not seem natural, but a string *is* a value of sorts. Each character in the string is represented in memory by a numeric ASCII code, so a string is really a series of special number codes that can be compared to other strings to see if they match (see Chapter 6).

signed to the variable **Alphabits** and the integer value **14** is *assigned* to the variable **AgeInYears**. Using the colon with the equal sign may seem like an extra burden, but the equal **(=)** sign is saved for use in Pascal comparison statements (for example, **IF x = 3 THEN WRITE('OK');**—which will be covered in Chapter 6) where we indeed mean *equals* and not *replaces*.

Declaring Variables

Now, in order to use a variable in Pascal, we need to do a special act called "declaring it" which means "write its name and define its type (so far, just **STRING** or **INTEGER**)". Variables are declared at the very beginning of a program, immediately after the **PROGRAM Name** and before the **BEGIN**. Listing 3-1 is an example of a program which uses variables and shows how they are "set up."

And here is a run of the program:

Did you know that it was only 66 years from the time the Wright Brothers first flew their airplane to when the first

man, Neil Armstrong, walked on the moon?

NOW YOU DO!

Pascal solves many of the problems of misplaced, misunderstood, or forgotten variables by requiring you to "declare" all of your variables. In essence, to declare a variable means: "I hereby announce that I am using a variable called **Name** in this program and it will be a such and such type." This may seem like a bother at first (all that extra typing!), but in the long run, you will really appreciate being able to look at the beginning of your program and find a list of all variables used. And when someone reviews your Pascal program 10 years down the road (or when you want to make some changes in a few weeks), they will know just where to look to find what the program's variables are and what their types are. And since you used *meaningful names,* they may even know what these variables represent!

The keyword

VAR

35

Listing 3-1.

```
PROGRAM Variables;

VAR     Astronaut                       : STRING;
        FirstFlightYear, MoonWalkYear,
        YearsElapsed                    : INTEGER;

BEGIN

  Astronaut := 'Neil Armstrong';
  FirstFlightYear := 1903;
  MoonWalkYear := 1969;
  YearsElapsed := MoonWalkYear - FirstFlightYear;

  GOTOXY(0,6);
  WRITELN('Did you know that it was only ',YearsElapsed,' years' );
  WRITELN('from the time the Wright Brothers first' );
  WRITELN('flew their airplane to when the first' );
  WRITELN('man, ',Astronaut,', walked on the moon?' );
  WRITELN;
  WRITELN('    NOW YOU DO!' );

END.
```

tells the computer that you are about to declare your variables. What follows this command is a list of the variables and their types. In the program **Variables**, there is one **STRING** variable (**Astronaut**) and three **INTEGER** variables (**FirstFlightYear, MoonWalkYear, Years-Elapsed**). Notice that there is nothing in the name of any of these variables which tells you what type they are. In BASIC, the $ in the name tells you it's a string variable, but there's usually nothing to help you decipher what kind of *numeric* variables you are dealing with—i.e., is it an integer or a real (a number with a decimal point). To find out the variable type in Pascal, just look at the section of the program in which these variables are declared—right after the word **VAR**. Easy, huh?

BY THE WAY . . .
Using *INTEGER*s or *REAL*s

Why bother worrying whether your numeric variable is an **INTEGER** or a **REAL**? After all, a number is a number! Well, **INTEGER**s take up less memory than **REAL**s. Also, calculations which use **INTEGER**s execute much faster than calculations using **REAL**s. On the other hand, **REAL**s are essential when working with monetary or scientific calculations. How would a bank survive if all the pennies were just ignored in a calculation. And we all know that there are a few scientific measurements which are greater than 32767 or between 0 and 1 (imagine measuring the vastness of the universe or the dimensions of an electron using

INTEGERs!). When using Pascal you must decide which number tool will be most effective and then declare your intentions!

Notice the way we formatted the **VAR** section in the previous program. This is mostly a matter of taste—there are no "hard core" rules about how you should set it up on the screen. It would have been correct to do it in any of the following ways:

```
VAR        Astronaut : STRING;
        FirstFlightYear : INTEGER;
        MoonWalkYear : INTEGER;
        YearsElapsed : INTEGER;
```

or

```
VAR     FirstFlightYear : INTEGER;
        Astronaut       : STRING;
        MoonWalkYear,
        YearsElapsed    : INTEGER;
```

or

```
VAR  Astronaut:STRING;
FirstFlightYear,MoonWalkYear,YearsElapsed:INTEGER;
```

and even

```
VAR Astronaut:STRING;FirstFlightYear,MoonWalkYear,
                        YearsElapsed:INTEGER;
```

Look over the above examples. Some are very clear; others are more difficult to decipher. Since neither spaces between words nor the number of lines you use robs you of precious memory, and since it is so much *easier* to understand a program that has been thoughtfully formatted, why not let your organizational and artistic abilities flow freely? Use lots of spaces and extra lines, and *make your programs look beautiful!*

 Uncle Pascal says: *A jalopy with a broken windshield, no back fender and a rusted out roof will probably get you where you're going, but I'd rather have a new Porsche!*

Just remember these essential ingredients when declaring variables:

1. The keyword **VAR** says "here comes the declarations."
2. The variable names go after **VAR**.
3. The variable type follows the variable name and is separated from it with a colon (:). (You may list all variables of the same type together, separated by commas, and then write the colon and the variable type.)
4. A semicolon goes at the end of the line after the variable type.

By the Way—How Big Is Your Screen?

Once upon a time, all crt displays were 80 characters wide by 24 lines high. When microcomputers came on the market, all this changed. Line lengths shrunk, mostly to allow people to use low cost television sets or monitors with their microcomputers. Two popular screen formats today are 64 characters by 16 lines and 40 characters by 24 lines. When writing your programs, keep that in mind and decide for what screen size format you will be writing. If you are writing a Pascal program for a screen that is 64 characters wide and someone with a 40 character wide screen wants to use it, that person will have to do quite a bit of conversion before the output looks good. All of the programs in this book are written so that their output during execution will fit on a 40 character by 24 line screen, such as the Apple II has. If you are using a 24 by 80 character screen, you can take two 40 character lines from our programs and make them into one 80 character line. If you are using a 16 by 64 character display, you may have to do some additional reformatting of our programs to *make the output look pretty.*

Now, let's look at the rest of the program, **Variables**. The first thing this program does after declaring its variables is to "stuff" the variables with fixed value information which in this case consists of string characters between apostrophes and numbers (integers here, with no decimal points). Again, notice the use of the colon equal sign combination (:=). After assigning the

string value 'Neil Armstrong' to the variable **Astronaut**, we assign the appropriate numeric dates to the variables **FirstFlightYear** (Wilbur and Orville's first successful flight) and **Moon-WalkYear** (the year Armstrong jumped off the ladder onto the dust of the moon). Then we get into the heavy math and have the computer calculate the difference between these two dates and place the value into the variable **YearsElapsed**.

The blank line that follows is just for appearance—to indicate a separate part of the program. (This could be imitated in BASIC using a series of REMark statements, and, in some BASICs, a series of colons or linefeeds.)

In the next part of the program, we are outputting the above information. First, we use a **GOTOXY** to place the cursor at the beginning of the seventh line in preparation for the first **WRITELN** statement. Now, look at this first **WRITELN** statement. Recall that we considered strings to be *separate elements* and that they can be separated by commas in a **WRITELN** statement. Variables are considered to be separate elements just as strings are. Therefore, commas are used to separate variables also. Note the space between the apostrophe preceding the numeric variable and the word **only** (it was only_'). Spaces are included within the apostrophes to keep the numeric variables from attaching to the end of a word. In some versions of BASIC, a space is automatically printed in front of all numbers (and in some BASICs, after the number). Pascal leaves the spacing up to you. No prepackaging here!

Again, we used spaces throughout **Variables** for increased clarity although none were really necessary. The spaces on either side of the := and the minus sign (—) are there for appearances only. *Pascal doesn't mind if you leave spaces out, but it goes against everything Uncle P is trying to tell us* (actually, everything N. Wirth is trying to tell us).

Initializing Variables

When a BASIC program is executed, all of the numeric variables are set to zero (i.e., in *most* BASICs when you type RUN). In addition, all string variables are set to *null* (empty) strings. Most versions of Pascal don't initialize their variables at all when the program is first run, so if you don't do it yourself, you may get some very strange results! Whatever garbage happens to be at the location in memory where the variable resides will appear in your variable. You won't discover the garbage until you try to print the variable or do a calculation with it. So, *always* initalize all your variables to the value you want them to start with, or to zero/null*.

Uncle Pascal says: Initialize all of your variables *explicitly* or suffer the consequences of GIGO (Garbage In = Garbage Out). *He who doesn't wash last night's dishes tastes last night's meal tonight!*

QUIZ—VARIABLES

True or False

1. The first 12 characters are significant in variable names.
2. STRING variables and INTEGER variables can easily be distinguished just by looking at their names.
3. Keep your variable names as short as possible to save memory.
4. Pascal initializes all variables to null or 0 at the beginning of each program run so you don't have to.
5. In Pascal, the symbol := means something different than the = symbol.

READLN

Perhaps the most critical part of any program is the part that allows a person to communicate

---

* You should initialize your variables in *any* computer language, even if the language does it for you.

with it during its execution. We say critical because when you are dealing with a real person who can do any number of crazy things (e.g., tap dance on the keyboard), your program must be ready to expect anything. This is not as simple as having your program output data to the screen, since you always know what will happen (except if your program has a bug, then you may be in for some surprises!). In the case of Pascal, inputting and interactiveness is much more picky than in BASIC.

So, let's create an interactive program and learn to surmount Pascal's pickiness. To be able to enter data while a Pascal program is running, we use the keyword:

READLN

This, of course, means "read a line of information." A line means "a bunch of characters (or numbers) which are terminated by a RETURN (carriage return)." Although this sounds suspiciously like BASIC's INPUT command, there are a few differences. First, in most BASICs you could write:

INPUT "What is your name? ";NAME$

Here's what happens:

What is your name? ▓
                    \ cursor

appears (with the cursor sitting one space away from the question mark) awaiting for your input and press of the RETURN key.

In Pascal, you can't print a "prompt" string and input a variable using a single command like this. Sorry . . . . The Pascal equivalent for writing a prompt string and inputting a variable would be:

See, no "LN" so we get the cursor where we want it

```
WRITE('What is your name? ');
READLN(Name);
```

Both versions (BASIC and Pascal) will look exactly the same on the screen when the program is executed.

READLN Error Traps

BASIC is much more forgiving of mistypes than Pascal, especially if you try to enter letters into a numeric variable using **READLN**. In BASIC, typing letters into a numeric variable INPUT will probably give an error message like:

> INPUT ERROR, RETYPE

or

> REDO FROM START

followed by a question mark on the next line and another chance to type the number correctly. In UCSD Pascal, if you try to type a letter into a numeric variable, the execution of the program halts entirely (it "bombs"), a cryptic error message appears, and the system reboots (imagine how the user would feel if this happened!). You must then restart the program from the beginning (this most definitely could have been better designed). This means that you must write your program so it can handle occurrences of bad input or you lose everything. It means you must learn about input testing and error recovery . . . we'll of course say more on this later.

 Make *sure* you protect against entering letters when Pascal is expecting a number! Uncle Pascal says: *Those who put oranges in apple crates will never end up with applesauce!*

READLN Revealed: An Input Example

Our next program (Listing 3-2) uses **READLN**. There are some new items in this longer Pascal

program—see if you can find them. And here is a sample run of this program. We will indicate all human inputs during a "run" of a program by *underlining* them.

Of course, Annie pressed the RETURN key here.

Hello there, what is your name? ANNIE

Oh yes, ANNIE, I should have known!

Tell me, how old are you? 29

Do you know that in 71 years you'll be 100 years old?!?

Press "RETURN" to end:

Comments

Let's start at the top. What you see on the first line following the program name (**Inputting**) is documenting information created with Pascal's version of the BASIC REMark statement—the *"paren-asterisk"* Comment. Comments should be used frequently to explain and document the program. They make it easier for someone to read the program like a book. To use comments, just follow two rules:

1. Start all comments with the two-character symbol (* —left parenthesis, asterisk
2. End all comments with the two-character symbol *) —asterisk, right parenthesis

Make sure that you don't add any spaces between the parenthesis and the asterisk! If you do, the two-character symbol will have become an illegal *three*-character symbol. Pascal also allows you to use the "curly brackets" { } instead of the (* *) symbol. However, some microcomputers don't have the curly brackets available on their keyboard, in which case you can't use them! For this reason, we'll use the "paren-asterisk" symbol throughout this book.

After the comment is the **VAR**iable declaration section. All variables used in this program are now declared. The **STRING** and **INTEGER** types are familiar, but what's that other one?

CHAR Variables

Next, in the program **Inputting**, you'll notice that a variable called **ClrScrnCode** has been declared as a new variable type, **CHAR**. A CHAR variable can hold only a single **CHAR**acter, *no more and no less*. If we were to say

Listing 3-2.

```
PROGRAM Inputting;

(* Program to demonstrate the use of READLN, COMMENTS,
    and how to clear the screen using the CHR function.   *)


VAR    Name, Continue : STRING;
       Age, Difference: INTEGER;
       ClrScrnCode     : CHAR;


BEGIN

   ClrScrnCode := CHR(12);    (* ASCII 12 is the Form Feed code which *)
                              (*  clears the screen on the APPLE II   *)

   WRITE(ClrScrnCode);           (* This line actually clears the screen *)

   WRITELN;
   WRITE('Hello there, what is your name? ');
   READLN(Name);
   WRITELN;
   WRITELN('Oh yes, ',Name,', I should have known!');
   WRITELN;
   WRITE('Tell me, how old are you? ');
   READLN(Age);

   Difference := 100 - Age;

   WRITELN;
   WRITELN;
   WRITELN('Do you know that in ',Difference,' years');
   WRITELN('you''ll be 100 years old?!?');
   GOTOXY(7,13);
   WRITE('Press "RETURN" to end: ');
   READLN(Continue);             (* Wait for press of RETURN key...       *)

   WRITE(ClrScrnCode);

END. (* Inputting *)
```

```
ClrScrnCode := '';
```
no space between apostrophes

in order to "empty out" the variable, we would get an error when the program was compiled. Likewise, if we tried

```
ClrScrnCode := 'FATCHANCE';
```

we would also get a compiler error because we are trying to squeeze more than one character into the variable. The only legal use of **CHAR** is when one and only one character is between the apostrophes, i.e.,

```
ClrScrnCode := 'X';
```

which would place the letter 'X' in the variable **ClrScrnCode.**

Uncle Pascal says: *One in a hole is par for this CHARs ("course"— Uncle P has an accent), all others go to Pitch and Putt.*

Using CHR to Clear the Screen

Now, in the first statement in our program following **BEGIN**, we did something special with the variable **ClrScrnCode.** Instead of a regular single character, we stored the special code which will clear the computer's screen when this variable is printed. To do this, we use the built-in **CHR**

routine. This is exactly like the CHR$ function available in most BASICs. Here's what it does. As you *may* know, each character that your computer recognizes has a special number code associated with it. This number is called the ASCII code (see Appendix D for a list of the computer's characters and their ASCII codes). The ASCII code for the capital letter A is 65, for the number 1, it is 49. Computers also have some characters which don't actually appear on the screen when they are printed, but perform some special function. For example, a line feed is such a nonappearing character; it has ASCII code 10 and causes the cursor to move down one line. A carriage return is an

ASCII 13. If your computer has a bell or buzzer, printing the code that corresponds to a Control G, ASCII 7, will sound it for you.

Most computers with a crt (television screen) have some special code to clear the screen. In some cases, it's a specific sequence of codes. Often, computers use ASCII 12 (control L), otherwise known as the Form Feed (FF) code. When this code is sent to a printer, the current page (form) will roll (feed) past and a new page will be ready for printing. On a crt, the screen will be erased in a flash. Check the operator's manual for your computer (or terminal or version of Pascal) to see what code(s) will clear the screen.

Now suppose we wish to have our Pascal program begin by clearing the screen. All we need to do is to have the program execute a **WRITE** with an ASCII 12 form feed character between the parentheses. Except there's a problem; namely, how do you get the form feed character into your program? There is no form feed key on the computer. The answer is simple. We use the handy **CHR** type routine* in Pascal that converts an ASCII number into its actual character, or in this case, its nonappearing function. When you write

```
ClrScrnCode := CHR(12);
```

the variable **ClrScrnCode** will "contain" the ASCII code for form feed. Now whenever our program executes:

```
WRITE(ClrScrnCode);
```

the screen will clear. Simple, clear, and best of all, self-descriptive even if you don't know ASCII (but do know Pascal)**.

Look to the right of the **CHR(12);** in the program and you'll find another comment. Comments can be placed *anywhere* in the program—between lines, after lines, before lines, in the middle of lines, etc. The only places they can't be used are within strings, keywords, or identifiers.

Notice that we used a **WRITE** instead of a **WRITELN** to ask the questions in the above program. This, of course, is to place the cursor after the question mark rather than on a separate line†.

Pascal's **READLN** does not automatically prompt you with a ? as some BASICs do. This means you must create your own prompt character (like : or ... or -) but you can use whatever prompt you like. Also, notice that we have a space following the question mark. Besides being more readable when the program is executed, this can also protect the program from a potential problem. Many times, when the cursor is placed immediately after the question mark (or prompt), a naive user will add a space or two in the beginning of the response (for neatness). In this case if that happened, the user's name would have a space or two as the first character(s). This would lead to an error if you were trying to match the user's input with a specific string ('__Brian' is *not* the same as 'Brian')*.

Further down the program, we input the **INTEGER** variable, **Age**. We used an **INTEGER** variable instead of a **STRING** variable because we will be using **Age** in a calculation (you can't use **STRING**s in numeric calculations, even if the characters that make up the string appear to be numbers). After the **Difference** is printed out, we center the phrase 'Press "RETURN" to end:' on the screen a few lines down. Look at how we use **READLN** to end the program. What is the purpose of the variable **Continue**? It's the variable which will "hold" the null or empty string (string with a length of zero) when the user presses RETURN**. The program ends with another screen clearing.

What Happened to Initializing Variables?—You may have noticed that the only variable we initialized in this program is **ClrScrnCode**. What about the rule to initialize all variables? Well, we are hereby introducing **READLN** as an alternative method to initialize variables. There is *no way* to get beyond a **READLN** without "initializing" the variable to something†. Even if the user just presses **RETURN**, the variable will be initialized to a null string.

PAGE—Built-in Screen Clearing

You may have wondered if there wasn't a more straightforward method of clearing the screen.

---

* CHR is a **CHAR** type routine because it will return a single character of type **CHAR**. Trying to use **CHR** to assign a value to a **STRING** type variable will yield a compiler error.

** You *could* say **WRITE(CHR(12))**; but that wouldn't be very descriptive.

† For those of you with ever-inquiring minds, the **LN** part of **WRITELN** actually causes the ASCII code for carriage return (13) and line feed (10) to be sent to the crt.

* It is possible to write the program in such a way that it will check for leading (or trailing) spaces—see "STRING FUNCTIONS" in Chapter 9 and Listing 10-3D.

** Actually, we could have left the variable **Continue** off and the effect wouldn't change; **READLN;** is a legal statement. The only difference is that any characters entered from the keyboard would be lost forever, since we aren't saving them in a variable.

† Or causing the program to "crash" by trying to enter a letter into a numeric variable.

Listing 3-3.

```
PROGRAM InputExperiment;

(* This is a program to test inputting a single
   CHARacter using both READLN and READ         *)

VAR    CharTest : CHAR;

BEGIN
  WRITE('Enter a string: ');
  READLN(CharTest);
  WRITELN('That was "',CharTest,'".');
  WRITELN;
  WRITE('And another: ');
  READ(CharTest);
  WRITELN('   That was "',CharTest,'".');
END.   (* InputExperiment *)
```

Well, there is. There's a built-in routine in Pascal which will automatically send the Form Feed character to your output device (crt, printer, or disk file—however, we will only cover the crt at this time). If you are using UCSD Pascal on an Apple computer, here is how you use **PAGE** to clear the screen:

```
PAGE(OUTPUT);
```

This is the method of screen clearing we will be using in this book from now on. If your version of Pascal won't clear your screen when you write **PAGE(OUTPUT);** in your program, then either use the method we introduced earlier (using **CHR** and the appropriate ASCII codes to clear your screen) or consult your Pascal manual.

READ—INPUT
WITHOUT PRESSING "RETURN"

You may have wondered if there is a **READ** command to go with the **READLN** just as there is a **WRITE** to go with **WRITELN**. Yes, Pascal lovers, there is. When entering **STRING**s and **INTEGER**s from the keyboard, there is almost no difference between the two. The differences are subtle and beyond the scope of this book. But when the variable type is **CHAR**, there's a big difference!

Try the following experiment. Enter the program shown in Listing 3-3. Now compile and run this program. During the execution of the program, you will discover that when using a **READLN** to enter data into a **CHAR** type variable, only the first letter that you typed is stored in the variable and there is *no* overflow error. But,

you can't use the backspace or delete key to correct that first letter typed. The computer will accept the first letter, then will wait for you to press RETURN before it goes on. Not very practical if you make a mistake during entry! However, when you use a **READ** to enter a **CHAR** type variable, the computer will accept the first typed letter, and then the program output will continue *on the same line without waiting for RETURN**! Here is a run of this program. Again, we are underlining the human input. In this example, <CR> indicates that the user pressed RETURN here.

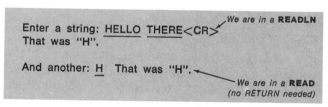

READ's ability to work without a RETURN can be a very valuable tool if you want to:

(A) save the user from having to press RE-TURN or
(B) collect only a single character input (for example, a "Y" instead of "YES").

As a general rule, you should use **READLN** when entering all variables *except* for **CHAR**s, then you should use **READ**.

Pascal Potholes Preview

So far we've said little about what would happen if you typed a number into a string variable. Well, we'll say a little about that now, but just as a preview.

---

* Much like the Applesoft "GET" statement, except that here the character is "echoed" or printed on the screen.

43

There is no real problem when you enter numbers in response to a request for string (letter) information since *any* keyboard character can be entered into a string—the computer will consider ANNIE and 99 to both be valid strings. In fact, $1,783,532.75 would be accepted without question as the name of a user! (Later we will see that it does, in fact, make much sense to input everything, including numbers, as strings.) But, as we have mentioned before, entering letters into a numeric variable will cause the computer to belch immediately.

Time to check your understanding.

QUIZ—INPUTTING

True or False

1. When using READLN, Pascal automatically provides you with a prompt character.

2. If you try to enter a letter into a numeric variable, Pascal will give you another chance.

3. Comments are a waste of space and time—after all, isn't it obvious what the program is supposed to do!?

4. The symbol (* is the same as the symbol (*.

5. CHAR type variables may be set to only *one* character.

6. READLN and READ act exactly the same way.

OTHER VARIABLE TYPES: REALS, BOOLEANS, LONG INTEGERS

You may be growing weary of all these variable types . . . bear with us—understanding them now will allow powerful Pascal features to make more sense later on.

REAL Variables

A REAL variable is a numeric variable that contains a decimal point. (No, there are no such things as "pretend," "unreal," or "make-believe" variables.) In most BASICs, as you may know, all numeric variables are reals unless you do something to change them to integers. Also, in BASIC, Scientific Notation format or E-format (see box) will only be used to output a REAL if that number is either too large or too small to be expressed using the available number of significant digits (also see box). In UCSD Pascal (and some other versions), *all* REALs are expressed using Scientific Notation. Here are some numbers that are printed from a BASIC which has 9 significant digits and a Pascal which has 6 significant digits (having only 6 significant digits can be a definite limitation).

BASIC (9 digit)	*Pascal* (6 digit)	
378.134	3.78134E2	
.043	4.30000E-2	
1	1.00000	*(all Scientific Notation output . . . don't go away!)*
671438915	6.71439E8	

1. How many significant digits the number has.
2. What those significant digits are.

First, let's explain what significant digits are. It has to do with how many digits of accuracy the number has. If you say that you are 34 years old, that number has 2 significant digits. Or you can say you are 34.04931506 years old (34 years and 18 days). This number has 10 significant digits. All you have to do is count the digits. The more significant digits you use, the more accurate the number is. In our Scientific Notation number (1.00 × 10⁹) we have 3 significant digits—the 1, and the 2 zeroes after the decimal point. Of course, the three significant digits of this number (1.00) could be replaced by any digit from 0 to 9 (yielding numbers from 0.00 to 9.99).

Since computers can't display the exponent above the line (yet), they print their numbers somewhat differently:

$$1.00E9$$

where the "E" stands for "times ten raised to the power of." All you have to do to convert a Scientific Notation number to a normal number is move the decimal point over to the right or left by the number of spaces indicated by the exponent. If you run out of significant digits, just add zeroes. To convert 3.578E6 to a decimal number, just move the decimal point 6 places to the right:

$$3.578E6 \rightarrow 3.578000 \rightarrow 3578000.$$

Numbers between 0 and 1 are very similar. You will recognize them by the negative sign in front of the exponent. To convert these numbers to decimal numbers, move the decimal point to the left instead of the right:

$$4.127E\text{-}5 \rightarrow 00004.127E\text{-}5 \rightarrow .00004127$$

BASIC's way of only using Scientific Notation when necessary may seem better to you. However, you should get familiar with E-Notation anyway—kind of like having to eat spinach. And for you spinach haters, we will be giving you a way to have the computer print *all* real numbers in a non-Scientific Notation format, later.

Earlier, we listed the numeric operators which could be used with **INTEGER**s (+ − * / DIV MOD). All of these operators can be used with **REAL**s *except* DIV and MOD. Note that a **REAL** can be combined with an **INTEGER** using the operators (+ − * /), but *the result will always be a REAL* (i.e., **INTEGER** + **REAL** = **REAL**, **REAL** / **INTEGER** = **REAL**). Also, two integers can be operated on by the Real Divide (/), but again *the result will always be interpreted as a REAL*, even if you expect the result to be an **INTEGER**. For example, 10 and 5 are both **INTEGER**s, but if you divide 10 by 5 using the real divide (10 / 5), the result will be 2.00000 (which is a **REAL**), *not* 2 (which is an **INTEGER**).

Pascal is particular about what *it* considers to be a **REAL**. Some versions of Pascal are more particular than others. UCSD Pascal, for example, is very tolerant about entering **REAL**s from the keyboard (practically any number will be accepted as a **REAL** if entered from the keyboard), but very *intolerant* when they are used inside the program. Here are the four rules to follow when using **REAL** numbers within a Pascal program:

1. All **REAL**s have decimal points. (Not necessary in UCSD Pascal.)
2. All **REAL**s have at least one number before the decimal point.
3. **REAL**s have at least one number after the decimal point (in most Pascals).
4. All exponents (when used) must be integers.

Here are some examples of legal Pascal **REAL**s:

123.012	1.000
0.12468	5.458E8
85 (in some Pascals)	−88.487E-9

Here are some examples of illegal Pascal **REAL**s:

.11458	(no digit before the decimal)
857.	(no digit after the decimal)
1274	(actually an **INTEGER**, some Pascals will accept this as a **REAL**)
8.44E8.4	(can only have integers for exponents)

If the **REAL** number you are using has more significant digits than your version of Pascal can handle, Pascal will just round off your number to a level of accuracy it can work with. We will use **REAL** variables in some programs in Chapter 5.

BOOLEAN Variables

A BOOLEAN variable type is kind of like a light switch—it can have only two different values. In the case of the light switch, these two values are ON and OFF. There isn't any position between ON and OFF (unless, of course, you have a dimmer switch—but that doesn't count!). The two *values* for a BOOLEAN variable are TRUE or FALSE*. BOOLEAN variables are used in "program control" when decisions to do one thing or another have to be made by the computer. Don't try to print out the value of a BOOLEAN variable using **WRITE** or **WRITELN** *or* input a BOOLEAN with **READ** or **READLN**—you'll just succeed in getting a compiler error (whoever heard of printing out a light switch, anyway!)†.

---

* TRUE and FALSE are built-in constant values, just as MAXINT is.

† "Standard Pascal" permits output but not input of BOOLEANs; UCSD Pascal permits neither.

BOOLEANs are for decision making only, not for i/o (input/output). We will cover this variable type in depth in Chapter 6—Program Control With Decision Making.

LONG INTEGER Variables

This is a special variable type that not all versions of Pascal have. It allows you to work with integers that are up to *36* digits long! Since this gives us *many* more significant digits to work with than **REAL** variables, **LONG INTEGERs** are used in place of **REALs** for most calculations where accuracy is vital. We will show you how to use **LONG INTEGERs** in Chapter 9.

Ordinal Types

Some of the variable types we introduced to you fall into a special category called *Ordinal Types,* mainly **INTEGERs**, **CHARs**, and **BOOLEANs**. The name "ordinal" comes from the fact that the possible values that these variable types can have are *ordered* in such a way that this order can be represented by an integer value.

Recall our explanation of ASCII values and the **CHR** function which changes the ASCII value to its appropriate character representation (presented earlier in this chapter). Well, there is another built-in routine which does just the opposite. It is called **ORD**. Remember we said that the ASCII value of the capital letter 'A' is 65. We can obtain this value directly by using **ORD**. Here is a program fragment using **ORD** (the variable i must be an **INTEGER**):

```
i := ORD('A');
WRITELN('The ordinal value (ASCII) of A is ', i);
```

Upon execution we get:

```
The ordinal value (ASCII) of A is 65
```

So, **ORD** returns the ordinal value (ordered position) of an ordinal variable type. 'A' is the 65th character in the set of ASCII characters so its ordinal value is 65.

Since the ordinal value of 'B' is 66, we can see that 'A' comes before 'B' (since 65 comes before 66). In fact, we can say that 'A' is **"less than"** 'B' because of their ordinal values.

ORD can be used with **BOOLEAN** values. Remember that **TRUE** and **FALSE** are values (type **BOOLEAN**) just as 214 is a value of type **INTEGER** and 'E' is a value of type **CHAR**:

```
i := ORD(FALSE);    i will be set to 0
i := ORD(TRUE);     i will be set to 1
```

This means that **FALSE** is *"less than"* **TRUE** (everyone knows that).

And finally, if **ORD** is used on an **INTEGER** value, the very same integer will be returned:

```
ORD(39)      will yield a 39
ORD(−1242)   will yield a −1242
```

QUIZ—OTHER VARIABLE TYPES

1. Which of the following are legal REALs?
   A. 5.012   E. 3
   B. .114678   F. 7.000
   C. 4.234E3.4 G. 87.45E-8
   D. 8.   H. −0.448

2. Convert these numbers to Scientific Notation.
   A. 12480000 C. −.000000001147
   B. 80   D. .55789

3. Convert these numbers to legal decimals.
   A. 8.04879E4 C. −9.4800E10
   B. 2.1448E-3 D. 5.148E-9

4. What are the two possible values for BOOLEAN variables?

5. True or false. Some of the digits in LONG INTERGERs can be to the right of the decimal point.

6. What is the ORDinal value of the following (for characters, you may use the ASCII chart in Appendix D)?
   A. '2'   D. TRUE
   B. 5   E. ' '(space)
   C. −875   F. ' = ' (equals)

Procedures the First Time Around

So far, all of the programs presented in this book have been relatively short—they all would fit on one or two crt screens. Recall the philosophy of Pascal that it is wiser to break a program into small modules, each with a specific purpose or function, than to write one large, long, and almost indeciperable program.

In this chapter, we will learn about small program modules or "units" which are called **PROCEDURE**s. A **PROCEDURE** module is short enough so that it usually fits completely on one or, at most, two screens. Each **PROCEDURE** of a program can have variables which are valid *only* within that procedure (called *local variables*) or we can define variables that are common to other procedures, called *global variables*.

BUILDING BLOCKS

Each of the programs we have written until this chapter were composed of a single section called a *block*. The block starts immediately after the **PROGRAM Name** (which actually gives the following block its name) and ends at the very end of the program (Fig. 4-1).

```
PROGRAM Name;

                            ┌─ The order in which these
                            │  appear is unimportant
    VAR     s  : STRING; ◄──┘
            i  : INTEGER;
            c  : CHAR;
            r  : REAL;
            b  : BOOLEAN;
    BEGIN
         :
      (* Body of PROGRAM *)
         :
    END.

                        ╲Block
```

Fig. 4-1. PROGRAM name block.

If you went ahead and tried to write a longer program before you read this chapter, you may have run into some difficulty with error messages. Sorry, *there is a limit to the size a block in a Pascal program can be**. The solution is to break the one large block into smaller blocks, each of which is no longer than one or two screensful. These smaller blocks are called **PROCEDURE**s. A Procedure looks almost exactly like a program (Fig. 4-2).

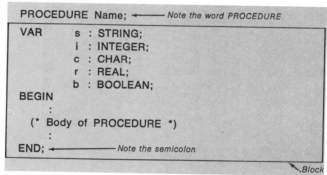

```
PROCEDURE Name; ◄──── Note the word PROCEDURE

    VAR     s  : STRING;
            i  : INTEGER;
            c  : CHAR;
            r  : REAL;
            b  : BOOLEAN;
    BEGIN
         :
      (* Body of PROCEDURE *)
         :
    END; ◄──────── Note the semicolon

                        ╲Block
```

Fig. 4-2. PROCEDURE name block.

There are only two major differences between the structure of a procedure and the structure of a program:

1. The keyword **PROCEDURE** is used in place of the keyword **PROGRAM**.
2. The semicolon terminates a procedure block instead of the period which is used for a program.

As you can see in this example, a procedure is also considered to be a block. Since programs can be made up of a number of procedures, we can have small blocks (procedures) within the larger block of the program. The program block is called the

---

* About 1200 bytes in Apple Pascal.

outer block, and the procedures are called the *inner blocks.* An example is illustrated in Fig. 4-3. Yes, we know it looks more complicated than our one block program, but hold on for now. First look at the end of the program where the procedures defined as inner blocks are used (Fig. 4-3). There is a comment which says this section is the "Main Program." Then the names of the **PROCEDURE**s appear (Part1, Part2, Part3) and then the final **END** (with its period). This section is the control section of the program. When the program is executed, the computer looks at

this list at the end (between **BEGIN** and **END**) and executes each procedure in order of appearance. The closest thing to **PROCEDURE**s in BASIC is the subroutine (GOSUB-RETURN). A definite advantage in Pascal (and one that shows GOSUBs to be less than perfect) is that each **PROCEDURE** has a name which is used to describe what the **PROCEDURE** does. Writing the name in the Main Program section (or elsewhere in the program) calls that procedure into action when the program is executed. This means that to understand what a program is supposed to do,

```
PROGRAM Name;
    VAR    s : STRING;
           i : INTEGER;
           c : CHAR;
           r : REAL;
           b : BOOLEAN;


    PROCEDURE Part1;
        VAR    i  : INTEGER;
        BEGIN
             :
          (* Body of PROCEDURE Part1 *)
             :
        END; (* Part1 *)



    PROCEDURE Part2;
        VAR    s  : STRING;
        BEGIN
             :
          (* Body of PROCEDURE Part2 *)
             :
        END; (* Part 2 *)



    PROCEDURE Part3;
        VAR    i  : INTEGER;
        BEGIN
             :
          (* Body of PROCEDURE Part3 *)
             :
        END; (* Part3 *)


    BEGIN   (* Main Program *)
        Part1;
        Part2;
        Part3;
    END.    (* Main Program *)
```

Fig. 4-3. Combining program and procedure blocks.

just look at the Main Program section at the end and read it just as you would an outline of a book or a flowchart for a computer program. The fantastic thing about Pascal is that this structure enables you to write very complicated programs without getting lost in the code—if the program is well written, you'll find a "summary" available for reference between **BEGIN** and the final **END**! Again, each **PROCEDURE** is like a subroutine that is called by just using its name in the program; no more trying to remember what GOSUB 9999 means!

Take a look at the next program (Listing 4-1) which is a new version of the program **Inputting** called **RevisedInputting**, rewritten to demonstrate **PROCEDURE**s. The program is simple enough so

that **PROCEDURE**s really aren't necessary, but we wanted to let you make a comparison between the two programs. The execution of the two versions will look exactly the same. Notice that the structure of the procedures is similar to the program structure we used previously. There is a **PROCEDURE Name** section (which looks like the **PROGRAM Name** section), the word **BEGIN**, the body of the procedure, and the word **END**. However, since it's only the **END** of the procedure, and not the end of the main program, we use a semicolon after the word **END** instead of a period. Comments are used to indicate which procedure has just ended. Use about 2 or 3 blank lines to separate procedures from each other.

As we said before, the first step to comprehending a Pascal program is to look at the end of the program and see a summary of what it will do. The first procedure to be called in our program **RevisedInputting** is named **ClearScreen**. Find this procedure at the beginning of the program. All it does is clear the screen using the **PAGE** statement. As we said before, we will be using **PAGE** in our programs from now on. (If **PAGE(OUTPUT);** doesn't work in your version of Pascal, just rewrite the **ClearScreen** procedure using the information from Chapter 3 on clearing the screen by writing an ASCII code.) We have essentially created a new customized Pascal statement especially for this program called **ClearScreen**. Whenever we write the word **ClearScreen** in this program, this procedure will be executed and the screen will be cleared. Seeing the procedure name, **ClearScreen**, in the program is much clearer than seeing **WRITE(CHR(12));** or even **PAGE(OUTPUT)**. Here's one of the "fundamental truths" of Pascal: *If Pascal doesn't have a specific command or routine to do what you want, you will eventually have the tools to create the command or routine yourself, then name it whatever you like.*

The next three procedures on the list, **GetName**, **GetAge**, and **Revelation**, are self-explanatory . . . look at them now. Finally, the **ClearScreen** procedure is called again and the program ends.

GLOBAL AND LOCAL VARIABLES

Take another look at the beginning of our **RevisedInputting** program, and compare it with the **Inputting** program of Chapter 3. You'll notice that only one of the four variables used in **RevisedInputting** (Difference) is declared at the beginning of the program. The rest of the variables are declared at the beginning of the proce-

Listing 4-1.

```pascal
PROGRAM RevisedInputting;

(* Program to demonstrate the use of PROCEDURES, READLN,
   COMMENTS, and how to clear the screen using PAGE.      *)

VAR    Difference: INTEGER;


PROCEDURE ClearScreen;

(* If PAGE(OUTPUT) won't clear your screen, use CHR to
   write the ASCII code which will clear your screen     *)

BEGIN
  PAGE(OUTPUT);
END; (* ClearScreen *)


PROCEDURE GetName;
VAR    Name : STRING;

BEGIN
  WRITELN;
  WRITE('Hello there, what is your name? ');
  READLN(Name);
  WRITELN;
  WRITELN('Oh yes, ',Name,', I should have known!');
END; (* GetName *)


PROCEDURE GetAge;
VAR    Age : INTEGER;

BEGIN
  WRITELN;
  WRITE('Tell me, how old are you? ');
  READLN(Age);

  Difference := 100 - Age;
END; (* GetAge *)


PROCEDURE Revelation;
VAR    Continue : STRING;
```

```
BEGIN
   WRITELN;
   WRITELN;
   WRITELN('Do you know that in ',Difference,' years');
   WRITELN('you''ll be 100 years old?!?');
   GOTOXY(7,13);
   WRITE('Press "RETURN" to end: ');
   READLN(Continue);
END; (* Revelation *)


BEGIN (* Main Program *)
   ClearScreen;
   GetName;
   GetAge;
   Revelation;
   ClearScreen;
END. (* RevisedInputting *)
```

dure in which they are used. *Each variable is valid only within the block (procedure) in which it is declared.* This means that in the **GetAge** procedure there is no such variable as **Name** and in the **Revelation** procedure there is no such variable as **Age**, etc. If a variable is declared within a procedure, it is only valid within that procedure. We say that a variable is *local* to the block in which it is declared—it has no influence outside that block. Then why, you may ask, is the variable **Difference** declared at the beginning of the program? Because this variable is used in more than one procedure, it must be declared at a higher level (outer block). Since all three procedures lie within the block in which **Difference** is declared, all three procedures can access this variable. We say that the variable **Difference** is *global* to the other procedures. A variable is global if it is valid in an inner block because it was declared in an outer block. We also say that the domain in which a variable is valid or accessible is called the *scope* of that variable. The scope of the variable **Difference** is the entire program. The scope of the variable **Age** is the procedure **GetAge**.

Side Effects

It's a very good practice to make variables as local as possible, to limit their scope to only the procedures in which they are needed. Recall the problem we mentioned which can occur in BASIC —when you change or update a specific section of a program, a bug appears in a totally remote part of the program. This is usually the result of a *side*

effect which is caused by reusing a variable which appeared in that remote corner of your program.

Look at the program in Listing 4-2, **Duplicate Names.** You'll notice that we declared the variable name **Sum** in the outer block and again the inner block. Even though the name is the same, these are *two separate and distinct variables.* Here is a run of this program:

```
1 + 1 = 2
5 + 5 = 10
Sum = 2
```

After clearing the screen, we add two ones together (1 + 1), store the result in **Sum**, and print the results on the screen. Then we call the **Add** procedure which places the sum of two 5s into **Sum** and prints out the result. However, since *this* **Sum** was declared in **Add**, it is *local* to this procedure—it is totally unrelated to the *global* **Sum** in the Main Program section. We can prove this when we return to the Main Program section and again print out the contents of **Sum**. It still has the sum of one plus one in it—calling **Add** had *no effect* on the global **Sum**. This shows the two **Sums** to be separate variables.

If an inner block uses an identifier (variable name) which was declared in an outer block, the outer block variable (global) becomes inaccessible to the inner block and the local variable "takes over." This is called *name precedence.* This means that if you declare some new variables in a procedure while you are modifying that procedure, *you don't have to worry about whether or not these variables' names were used elsewhere in the program!* When there is any question as to which variable is in effect, the most local variable always wins.

Listing 4-2.

```
PROGRAM DuplicateNames;
VAR    Sum : INTEGER;


PROCEDURE ClearScreen;

BEGIN
  PAGE(OUTPUT);
END;  (* ClearScreen *)


PROCEDURE Add;
VAR    Sum : INTEGER;

BEGIN
  Sum := 5 + 5;
  WRITELN('5 + 5 = ',Sum);
END;  (* Add *)


BEGIN  (* Main Program *)
  ClearScreen;
  Sum := 1 + 1;
  WRITELN;
  WRITELN('1 + 1 = ',Sum);
  Add;
  WRITELN('Sum = ',Sum);
END.  (* DuplicateNames *)
```

On the other hand, if you make use of global variables when modifying a procedure, you still must watch out for side effects!

A Stolen Procedure

Take another look at the **DuplicateNames** program. The first procedure called by the Main Program is an old friend of ours, the **ClearScreen** procedure. It's the same procedure we used in the **RevisedInputting** program. We stole it! It is possible to save a library of often used procedures like this one on a disk. When you want to use one, just load it in as you are editing your program. (Hopefully, the Editor you are using allows you to "append" like this.) Each procedure is thought of in terms of its overall generality . . . make it as universal as possible so you can use it everywhere!

PROCEDURES CALLING PROCEDURES

How about having one procedure which calls another procedure? Consider the example shown in Listing 4-3. Here is a run of this program.

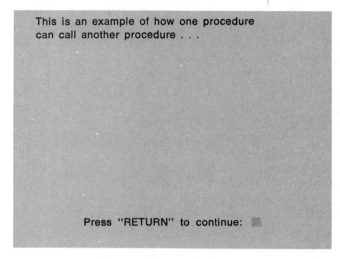

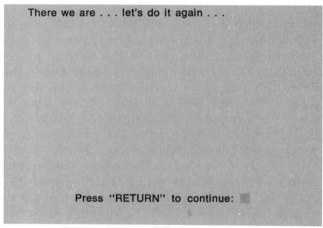

When one procedure calls another, it is important to pay attention to the order in which they appear in the program. The compiler has to know what an identifier means in order to compile its corre-

sponding code into the program later on. In this case, the **ClearScreen** procedure is defined first so that when the computer sees the word **Clear-Screen** later in the **Continue** procedure, it knows exactly what to do. If we were to reverse the order of these two procedures, the compiler would see the word **ClearScreen** and not know what it means, then it would tell you that there is an "Undeclared Identifier"*. *You can think of procedure names as new vocabulary keywords or commands for the computer and the actual procedure as the* *definition of these words*. The compiler has to have the word in its vocabulary *before* it can use it to define *another* vocabulary word! It's not smart enough to scan the rest of the program for hints. Too bad! If none of the procedures are called by any of the other procedures, then the order in which they appear in the program isn't critical for the program to run. But following the order in which the procedures are called is desirable for increased clarity and readability**.

---

* There is a way to get around this problem with the **FORWARD** reference—see Chapter 8.

** It's possible for a procedure to call itself! This is called *recursion* and is an advanced topic you can wrangle with in other books.

NESTED PROCEDURES

It is possible to have one procedure nested within another procedure. The example in Listing 4-4 tries to shed some light on this country's taxation scheme. The United States is divided up into states which are divided up into counties which often have a bunch of cities in them. As you can see, there are a number of block levels in this "program"—four to be exact. Here is a diagram to help you see the blocks:

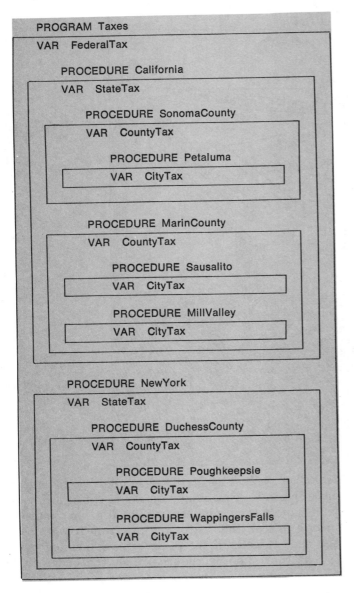

The outermost block is the entire program—the only variable which is global to the entire program is **FederalTax**, which, as we all know, *everyone* has to pay. No matter where you live in this program, **FederalTax** is valid and (unfortunately) accessible. The next block level has two state pro-

cedures, **California** and **NewYork**. **StateTax** for **California** is payable anywhere within the **California** procedure but not within the **NewYork** procedure. These two procedures both have a variable named **StateTax**, but these are two separate variables. The money that goes into **NewYork's StateTax** will not accidentally find its way into **California's StateTax**.

Within **California** and **NewYork** are a number of counties. In **California**, the next block level has two procedures—**SonomaCounty** and **MarinCounty**. Again, both of these procedures have a variable with the same name, **CountyTax**, and these are two distinct variables. People in **SonomaCounty** and **MarinCounty** have to pay their **CountyTaxes**, **California StateTaxes**, and, of course, their **FederalTaxes**.

Finally, the innermost blocks are made up of the cities and again we are using a number of totally distinct **CityTax** variables. So, the lucky residents of **MillValley** get to pay **MillValley CityTax** (local to their block level), **MarinCounty CountyTax** (global to their block level), **California StateTax** (global to their block level), and, of course, U.S. **FederalTax** (global to all blocks). **MillValley** taxpayers don't have to pay city, county or state taxes that do not have any scope in **MillValley** (e.g., **WappingersFalls**, **SonomaCounty**, or **NewYork**).

Looking at this from the other direction, the variables of the inner blocks have no validity in the outer blocks. If a **Poughkeepsie** resident tries to send his **CityTax** to the U.S. Government (outer block), the IRS will eventually figure out that it is not **FederalTax** and send it back with a polite note of correction (Compiler Error).

Keep track of the scope of your variables! Uncle Pascal says: *If I try to spend my francs in a Denver Doughnut shop, I won't even end up with holes!**

QUIZ

True or False

1. If a procedure is less than one screenful, it is probably too short.

2. It is not really necessary to use procedures when a program gets very large.

3. Follow the same Pascal variable naming rules when you name your procedures.

---

* Note from the authors to the readers: Sorry, but the deal we made with Uncle Pascal was a package deal—we either had to take "all his witticisms or nothing."

Listing 4-3.

```
PROGRAM PagingDemo;

PROCEDURE ClearScreen;
BEGIN
  PAGE(OUTPUT);
END;  (* ClearScreen *)

PROCEDURE Continue;
VAR    Cont : STRING;

BEGIN
  GOTOXY(5,22);
  WRITE('Press "RETURN" to continue: ');
  READLN(Cont);
  ClearScreen;
END;  (* Continue *)

BEGIN  (* Main Program *)
  ClearScreen;
  WRITELN('This is an example of how one procedure');
  WRITELN('can call another procedure...');
  Continue;
  WRITELN('There we are... let''s do it again...');
  Continue;
  GOTOXY(11,10);
  WRITELN('Good bye for now!');
END.  (* PagingDemo *)
```

Listing 4-4.

```
PROGRAM Taxes;
VAR    FederalTax : REAL;

PROCEDURE California;
VAR    StateTax : REAL;
  PROCEDURE SonomaCounty;
  VAR    CountyTax : REAL;
    PROCEDURE Petaluma;
    VAR    CityTax : REAL;
    BEGIN
      :
    END;  (* Petaluma *)

  BEGIN  (* SonomaCounty *)
    Petaluma;
  END;  (* SonomaCounty *)

  PROCEDURE MarinCounty;
  VAR    CountyTax : REAL;
    PROCEDURE Sausalito;
    VAR    CityTax : REAL;
    BEGIN
      :
    END;  (* Sausalito *)
```

```
   PROCEDURE MillValley;
   VAR    CityTax : REAL;
   BEGIN
        :
   END;  (* MillValley *)

 BEGIN  (* MarinCounty *)
   Sausalito;
   MillValley;
 END;  (* MarinCounty *)

 BEGIN  (* California *)
   SonomaCounty;
   MarinCounty;
 END;  (* California *)

 PROCEDURE NewYork;
 VAR    StateTax : REAL;
   PROCEDURE DuchessCounty;
   VAR    CountyTax : REAL;
     PROCEDURE Poughkeepsie;
     VAR    CityTax : REAL;
     BEGIN
          :
     END;  (* Poughkeepsie *)

     PROCEDURE WappingersFalls;
     VAR    CityTax : REAL;
     BEGIN
          :
     END;  (* WappingersFalls *)

   BEGIN  (* DuchessCounty *)
     Poughkeepsie;
     WappingersFalls;
   END;  (* DuchessCounty *)

 BEGIN  (* NewYork *)
   DuchessCounty;
 END;  (* NewYork *)

 BEGIN  (* Main Program *)
   California;
   NewYork;
 END.  (* Taxes *)
```

4. One procedure can call another procedure.

5. Pascal automatically scans the entire program for the definition of a procedure before it gives you an error message during compilation.

6. If a variable is global, it can't be a local variable.

7. If two variables in different block levels have the same name, the one in the outermost block is active and the one in the innermost block is ignored.

chapter 5

Program Control With Loops

Up to now, all of the programs have been very simple, even though they may have been somewhat lengthy. We say "simple" because when they were run, they just started by executing the first statement, then the second statement, the third, and so on until all statements were executed. Kind of like dropping a stone off of a building—it keeps falling and passing floors until it hits the ground. The stone doesn't say, "I think I'll go back up to the fourth floor and do that again!" or "I'm going to jump off of this building 23 times or until it starts to rain." There is no change in direction, no repetition, or no decision to make. It just *drops*.

So much for stones. Computers are somewhat more "intelligent"—they can make decisions of a sort. This chapter and the following two chapters will show you how to put some intelligence into your programs. In this chapter, we will introduce you to the use of the **FOR** loop and a Loan Payment Program.

THE FOR STATEMENT

*The **FOR** statement is used to make a statement (or series of statements) execute a specific number of times.* It is similar to BASIC's FOR-NEXT statements. Consider the following BASIC and Pascal examples:

BASIC	Pascal
10 FOR I=1 TO 20	FOR i := 1 TO 20 DO
20 PRINT I	WRITELN(i);
30 NEXT I	

Both examples will do exactly the same thing when they are executed. Note the differences between the two. The main differences are that Pascal doesn't have an equivalent to NEXT and

BASIC lacks a **DO**. The exact structure for the Pascal **FOR** statement is:

FOR control-value := initial-value TO final-value DO
    statement;

where all of the values (**control, initial, final**) are of the same *ordinal* type; we'll just cover type **INTEGER** for now. These values can also be expressions (e.g., x + 5), but the expression is *only evaluated once* when the **FOR** statement begins execution. If the value of the **final-value** expression changes during the execution of the loop, Pascal will just not care.

The word **statement** can be an assignment statement (**Food** := 'okra';), a procedure name (to call a procedure), or any other executable Pascal statement—even another **FOR** loop!*

Here is the way the **FOR** loop works:

1. The **control-value** is automatically initialized to the **initial-value**.
2. Pascal checks to make sure that the **control-value** is *not larger* than the **final-value**. If it *is* larger, the **FOR** loop is terminated and the next statement is executed.
3. The **statement**** (or body of the loop) is executed.
4. The **control-value** is incremented by one.
5. Go to #2

Many BASIC users make use of the fact that the value of the **control-value** (or index) will be set to one greater than the **final-value** when the **FOR**

---

* See examples of *nested* **FOR** loops in Chapter 10, page 147.

** Note that only one statement is under the control of the **DO** loop. We'll cover multiple statements in the upcoming Compound Statement section.

NumberOfLaps:=10;
FOR i:=1 TO NumberOfLaps DO
  Lap;

loop terminates. In Pascal, the value of the **control-value** is *undefined* at the termination of the loop, so don't depend on it in your programs.

Now for some practical programs using the **FOR** statement. Let's say we want Pascal to add all of the integers from 1 to 10. We could do it this way:

```
Sum := 1 + 2 + 3 + 4 + 5 + 6 + 7 + 8 + 9 + 10;
  WRITELN(Sum);
```

but that's kind of awkward, especially if we want to later add together all of the integers from 1 to 100! It is important to *generalize your program code* whenever possible. So, using **FOR** we get the program shown in Listing 5-1.

The output for this program is:

```
        The sum of the integers from 1 to 10
        is 55
```

By using a variable in place of the 10 and using **READLN**, we can make this loop (called a

summation) into an interactive program (Listing 5-2).

Here are a couple of executions of this program:

```
(1) Enter the top value: 100

        The sum of the integers from 1 to 100
        is 5050

(2) Enter the top value: 250

        The sum of the integers from 1 to 250
        is 31375
```

Let's learn more about looping in Pascal through its use in mathematics.

Exponents in Pascal

Let's say we have a number that we want to multiply by itself (squared):

$$3 * 3$$

Now let's multiply it by itself once more (cubed):

Listing 5-1.

```
PROGRAM AddIntegers1;

VAR    i, Sum : INTEGER;

BEGIN
  Sum := 0;
  FOR i := 1 TO 10 DO
    Sum := Sum + i;
  WRITELN('The sum of the integers from 1 to 10' );
  WRITELN('  is ',Sum);
END.  (* AddIntegers1 *)
```

3 * 3 * 3

In BASIC, either of these operations could be done with the exponentiation operator ($\uparrow$), as indicated in these examples:

$$3 \uparrow 2 \quad \text{is the same as } 3*3$$
$$3 \uparrow 3 \quad \text{is the same as } 3*3*3$$

Unfortunately, Pascal does not have a built-in exponentiation operator (much gritting of teeth). It would be simple to just multiply the numbers times themselves using the $*$ operator if we only want to square or cube the number. But what about 3.45^{10}? Or what about when the exponent is to be entered via the keyboard as a variable? The answer is a Pascal program which uses a **FOR** statement to *simulate* the exponentiation operator. It is based on the fact that raising a number to a certain power is really just a series of consecutive multiplications of that number times itself (Listing 5-3).

Here is a sample run of the program:

```
Enter the base number: 1.28
Enter the exponent: 18

The final result:
  1.28000 ↑ 18 = 8.50707E1
```

Here is how it works. The first step is to input the data. Next, we set the variable **Temp** to 1. This variable will hold the temporary products of the consecutive multiplications. When the **FOR** loop is finished, the final value will be in **Temp**. This routine will handle any positive integer exponent, including 0. If the exponent is 0, then the **FOR** loop will not cycle at all, since the initial value (1) will start out greater than the final value (0). This will not yield an error in our result—the value in **Temp** will remain unchanged (1). This is as it should be since any number raised to the 0 power is 1:

$$X^0 = 1$$

What will happen if you use a negative exponent? The same thing as using a 0 for the exponent. It

Listing 5-2.

```
PROGRAM AddIntegers2;

VAR    i, Sum, TopValue : INTEGER;

BEGIN
  WRITE('Enter the top value: ');
  READLN(TopValue);
  WRITELN;

  Sum := 0;
  FOR i := 1 TO TopValue DO
    Sum := Sum + i;

  WRITELN('The sum of the integers from 1 to ',TopValue);
  WRITELN('  is ',Sum);
END.  (* AddIntegers2 *)
```

Listing 5-3.

```
PROGRAM Exponentiation1;

VAR    Number, Temp : REAL;
       Power, i     : INTEGER;

BEGIN
  WRITE('Enter the base number: ' );
  READLN(Number);
  WRITE('Enter the exponent: ' );
  READLN(Power );
  WRITELN;

  Temp := 1;

  FOR i := 1 TO Power DO
    Temp := Temp * Number;

  WRITELN;
  WRITELN('The final result:' );
  WRITELN('    ',Number,'↑',Power,'  =',Temp );
END.  (* Exponentiation1 *)
```

won't bomb out, but it also won't give us the right answer. If you try to enter a real number as the exponent, Pascal will either ignore everything after the decimal point or "bomb out" (depending on which version of Pascal you have).

VARIATIONS ON *FOR*

Before we go on, we want to introduce some variations on the **FOR** loop.

Looping With DOWNTO

The first variation will allow you to count backwards by *decrementing* the **control-value**:

```
FOR control-value := initial-value DOWNTO final-value DO
   statement;
```

Just substitute the word **DOWNTO** for the word **TO** and make sure that your **initial-value** is *larger* than your **final-value** (or the computer will skip the **FOR** loop). Here is an example that will count backwards from 20 to 1:

```
FOR i := 20 DOWNTO 1 DO
   WRITELN(i);
```

Counting by Twos

Unfortunately, Pascal doesn't have a built-in method to count by a specific step as BASIC does. Here is a loop which counts by twos:

```
FOR i := 1 TO (100 DIV 2) DO
   WRITELN(i * 2);
```

On execution, we'd get:

```
2
4
6
8
:
:
100
```

A more general formula to count from **Start** to **Finish** by **Step** is:

```
FOR i := Start TO (Finish DIV Step) DO
   WRITELN(i * Step);
```

Counting Without Numbers

The third variation may sound a little strange to those of you who grew up on BASIC. It allows you to *count with letters* instead of with integer numbers.

Recall that we said that the values in a **FOR** statement must be of the "same *ordinal* type." This means that in addition to using **INTEGER**s, we can use **CHAR**s (or even **BOOLEAN**s). The program in Listing 5-4 will print the letters of the alphabet on the screen in order, and then in reverse order.

Here is a run of this program:

```
Here is the alphabet:
ABCDEFGHIJKLMNOPQRSTUVWXYZ

And here is the alphabet backwards:
ZYXWVUTSRQPONMLKJIHGFEDCBA
```

Listing 5-4.

```
PROGRAM AlphaWrite;
VAR    Ch : CHAR;

BEGIN
  WRITELN('Here is the alphabet:');
  FOR Ch := 'A' TO 'Z' DO
    WRITE(Ch);

  WRITELN;
  WRITELN;

  WRITELN('And here is the alphabet backwards:');
  FOR Ch := 'Z' DOWNTO 'A' DO
    WRITE(Ch);
END.    (* AlphaWrite *)
```

Of course, you aren't confined to just using the letters of the alphabet. The **initial** and **final** values can be *any* ASCII character.

We aren't sure why you would want to use **BOOLEAN** variables as the values in a **FOR** statement, but it can be done as shown in Listing 5-5.

Listing 5-5.

```
PROGRAM BooleanWrite;
VAR    Boo : BOOLEAN;

BEGIN
  FOR Boo := FALSE TO TRUE DO
    WRITELN(ORD(Boo));
END.    (* BooleanWrite *)
```

And the run of this program:

```
0
1
```

We are writing out the **ORD**inal value of the variable **Boo** because if you try to write out the variable itself (**WRITELN(Boo);**) you will just get a compiler error. **BOOLEAN** variables are used for logic flow (as you will discover in the upcoming **IF-THEN** section of Chapter 6), and not for data input/output (in UCSD Pascal).

COMPOUND STATEMENTS

You might be wondering what to do if you have more than one statement that you want to execute a certain number of times. In BASIC, it's simple—everything between the FOR line and the NEXT line will be repeated. Let's say we wanted to observe the computer's progress as it did a summation. Look at the following example:

```
Sum := 0;
FOR i := 1 TO 10 DO
  WRITELN(Sum);
  Sum := Sum + i;
```

The output will be a series of zeroes because only the **WRITELN** statement is under the control of the **FOR** loop (even though the indentation we used may lead you to believe otherwise). This brings us to the Pascal *Compound Statement*. Here it is:

```
BEGIN
  statement 1;
  statement 2;
      :
      :
      :
  statement n;
END;
```

That looks strangely like the innards of a Pascal program or procedure. The words **BEGIN** and **END** are not statements. They are reserved words with a special function called *delimiters*. They actually show the **BEGIN**ning and **END**ing limits of the compound statement. A compound statement is treated in exactly the same way as a single statement and can be used *in place* of a single statement. Therefore, wherever you see the word "statement" in our syntactical descriptions, you may use a compound statement. The example from the beginning of this chapter becomes:

```
Sum := 0;
FOR i := 1 TO 10 DO
  BEGIN
    WRITELN(Sum);
    Sum := Sum + i;
  END;
```

And the general **FOR** statement becomes:

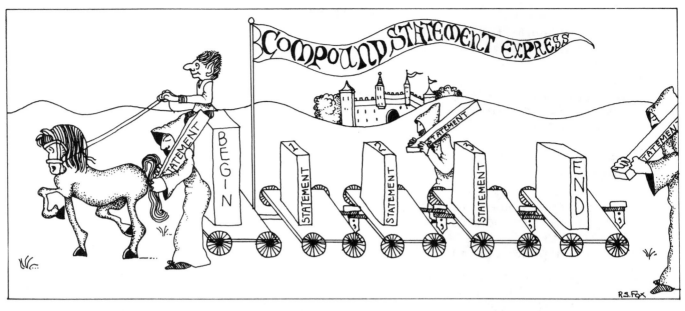

```
FOR control-value := initial-value TO final-value DO
  BEGIN
    statement 1;
    statement 2;
        :
        :
        :
    statement n;
  END;
```

 Everything between the **BEGIN** and the **END** will be under the control of the **FOR** statement. As Uncle Pascal says: *Where the trunk and tail go, so goes the elephant!*

BY THE WAY . . .
More on Semicolons

There is a rule in Pascal that all statements must have a semicolon after them. Since the word **BEGIN** isn't a *statement* (it's a delimiter), that explains why it doesn't have a semicolon following it. But what about the word **END**? It too is a delimiter. The answer lies in the fact that a compound statement is treated exactly like a single statement. Since a single statement requires a semicolon following it, so does a compound statement. This means that the semicolon following **END** is actually the semicolon that is following the entire compound statement.

Semicolons are used to separate successive Pascal statements. So, if **END** *isn't* a statement, why do we need to have a semicolon between the last statement in a compound statement and the delimiter **END**? The answer is *we don't!* The last semicolon before an **END** is optional. We have been using a semicolon in this position to make things easier for you to remember. Both of the following examples are correct:

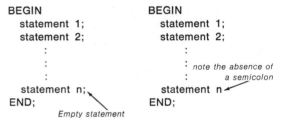

```
BEGIN                    BEGIN
  statement 1;             statement 1;
  statement 2;             statement 2;
      :                        :
      :                        :  note the absence of
      :                        :      a semicolon
  statement n;             statement n
END;                     END;
      Empty statement
```

This may seem surprisingly inconsistent for a structured language like Pascal. AHA! There is really no inconsistency here. This is because there is something called an *empty statement* following **statement n**; in the first example, and the semicolon is *separating* **statement n** from the empty statement. The reason you can't see the empty statement is that it is IN-VISIBLE. The empty statement was apparently invented just so the semicolon before an **END** would be optional. Uncle Pascal would just *love* it! All this time you have been writing invisible empty statements in your programs and you didn't even know it!

The truth is that we could place an empty statement after the delimiter **BEGIN** and no problem would be reported:

```
            empty statement
  BEGIN;
    statementl;
        :
        :
```

But the convention is to not do this so we won't. However, we *will* continue to write empty statements in our sample programs (alas, poor typesetter). We mention this here to clear up the apparent inconsistency and to explain why Pascal programs from other sources may not have the semicolon immediately before **END**.

Using the Compound Statement

Let's take the exponentiation program and use a compound statement. Listing 5-6 shows a mod-

Listing 5-6.

```
PROGRAM Exponentiation2;

VAR    Number, Temp : REAL;
       Power, i     : INTEGER;

BEGIN
  WRITE('Enter the base number: ');
  READLN(Number);
  WRITE('Enter the exponent: ');
  READLN(Power);
  WRITELN;

  Temp := 1;

  FOR i := 1 TO Power DO
    BEGIN
      Temp := Temp * Number;
      WRITELN(Number,'↑',i,' =',Temp);
    END;

  WRITELN;
  WRITELN('The final result:');
  WRITELN('    ',Number,'↑',Power,' =',Temp);
END.  (* Exponentiation2 *)
```

ification which will allow you to observe the progress of the consecutive multiplications. Here is a sample run of this program:

```
Enter the base number: 1.41421
Enter the exponent: 6

1.41421 ↑ 1 = 1.41421
1.41421 ↑ 2 = 1.99999
1.41421 ↑ 3 = 2.82841
1.41421 ↑ 4 = 3.99996
1.41421 ↑ 5 = 5.65678
1.41421 ↑ 6 = 7.99988

The final result:
1.41421 ↑ 6 = 7.99988
```

The number we used as the "base number" in this example may look familiar to you. It is the square root of 2. Take a look at the result we get when we square 1.41421—it's almost 2.0, but not quite. Now take a look at the results for our base number raised to the fourth and sixth powers. The answers to these calculations should be 4.0 and 8.0, respectively. This is what happens when you start out with a number with a small accuracy error in it and then work with it. The error in accuracy gets larger and larger. This means you can't trust your computer's calculations to be perfectly accurate when you are working with **REAL** numbers, especially small **REAL**s. The solution is to use a combination of **LONG INTEGER**s (which can have up to 36 digits of accuracy) and **STRING**s. We will show you how to do this in Chapter 9.

BY THE WAY . . .
Changing the *control-value* During Execution

In some versions of BASIC it is admissible to change the value of the **control-value** (index) within the FOR loop. This might be done to force the loop to terminate prematurely by setting the **control-value** to the **final-value**. It is important that you *never* try to do this in Pascal (Uncle Pascal *hates* to leave something unfinished.) For example, this is *incorrect:*

```
FOR i := 1 TO 100 DO
  BEGIN
    Count := Count + i;
    i := i + 10;       ←——— Wrong! (Changing the
  END;                        control-value)
```

THE LOAN PAYMENT PROGRAM

We will now present a program which you will find extremely valuable in these times of outrageous interest rates. You can use it to help talk yourself out of applying for a loan or make sure you don't let your charge card get out of hand!

Most people have had to take out a loan from a bank, credit union, or other lending institution at one time or another. Have you ever wondered how the bank figures your monthly payment? Or did you ever wish you could check to see if their figures were right? This next program uses everything we have learned so far to calculate the regular payment on a loan.

The banks figure out your regular loan payments by using special tables of figures. There is also a special formula that tells you how much your regular payments should be to pay off your debt. It's called an *amortization loan* formula and it looks like this:

$$RegularPayment = \frac{Principal \times InterestPerPeriod}{1 - (InterestPerPeriod + 1)^{-NumberOfPayments}}$$

Don't Go Away! Before you say "Oh Nooo!" and close the book, we want you to know that it's not necessary to understand this formula in order to follow our next program example. If you like math, then enjoy! Otherwise, skim the explanations on the Loan Formula and center on our discussion of the program itself.

The Formula

What the formula says is this: Take the total amount borrowed (the principal), the interest rate, and the length of time you have in which to pay back the loan, then perform the calculations to obtain the regular payment. The interest rate (**InterestPerPeriod**) is not the yearly rate. It is calculated by dividing the yearly interest rate (called **AnnualInterest** rate) by the number of **PaymentsPerYear**. The total **NumberOfPayments** is found by multiplying the number of **Payments-PerYear** by the number of years of the term (**TermInYears**). What follows is a program based on this formula called **Loan1** (Listing 5-7). First, here are a couple of sample runs of the program. The first might be for a car loan (this book is being written during a period of high interest rates; we hope that they are *much* lower now!). The second run is an example of what you would have to pay if you were buying a $100,000 house and financing 80% of it (20% down).

```
(1)      ** LOAN PAYMENT **

  Enter amount of loan: 4000
  Enter the annual interest: 20
  Enter payments per year: 12
  Enter term in years: 5

  Regular payment = $ 1.05976E2

  That's all folks . . . BYE
```

```
(2)      ** LOAN PAYMENT **

  Enter amount of loan: 80000
  Enter the annual interest: 15
  Enter payments per year: 12
  Enter term in years: 30

  Regular payment = $ 1.01155E3

  That's all folks . . . BYE
```

The Program

The first step in our program is to clear the screen. Next, in the **GetData** procedure, we input our **Principal**, **AnnualInterest** rate, number of **PaymentsPerYear**, and the **TermInYears**. The next procedure, **Calculate**, is the most important section of the program. The first thing you'll notice is that we included a version of the exponentiation routine (introduced earlier in this chapter) as a nested procedure called **Power**. We did this to make **Power** *local* to the **Calculate** procedure. Yes, procedures can be thought of as *local* or *global* just as variables can. Since **Power** is local to **Calculate**, no other procedure can call **Power**. The same rule that holds for variables holds for procedures—it's wise to make them as local as possible. Since the only procedure in this program which accesses **Power** is **Calculate**, we decided to place **Power** within **Calculate** so that all of **Calculate**'s variables become global (accessible) to **Power** without having to be global to the entire program, thus protecting them from accidental tampering.

After the **InterestPerPeriod** and the **NumberOfPayments** are calculated, the nested procedure **Power** is called. To make this procedure clearer, we are setting **x** to the base number (the number to be raised by an exponent) and **y** to the exponent. The variable **Temp** will contain the result.

Next, we'll calculate the **RegularPayment**. If you look at our loan formula, you'll notice that it calls for us to raise a number by a negative exponent. You'll recall that our exponentiation routine can't do this. Raising a number to a negative exponent is the same as raising the number to a positive exponent and then dividing the result into 1.

$$N^{-e} = \frac{1}{N^e}$$

or

$$5^{-3} = \frac{1}{5^3} = \frac{1}{125} = 0.008$$

So, this is what we are doing.

Finally, we print out our result in the **Print-Answer** routine, and then exit the program with **END**.

EXPANDING A PROGRAM

There is an old computer proverb which states that the closer a program is to being completed, the more extremely important things you will discover to add to it. No problem—adding to or revising a Pascal program is actually quite a simple task, because of Pascal's modularity. For example, consider an enhancement of the loan program that computes the actual total interest you are paying on the amount borrowed. In order to calculate this, we must first find the total amount that is to be paid to the bank by multiplying the regular payment by the total number of payments. Then subtract the actual principal that was borrowed. What is left is the amount of the loan which is going toward the interest. Here is the formula:

```
TotalInterest :=
    RegularPayment * NumberOfPayments — Principal;
```

This formula can be inserted at the end of the **Calculate** procedure, and the output of this new information can be inserted at the end of the **PrintAnswer** routine using the editor. (Of course, don't forget to declare **TotalInterest** as a **REAL** variable!) Before we show you the revised loan program, here is one more modification, a new way to output information.

Formatted Printing

Our loan payment program works well enough, but the output is in Scientific Notation.

 Uncle Pascal says: *Who wants to look at dollar amounts that remind us of a nuclear physicist's nightmare!*

Fortunately, Pascal has a way to specify how the output of numerical values will look. Here is the general format of this new technique called **Formatted Printing**:

```
WRITELN(Variable : field-length : places-after-decimal);
```

Field-length indicates how many spaces, *including the decimal,* you want to reserve on the screen for the output of your variable. The second number, **places-after-decimal**, is optional. It specifies how many places after the decimal point you want to be displayed. These two numbers can either be numbers (e.g., 5, 2, 10), **INTEGER** variables

(e.g., **i**, **Spaces**), or expressions which reduce to an integer value (e.g., **i** + 9, **Space** ∗ **Tab**):

```
WRITELN(Alimony : 12 : 2);        Using numbers
WRITELN(Pi: DecPlaces + 2 : DecPlaces);
                                  Using variables
                                  and expressions
                                  DecPlaces must be
                                  INTEGER
WRITELN(Display : Tab + 10);      Expression—no
                                  places-after-decimal
```

If the variable you are outputting is *shorter* than the allowed places for **field-length**, the extra spaces (columns) will be filled with spaces *to the left of the number:*

```
Num := 12.113;
WRITELN('The number is —', Num : 9 : 3);
```

The output of this statement looks like this:

```
The number is —      12.113
```

There are three blank spaces before the number because nine spaces were reserved for **Num** and it only needed six (count the decimal point).

If your number is *too large* to fit into the space allowed for **field-length**, it will be displayed in Scientific Notation.

In the case of our loan payment program, we want the final answer to be in dollars and cents, so we will change the output line in the **PrintAnswer** procedure to:

```
WRITELN('Regular payment = $',Payment : 7 : 2);
```

This means reserve seven spaces for the variable **Payment**: four spaces before the decimal point

Listing 5-7.

```
(*================================================*)
(*                                                *)
(* Program Language: PASCAL                       *)
(* Program Title: Loan Payment - version 1        *)
(* Subtitle:   Quick and dirty first attempt.  Has *)
(*             crummy E-Notation output.          *)
(*                                                *)
(* Author:     Mitch Waite                        *)
(* Program Summary:  Calculates the regular payment *)
(*             on a loan.                          *)
(*                                                *)
(*================================================*)


PROGRAM Loan1;

VAR   Principal, AnnualInterest,
      RegularPayment               : REAL;
      PaymentsPerYear, TermInYears : INTEGER;




PROCEDURE ClearScreen;

BEGIN
  PAGE(OUTPUT);
END; (* ClearScreen *)




PROCEDURE GetData;

BEGIN
  ClearScreen;
  WRITELN('            ** LOAN PAYMENT **');
  WRITELN;
  WRITELN;
  WRITE('Enter amount of loan: ');
  READLN(Principal);
  WRITE('Enter the annual interest: ');
  READLN(AnnualInterest);
  WRITE('Enter payments per year: ');
  READLN(PaymentsPerYear);
  WRITE('Enter term in years: ');
  READLN(TermInYears);
END; (* GetData *)
```

```
  PROCEDURE Calculate;
  VAR    Temp, InterestPerPeriod : REAL;
         NumberOfPayments        : INTEGER;

    PROCEDURE Power;
    VAR    x    : REAL;
           y, i : INTEGER;
    BEGIN
      x := InterestPerPeriod + 1;      (* Routine which will       *)
      y := NumberOfPayments;           (* raise x to the y power,  *)
      Temp := 1.0;                     (* that is, x↑y   (x >= 0)  *)
      FOR i := 1 TO y DO               (* Answer is in Temp        *)
        Temp := Temp * x;
    END;  (* Power *)

  BEGIN (* Calculate *)
    InterestPerPeriod := (AnnualInterest / 100) / PaymentsPerYear;
    NumberOfPayments := PaymentsPerYear * TermInYears;

    Power;

    RegularPayment := Principal * InterestPerPeriod / (1 - 1 / Temp);
  END; (* Calculate *)




  PROCEDURE PrintAnswer;

  BEGIN
    WRITELN;
    WRITELN;
    WRITELN('Regular payment = $',RegularPayment);
    WRITELN;
    WRITELN;
  END; (* PrintAnswer *)




  BEGIN (* Main Program *)
    GetData;
    Calculate;
    PrintAnswer;
    WRITELN('That''s all folks...BYE' );
  END. (* Loan1 *)
```

Listing 5-8.

```
PROGRAM Loan2;

VAR   Principal, AnnualInterest,
      RegularPayment, TotalInterest : REAL;
      PaymentsPerYear, TermInYears   : INTEGER;


(*                              :                          *)
(*                              :                          *)
(*            This part of program is the same as before   *)
(*                              :                          *)
(*                              :                          *)


    TotalInterest := RegularPayment * NumberOfPayments - Principal;
END; (* Calculate *)



PROCEDURE PrintAnswer;

BEGIN
  WRITELN;
  WRITELN;
  WRITELN('Regular payment = $',RegularPayment : 7 : 2);
  WRITELN;
  WRITELN('Total  interest on loan = $',TotalInterest : 7 : 2);
  WRITELN;
  WRITELN;
END; (* PrintAnswer *)



BEGIN (* Main Program *)
  GetData;
  Calculate;
  PrintAnswer;
  WRITELN('That''s all folks...BYE' );
END. (* Loan2 *)
```

(dollars), one for the decimal point, and two spaces after the decimal point (cents). A nice feature of formatted printing is that it automatically rounds off the number. This format (7:2) is set up for the six significant digits which is the most that Apple Pascal (UCSD) can handle. If your Pascal has more than six significant digits, just increase the **field-length** appropriately.

If you want to use formatted printing for **INTEGER**s or **STRING**s, then *do not use the second number for places after the decimal* (there *is* no decimal in **INTEGER**s or **STRING**s) or you will get a compiler error. When using formatted printing with **INTEGER**s, if you don't reserve enough

space for the value, that is, if the value is longer than the **field-length**, the formatted printing information will be ignored and the value will be displayed in full. If you use it with **STRING**s, the **STRING** will be chopped off to *make* it fit within the **field-length**:

```
Complaint := 'I am too long';
WRITELN(Complaint : 8);
```

This statement will print only the first eight letters:

```
I am too
```

Tabbing With Formatted Printing—Formatted printing can be used as a makeshift TAB function. Look at how we are using it to center the title of the program in the **GetData** in the following version of the Loan Payment program, **Loan2**. Since the heading is 18 characters long and the screen width we are using is 40 characters long, we want to place 11 blank spaces before the heading and 11 blank spaces after it (11 + 18 + 11 = 40) in order to center it on the screen. We reserved 29 spaces for the heading. Since the heading is only 18 characters long, the 11 extra spaces we reserved will be placed *in front* of the heading—and there we have it!

Listing 5-8 contains the revised loan payment program.

Here are two sample runs of the revised program using the same data that we used in our runs of **Loan1**:

```
(1)      ** LOAN PAYMENT **

      Enter amount of loan: 4000
      Enter the annual interest: 20
      Enter payments per year: 12
      Enter term in years: 5

      Regular payment = $ 105.98

      Total interest on loan = $2358.54

      That's all folks . . . BYE

(2)      ** LOAN PAYMENT **

      Enter amount of loan: 80000
      Enter the annual interest: 15
```

```
      Enter payments per year: 12
      Enter term in years: 30

      Regular payment = $1011.55

      Total interest on loan = $284160.

      That's all folks . . . BYE
```

Whew! That's a lot of interest!! You'll notice that since we are using a version of Pascal that has only six significant digits, there are no zeroes after the decimal point in the answer to **Total interest on loan** in the second run of the program. This means, of course, that the answer isn't exact. Six digits of accuracy might be tolerable for your own use, but not for a business. The solution is to use the variable type, **LONG INTEGER**, which is covered in Chapter 9. If you are interested in learning more about the inaccuracies of the loan formula, see Appendix G.

QUIZ

True or False

1. If the initial value in a FOR statement is smaller than the final value, the program will "bomb out."

2. The words BEGIN and END are called "delimiters" because they show the limits of a compound statement.

3. If there is a discrepancy between the results you get from running the LOAN PAYMENT program and what the bank says, the bank is probably wrong.

4. If your version of Pascal has six significant digits of accuracy, you can get it to display more than six digits by using formatted printing.

5. Formatted printing can be used for STRINGs and INTEGERs as well as REALs.

chapter 6

Program Control With Decision Making

In this chapter we will continue our introduction of program control with *IF-THEN* and *IF-THEN-ELSE*. We will be presenting a useful Metric Conversion Program at the end of this chapter.

THE *IF-THEN* DECISION MAKER

Here is another familiar statement for those who are familiar with BASIC. Pascal's **IF-THEN** is very much like BASIC's. **IF-THEN** allows you to check a condition to see whether it is TRUE or FALSE and then do something if it is TRUE. The format of the statement is:

```
IF condition THEN statement;
```

What's a Condition?

A condition can result in a value which is either TRUE or FALSE. It can't be maybe, kind of, or usually. Does something here sound familiar? Yes, conditions are *Boolean* values—they all evaluate to a Boolean quantity, either TRUE or FALSE. A condition is often a *Boolean expression*, a comparison of two values using the relational operators:

=	equals
<	less than
>	greater than
<=	less than or equal to
>=	greater than or equal to
<>	not equal to

Here are some examples of Boolean expressions that evaluate to a TRUE or FALSE Boolean result:

a < b	FirstName = 'Louis'
Days = 30	Month <> 'December'
Denominator > 0.0	Choice <= 8

We will call these expressions "simple" Boolean expressions because only one comparison is made in each of them. Again, don't mix up the use of the two equal signs (=) above with the assignment symbol (:=). The equal sign means "exactly equivalent to" while the assignment symbol reads "is replaced by" or "becomes." Also, it is important to pay close attention not to mix variable types in a Boolean Expression (i.e., don't compare **INTEGER**s with **REAL**s or **STRING**s with **CHAR**s).

Here are some examples of **IF-THEN** statements. The statement following the **THEN** will *only* be executed if the condition after **IF** evaluates as TRUE. If it evaluates as FALSE, the statement part of the **IF-THEN** will be skipped and the next statement in the program will be executed.

```
IF Guess < RandomNumber THEN
    WRITELN('Your guess was too low!');

IF Password <> 'KNOCK KNOCK' THEN
    WRITELN('No way, Charlie!');

IF DaysInMonth = 28 THEN
    Month := 'February';
```

Notice our use of equals (=) and assigned (:=) in the last example.

IF-THEN With Compound Statements

As in the **FOR** statement, the statement part of **IF-THEN** can be a compound statement. For example:

```
IF Response = 'NO' THEN
    BEGIN
        WRITELN('Your answer was correct!');
        Score := Score + 10;
        WRITELN('Your total score is now ',Score);
    END;
```

70

Boolean Variables as the Condition

Instead of using a Boolean expression as the condition, you can use a simple Boolean variable:

```
IF ErrorFlag THEN
    WRITELN('There was an error, please try again.');
```

The value of **ErrorFlag** is evaluated in the same way our simple expressions are evaluated. The message will be printed *only* if the value of the Boolean variable, **ErrorFlag**, is TRUE. Another way to write this is:

```
IF ErrorFlag = TRUE THEN
    WRITELN('There was an error, please try again.');
```

The outcome of these two examples will be the same; the first example is actually a shorthand way of writing the second example.

The important thing to remember is that the condition in an **IF-THEN** must evaluate to either TRUE or FALSE. Uncle Pascal says: *You might be able to keep dry in the rain, but when you take a bath you get wet!*

AND, OR, and NOT

These three functions are sometimes called Boolean operators or logical operators. This is because they operate "logically" on Boolean variables or expressions.

What follows are the "Truth Tables" for the logical operators, AND, OR, and NOT (Fig. 6-1). In these tables, **Alpha** and **Beta** are both **BOOLEAN** variables (i.e., TRUE or FALSE). To use the tables, check to see what the values for **Alpha** and **Beta** are, then what the values will be when operated on by the logical operator.

As you can see, when Alpha and Beta are operated on by AND, *both* variables have to be TRUE for **Alpha AND Beta** to be TRUE. If either of the variables is FALSE, then the result will be FALSE. When OR is the operator, the result will be TRUE if *either* variable is TRUE. The result will be FALSE only if both variables are FALSE. NOT is different from the other two operators in that it doesn't make a comparison— it combines with the variable to give the opposite value of the variable. If Alpha is TRUE, then **NOT Alpha** is FALSE. If Alpha is FALSE, then **NOT Alpha** is TRUE.

We said that the Boolean Operators can also be used on Boolean expressions. This can be done by making the expression look like a single Boolean value. All you have to do is surround the expression with a pair of parentheses. We will call this a "complex" Boolean expression since it is

... which horse should I buy? The black stallion **OR** the Palomino but **NOT** the one with the buck teeth, **AND** for sure **NOT** the one used to slay dragons, **OR** maybe that dark horse with the feathers, **AND/OR** the little pony...

BOOLEAN STABLES

made up of two or more "simple" Boolean expressions operated on by a Boolean operator:

(Answer = 'YES') OR (Answer = 'Y')

Alpha	Beta	Alpha AND Beta
TRUE	TRUE	TRUE
TRUE	FALSE	FALSE
FALSE	TRUE	FALSE
FALSE	FALSE	FALSE

Alpha	Beta	Alpha OR Beta
TRUE	TRUE	TRUE
TRUE	FALSE	TRUE
FALSE	TRUE	TRUE
FALSE	FALSE	FALSE

Alpha	NOT Alpha
TRUE	FALSE
FALSE	TRUE

Fig. 6-1. Truth tables for AND, OR, and NOT.

This example will evaluate as TRUE if the string variable **Answer** contains either the string 'YES' or the string 'Y' (if *either* expression within the parentheses evaluates as TRUE). Going one step further:

(Answer = 'YES') OR (Answer = 'Y') OR (Answer = 'SURE')

If any of the single expressions within the parentheses are TRUE, the entire complex expression will be evaluated as TRUE. In fact, your expression can be made up of as many smaller expressions as you like:

(EXP1) OR (EXP2) OR (EXP3) OR . . . OR (EXPn)

The same holds true for AND:

(EXP1) AND (EXP2) AND (EXP3) AND . . . AND (EXPn)

You must use parentheses to surround each expression in a complex expression. Uncle Pascal says: *Placing your potatoes in a sack will make for easier handling.*

Here is an example of using AND in a complex expression:

```
(FirstName = 'Seth') AND (Age = 34)
   AND (SocialSecurity = '555-66-7777')
```

This entire expression will only be evaluated as TRUE if *ALL* of the simple expressions within the parentheses are TRUE. Notice that even though this is a *single* expression, we split it up into two lines. It is fine to break *expressions* up into multiple lines.

Notice also that **Age** is an integer, whereas all the other variables are strings. However, we are not mixing variable types since each expression within the parentheses is evaluated separately as TRUE or FALSE. (Bet you thought you caught us in a contradiction!)

Let's put this last example into an **IF-THEN** statement:

```
IF (FirstName = 'Seth')
   AND (Age = 34)
   AND (SocialSecurity = '555-66-7777') THEN
      WRITELN('OK, Seth, you pass. Begin entering data.');
```

By surrounding the entire condition section of the above example with an additional set of parentheses, it too can be operated on:

```
                  beginning parenthesis
IF NOT ((FirstName = 'Seth')
   AND (Age = 34)
                                    ending parenthesis
   AND (SocialSecurity = '555-66-7777')) THEN
      BEGIN
      WRITELN('ILLEGAL ENTRY.');
      WRITELN('Someone is tampering with the data.');
      END;
```

The way the computer figures this one out is by evaluating the expressions starting with the one within the innermost set of parentheses and working its way out, level by level. In this example, there are three levels to be evaluated:

Level 1—the three expressions surrounded by the parentheses (e.g., (**FirstName** = 'Seth'), etc.)
Level 2—the Level 1 expressions connected by **AND**s
Level 3—the Level 2 expression operated on by **NOT**

If any of the Level 1 expressions are FALSE, then the Level 2 expression will also be FALSE. If the Level 2 expression is FALSE, then the Level 3 expression will be TRUE (the logical operator NOT operating on the level 2 expression yields the opposite value). If Level 3 is TRUE, then the Compound Statement will be executed.

Using Parentheses for "Precedence of Evaluation"

Parentheses are also used to make sure the computer evaluates the expression in the correct order. Let's say that we have a program that tabulates certain personal information about a certain group of people. And let's say we wanted to count the number of men who had been either married or had lived with someone (**LWS**) before. Consider the following two statements:

```
(A) IF (Sex = 'MALE') AND (Married > 0) OR (LWS > 0)
       THEN Counter1 := Counter1 + 1;

(B) IF (Sex = 'MALE') AND ((Married > 0) OR (LWS > 0))
       THEN Counter1 := Counter1 + 1;
```

These two statements will be evaluated differently because there is an extra set of parentheses in (B). What we really want the computer to do is to check to see if this person is a man, *then* check to see whether or not he has ever been married or lived with someone (if he has, the variables, **Married** or **LWS**, will be greater than zero). If so, then increment the counter by one.

Let's say that we were checking a woman who is married and lived with someone once before. The computer would evaluate statement (A) in the following way:

Level 1—Check each simple expression within the parentheses:

```
(Sex = 'MALE')  → FALSE

(Married > 0)   → TRUE

(LWS > 0)       → TRUE

IF (FALSE) AND (TRUE) OR (TRUE) THEN . . .
```

Level 2—Carry out the logical operations on the Level 1 results (use the previous truth tables):

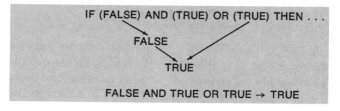

A FALSE ANDed with a TRUE yields a FALSE, but when this FALSE is ORed with a TRUE, the final result is TRUE.

Since this person is a woman, we want the statement to evaluate as FALSE regardless of the other data, so statement (A) will yield incorrect results.

When an extra set of parentheses are added, as in statement (B), the statement does what we want it to:

Level 1—Evaluate the **Married** and **LWS** variables:

```
              (Married > 0) → TRUE

              (LWS > 0)  →  TRUE

IF (SEX = 'MALE') AND ((TRUE) OR (TRUE)) THEN . . .
```

Level 2—Evaluate the **Sex** variable. Separately evaluate the results of Level 1:

```
       (Sex = 'MALE') → FALSE

IF (FALSE) AND ((TRUE) OR (TRUE)) THEN . . .
                        ↘      ↙
                        TRUE

           TRUE OR TRUE → TRUE
```

Level 3—AND the results of Level 2:

```
IF (FALSE) AND (TRUE) THEN . . .
         ↘        ↙
         FALSE

  FALSE AND TRUE → FALSE
```

Statement (B) works because we are no longer giving equal importance to all three expressions. What we have just demonstrated is called precedence of evaluation. *First the* **NOTs**, *then the* **ANDs**, *and finally the* **ORs** *will be evaluated in a Boolean expression unless parentheses are used to indicate that a specific section should be evaluated first.* When parentheses are used, the expression within the innermost set will be evaluated first.

Take a look at the following example:

```
IF (Sex = 'MALE') THEN
  IF (Married > 0) OR (LWS > 0) THEN
    Counter1 := Counter1 + 1;
```

The end result of this statement will be exactly the same as example (B). However, this example is probably more efficient simply because the computer doesn't have to waste its time evaluating the **Married** and **LWS** variables if the first part is FALSE—it will just drop down to the next statement. In example (B), *everything* in the statement had to be evaluated before the computer could make its decision.

IF-THEN-ELSE

This statement is actually a variation on **IF-THEN**. Its syntax is:

```
IF condition THEN statement1 ELSE statement2;
```

It says "if the condition is TRUE, then execute **statement1**, *otherwise* execute **statement2** (when the condition is FALSE)." *Either* **statement1** *or* **statement2** will be executed—never both, never neither. This gives us an alternative path to follow if the condition is FALSE (the **ELSE** section), whereas the "plain vanilla" **IF-THEN** "fell through" to the next statement when FALSE.

Again, the **condition** can be anything from a simple Boolean variable to a complex Boolean expression, and the **statements** (**1 and 2**) can be compound statements.

Notice that there is only one semicolon in the entire **IF-THEN-ELSE** statement and that it's located at the very end. *Do not place semicolons after* **statement1** *or you will get a compiler error.*

How Do We Use *IF-THEN-ELSE*

Let's say you were ordering a sandwich and could choose either wheat bread or rye bread. Listing 6-1 shows how a program could handle this situation.

Here are a couple of runs of this program:

```
(1) What kind of bread do you want on your
    sandwich, WHEAT or RYE? WHEAT

    One turkey on WHEAT, coming up--

(2) What kind of bread do you want on your
    sandwich, WHEAT or RYE? RYE

    Catch the Rye Bread, here it comes . . .
```

Pretty simple! If the person types WHEAT, the Wheat statement is executed, otherwise the Rye statement is executed. But, what happens if we have one of those customers who is picky and hard to please?

```
What kind of bread do you want on your
sandwich, WHEAT or RYE? PUMPERNICKEL

Catch the Rye Bread, here it comes . . .
```

The program can't handle that response. It assumes that if it isn't wheat, it's rye. In Listing 6-2 is a revised version of the program which corrects the problem.

And a run of the program:

Listing 6-1.

```
PROGRAM ChooseBread1;

VAR    BreadType : STRING;

BEGIN
  WRITELN('What kind of bread do you want on your');
  WRITE('  sandwich, WHEAT or RYE? ');
  READLN(BreadType);
  WRITELN;

  IF BreadType = 'WHEAT' THEN
    WRITELN('One turkey on WHEAT, coming up--')
  ELSE
    WRITELN('Catch the Rye Bread, here it comes...');
END. (* ChooseBread1 *)
```

```
What kind of bread do you want on your
  sandwich, WHEAT or RYE? PUMPERNICKEL

Sorry Bub, we're all out of PUMPERNICKEL
```

In this program, first the computer tries for a match with WHEAT. If it fails, it tries for a match with RYE. If it fails again, the "Sorry Bub ..." message is printed out. If there were more options to check out, we could just add more ELSEs:

```
IF condition1 THEN
   statement1
ELSE IF condition2 THEN
   statement2
ELSE IF condition3 THEN
   statement3
ELSE
   :
   :
   :
```

```
ELSE              ——semicolon at very end
   statementN;
```

Again, notice where in the **IF-THEN-ELSE** statement the semicolon is placed. There is only one of them and it is at the very end. Also, notice how we handled the indentation of this statement. Indenting it this way makes it easier to follow the logic.

Shown in Listing 6-3 is a program which uses compound statements in the **IF-THEN-ELSE** statements.

Here are three sample runs of the program from Listing 6-3:

```
(1)  Hello there good looking!
     What's your name? DONALD

     Oh, DONALD, it's been years!!!
```

Listing 6-2.

```
PROGRAM ChooseBread2;

VAR    BreadType : STRING;

BEGIN
  WRITELN('What kind of bread do you want on your');
  WRITE('  sandwich, WHEAT or RYE? ');
  READLN(BreadType);
  WRITELN;

  IF BreadType = 'WHEAT' THEN
    WRITELN('One turkey on WHEAT, coming up--')
  ELSE
    IF BreadType = 'RYE' THEN
      WRITELN('Catch the Rye Bread, here it comes...')
    ELSE
      WRITELN('Sorry Bub, we''re all out of ',BreadType);
END. (* ChooseBread2 *)
```

Listing 6-3.

```
(*===============================================*)
(*                                               *)
(* Program Language: PASCAL                      *)
(* Program Title: Advances                       *)
(* Subtitle:  How to use IF-THEN-ELSE to get your *)
(*            computer to be fresh to you.       *)
(*                                               *)
(* AUTHOR:    Annie Fox                          *)
(*            Pascal version by David Fox        *)
(*                                               *)
(* Program Summary:  Accepts data from the keyboard *)
(*            to use in making simple decisions. *)
(*                                               *)
(*===============================================*)



PROGRAM Advances;

VAR  Name : STRING;



PROCEDURE ClearScreen;

BEGIN
  PAGE(OUTPUT);
END; (* ClearScreen *)




PROCEDURE GetName;

BEGIN
  WRITELN('Hello there good looking!');
  WRITE('What''s your name? ');
  READLN(Name);
  ClearScreen;
  WRITELN('Oh, ',Name,', it''s been years!!!');
  WRITELN;
END; (* GetName *)
```

```
PROCEDURE GetEyecolor;
VAR    Eyecolor : STRING;

BEGIN
  WRITELN('Forgive me for forgetting, but what');
  WRITE('  color are your eyes? ');
  READLN(Eyecolor);
  ClearScreen;
  IF Eyecolor = 'BLUE' THEN
    BEGIN
      WRITELN('Ah, yes, ',Name,', they are as blue as');
      WRITELN('  the summer sky.');
    END
  ELSE
    IF Eyecolor = 'BROWN' THEN
      BEGIN
        WRITELN('AH, ',Name,', they are as lovely as');
        WRITELN(' brown velvet.');
      END
    ELSE
      BEGIN
        WRITELN('Of course, ',Name,', and very beautiful');
        WRITELN(Eyecolor,' eyes, I might add.');
      END;
  WRITELN;
END; (* GetEyecolor *)




PROCEDURE GetMaritalStatus;
VAR    Married : STRING;

BEGIN
  WRITELN('Tell me, my dear ',Name,',');
  WRITE('  are you married? ');
  READLN(Married);
  ClearScreen;
  WRITELN;
  WRITELN;
  IF Married = 'YES' THEN
    WRITELN('I might have known.....SIGH.')
  ELSE
    IF Married = 'NO' THEN
      WRITELN('OH HAPPY DAY!!!!!!!')
    ELSE
      BEGIN
        WRITELN('If you can''t make up your mind now, then');
        WRITELN('I''ll check back with you in 5 MINUTES!');
      END;
END; (* GetMaritalStatus *)
```

```
BEGIN (* Main Program *)
  ClearScreen;
  GetName;
  GetEyecolor;
  GetMaritalStatus;
END. (* Advances *)
```

Forgive me for forgetting, but what
  color are your eyes? BLUE

Ah, yes, DONALD, they are as blue as
  the summer sky.

Tell me, my dear DONALD,
  are you married? YES

I might have known.....SIGH.

(2) Hello there good looking!
    What's your name? HOPE

Oh, HOPE, it's been years!!!

Forgive me for forgetting, but what
color are your eyes? BROWN

Ah, HOPE, they are as lovely as
  brown velvet.

Tell me, my dear HOPE,
  are you married? NO

OH HAPPY DAY!!!!!!!

(3) Hello there good looking!
    What's your name? ELIZABETH

Oh, ELIZABETH, it's been years!!!

Forgive me for forgetting, but what
  color are your eyes? VIOLET

Of course, ELIZABETH, and very beautiful
  VIOLET eyes, I might add.

Tell me, my dear ELIZABETH,
  are you married? SOMETIMES

If you can't make up your mind now, then
I'll check back with you in 5 MINUTES.

The first two procedures are already familiar
to you. In the procedures, **GetEyeColor** and **Get-MaritalStatus**, we see a variation on the **Choose-Bread2** program. The main difference is that compound statements are used throughout. Once again, notice how semicolons are used in the **IF-THEN-ELSE** statement. The compound state-

ments have semicolons at the end of each statement (as always), but the delimiter, **END**, in these compound statements doesn't have semicolons following it—except for the last **END** in the statement, and its semicolon is really the semicolon that belongs at the very end of an **IF-THEN-ELSE** statement.

The variable **Name** is the only one which has to be global since it is used in more than one procedure. The other two variables are local since they are only used locally.

Take a look at this next statement and figure out how the computer will interpret it:

```
IF Reply = 'Y' THEN IF Sum = 0 THEN Sum := Sum +1
ELSE Sum := 0;
```

Does the **ELSE** belong to the first **IF-THEN** or the second **IF-THEN**? We didn't properly indent this statement to make the problem more obvious. Here are two possible ways of indenting this statement. Although both will execute exactly the same, only one of them clearly shows the correct logic flow:

```
(A) IF Reply = 'Y' THEN        (B) IF Reply = 'Y' THEN
      IF Sum = 0 THEN                IF Sum = 0 THEN
        Sum := Sum +1                  Sum := Sum + 1
    ELSE Sum := 0;                 ELSE Sum := 0;
```

The indentation in the second example (B) illustrates the logic flow more accurately. Just remember that **ELSE** always goes with the most recent **IF-THEN**.

Indent your programs to illustrate the logic flow. Uncle Pascal says: *He who pens his treasure map with closed eyes will find his way back to naught!*

METRIC CONVERSION PROGRAM

We will now introduce a practical application of **IF-THEN-ELSE**. We have all heard of the intended adoption of the Metric System of Measurement by the world at large. Many manufacturers of prepared food are printing both the English (the system we grew up with) and metric quantities on their products. Although this transition may seem to be difficult, there are many advantages to the metric system, which is always based upon the number 10. The measurements in the English system are not based on a number system but on tradition. Why are there 12 inches to a foot or 3 feet to a yard or 5,280 feet to a mile? We can guarantee that a group of scientists *did not* sit down together and create the English system as an experiment in logical thinking! The task of converting a length from yards to miles requires that two conversion factors be used. First, we must convert the length to feet, and then from feet to miles. The metric system, based on ten, allows very simple conversion of lengths either measured in centimeters, meters, or kilometers. All we need to do is to multiply or divide by a power of ten (10, 100, 1000, etc.) to perform the conversion. This then requires only that the decimal point be moved either to the right for multiplication, or to the left for division. For example, let us convert 500 meters to kilometers. First of all, we need to know the fact that 1 kilometer is equal to 1,000 meters. This is conveniently indicated by the prefix "kilo" meaning thousand. Therefore, to convert meters to kilometers, we simply divide by 1,000, or move the decimal point three places to the left. So, 500 meters is equal to .500 kilometer, or exactly half a kilometer.

During the worldwide struggle to convert from the English system to the metric system, the major problem is that the new units don't seem to have the inherent "sense" that the old ones did. How long *is* half a kilometer? Being conditioned to the old concepts of feet, yards, and miles, we find it hard to conceive of half a kilometer. But this is only due to our being unfamiliar with the metric terms. The children who are being brought up on metric would think that the *English* system didn't have any "inherent sense." With a little practice, we can easily adapt to the metric system. In the meantime, we can use Pascal to write a simple program that converts the English measurements which we are now using to metric measurements (Listing 6-4).

There are essentially three main parts to this program: the section which displays the menu (**MenuDisplay**), the section which accepts your selection (**Selection**), and the section which does the actual conversions (actually three procedures, **InchesToCentimeters**, **PoundsToKilograms**, **QuartsToLiters**).

Creating Constants

First, take a look at the beginning of the three procedures, **InchesToCentimeters, PoundsToKilo-** grams, and **QuartsToLiters**. You'll see a new keyword there called **CONST**. The **CONST**ant declaration does two jobs at once—it *declares* a constant name (which will be used in the block in which it is declared) and then assigns this constant a "permanent" value. A **CONST**ant will retain its value for the life of the program—its value cannot be changed once it is assigned. The constant declarations are always located after the block name and before the **VAR**iables are declared (if you have any variables). This means they can be global for the entire program or local, just as variables can be. Constants can be used wherever variables or values are used. There are some definite advantages to using constants:

1. It improves program legibility to see a name throughout the program (using **Pi** is clearer than using 3.14159).
2. If you want to *change* the value of a constant, it is much easier to make one edit at the beginning of the program (or block) than to search through the whole program to change a number each time that it occurs.
3. You know exactly where to look if you want to find out what the value of the constant is (at the beginning of the block).

Here is the format for constants:

```
CONST   Name1 = value;
        Name2 = value;
          :
        NameN = value;
```

Note that we use an equal sign here rather than the assigned symbol (:=). This is because we really are making the constant *equal* to its value. From the point of declaration on, the constant *is* the value—we just changed its name. The value can be an **INTEGER**, a **REAL**, a **CHAR**, a **STRING**, or **BOOLEAN**.

When should you use constants? Whenever any of the following conditions are met:

1. The clarity of a program needs to be improved.
2. The value will be used frequently in the program.
3. You plan to edit your program to *change* the value at a future date.
4. The value will remain "constant" throughout the program.

In our metric conversion program, we used constants to improve the clarity of the program.

Listing 6-4.

```
(*=================================================*)
(*                                                 *)
(* Program Language: Pascal                        *)
(* Program Title: Metric Conversion Program #1     *)
(* Subtitle:  Program to convert from English to   *)
(*            Metric units.                        *)
(*                                                 *)
(* Author:     Mitch Waite / David Fox             *)
(* Program Summary:  Demonstrates the use of a menu*)
(*            using IF-THEN, introduces CONSTants   *)
(*                                                 *)
(*=================================================*)


PROGRAM MetricConversion1;


PROCEDURE ClearScreen;

BEGIN
  PAGE(OUTPUT);
END; (* ClearScreen *)



PROCEDURE Continue;
VAR    Cont : STRING;

BEGIN
  GOTOXY(6,22);
  WRITE('Press "RETURN" to continue: ');
  READLN(Cont);
  ClearScreen;
END;  (* Continue *)




PROCEDURE InchesToCentimeters;
CONST   CentConst = 2.54;        (* CONSTants come before VARiables *)
VAR     Inches, Centimeters : REAL;

BEGIN
  ClearScreen;
  GOTOXY(9,2);
  WRITELN('INCHES TO CENTIMETERS');
  GOTOXY(0,5);
  WRITE('Enter length in inches: ');
  READLN(Inches);
  Centimeters := CentConst * Inches;
  WRITELN;
  WRITELN(Inches:7:3,' inches is equal to');
  WRITELN(Centimeters:7:3,' centimeters.');
  Continue;
END;  (* InchesToCentimeters *)
```

```
PROCEDURE PoundsToKilograms;
CONST   KiloConst = 0.4536;
VAR     Pounds, Kilograms : REAL;

  BEGIN
    ClearScreen;
    GOTOXY(10,2);
    WRITELN('POUNDS TO KILOGRAMS');
    GOTOXY(0,5);
    WRITE('Enter weight in pounds: ');
    READLN(Pounds);
    Kilograms := KiloConst * Pounds;
    WRITELN;
    WRITELN(Pounds:7:3,' pounds is equal to');
    WRITELN(Kilograms:7:3,' kilograms.');
    Continue;
END;  (* PoundsToKilograms *)




PROCEDURE QuartsToLiters;
CONST   LiterConst = 0.9463;
VAR     Quarts, Liters : REAL;

BEGIN
    ClearScreen;
    GOTOXY(12,2);
    WRITELN('QUARTS TO LITERS');
    GOTOXY(0,5);
    WRITE('Enter volume in quarts: ');
    READLN(Quarts);
    Liters := LiterConst * Quarts;
    WRITELN;
    WRITELN(Quarts:7:3,' quarts is equal to');
    WRITELN(Liters:7:3,' liters.');
    Continue;
END;  (* QuartsToLiters *)




PROCEDURE MenuDisplay;

BEGIN
    ClearScreen;
    GOTOXY(5,2);
    WRITELN('* METRIC CONVERSION PROGRAM *');
    GOTOXY(0,6);
    WRITELN('1 - Inches to Centimeters');
    WRITELN('2 - Pounds to Kilograms');
    WRITELN('3 - Quarts to Liters');
    WRITELN;
    WRITELN('0 - To END the program');
END;  (* MenuDisplay *)
```

```
PROCEDURE Selection;
VAR      Select : CHAR;

BEGIN
   GOTOXY(0,12);
   WRITE('Enter your selection: ');
   READ(Select);

   IF Select = '1'  THEN InchesToCentimeters
      ELSE IF Select = '2'  THEN PoundsToKilograms
         ELSE IF Select = '3'  THEN QuartsToLiters;
END;  (* Selection *)



BEGIN  (* Main Program *)
   MenuDisplay;
   Selection;

   ClearScreen;
   GOTOXY(13,7);
   WRITELN('Bye for now...');
END.  (* MetricConversion1 *)
```

How the Program Works

First, let's look at a sample run of the program:

```
       * METRIC CONVERSION PROGRAM *



  1 - Inches to Centimeters
  2 - Pounds to Kilograms
  3 - Quarts to Liters

  0 - To END the program

  Enter your selection: 2
```

```
             POUNDS TO KILOGRAMS


  Enter weight in pounds: 126

  126.000 pounds is equal to
  57.154 kilograms.



            Press "RETURN" to continue: []
```

```




             Bye for now . . .
```

The first procedure called by the program is the **MenuDisplay** procedure. It clears the screen and displays a *menu of choices*, much like a restaurant menu does.

The next procedure is the **Selection** procedure. This procedure is the "waitress" of the program. It "takes your order" and sends it on to the "chef." This waitress is a little rude, however. If you don't make a proper selection on the menu, she turns her back and walks away (the program ends). Actually, she could be much worse. If the variable **Select** were an **INTEGER** variable and you entered a letter, she would probably dump a glass of water in your lap (the program would bomb) before she walked away. She *is* efficient enough to accept your request without your having to type in the entire name. And you don't even have to press RETURN. Typing the appropriate number is all that is necessary (remember **READ** and **CHAR** variables?). We'll provide a waitress with more class in the **REPEAT-UNTIL** section of the next chapter.

Once you make your choice, the waitress will call out your order to the chef (call the appropriate conversion procedure). This is a very special chef—he not only comes to your table and asks for your ingredients before he makes the dish (accepts the value to be converted), but he delivers your meal to you (prints out the answer)! You'll notice that the only differences between the three conversion procedures are:

1. The title printed at the top of the screen.
2. The constants which are used.
3. The prompts asking you for your input.

The structure of each is identical. After the screen is cleared and the heading is centered near the top, you are prompted to enter the value to be converted. This value is then multiplied by the conversion constant. The result is displayed on the screen. Note the formatting of the **REAL** variables in the **WRITELN** statements. Finally, the procedure **Continue** is called. It waits for you to press RETURN, then clears the screen. The "waitress" then comes back and says good-bye.

To add additional conversion choices is fairly simple; just update the menu display and selection procedures with the new choice, and add a new procedure to do the conversion.

QUIZ

True or False

1. There are three possible values the condition in the *IF-THEN* statement can take—TRUE, FALSE, and SOMETIMES.

2. A condition can be a single variable or a complex Boolean expression.

3. When a condition is made up of a series of Boolean expressions, Pascal will evaluate them in the order they are written.

4. There is no way to change the order in which Pascal evaluates a complex Boolean expression.

5. The only way to tell which *IF-THEN* a certain *ELSE* is referring to is by looking at the way the statement is indented.

chapter **7**

Further Control

The three statements that we will introduce in this chapter, *WHILE, REPEAT-UNTIL,* and *CASE,* have no exact equivalents in most BASICs. Having these statements makes Pascal more flexible when working with program control. First, we will cover two statements which allow you to use Boolean expressions to control the repetition of a series of statements.

THE *WHILE* STATEMENT

Using **WHILE** in your program will allow you to have a statement (or series of statements) repeat *while* a certain condition is TRUE. The syntax is:

```
WHILE condition DO
   statement;
```

The condition is a Boolean value and can be a Boolean variable or a Boolean expression. All the rules for conditions which we described in the **IF-THEN** section of Chapter 6 are valid here. Of course, the **statement** can be a compound statement.

Listing 7-1 shows a program in which **WHILE** is used to make the computer count from 1 to 100. Unfortunately, if you try to execute this program, you will have to trust your computer to count all the way to 100 by itself—nothing will appear on your screen except the message 'Done . . .' because the variable, **Count**, is never printed out. In Listing 7-2 is the same program but with a compound statement. This program will, of course, print out the numbers from 1 to 100 so you can keep your computer honest. We won't show you how this program looks on execution—you may try it out for yourself.

WHILE Explained

Here are the steps the computer went through when in **WhileDemo2**:

1. **Count** is initially set to 1.
2. The **WHILE** statement checks the current value of **Count**. If the condition is TRUE (**Count** is less than or equal to (<=) 100), then the compound statement is executed once. If the condition is FALSE (**Count** is greater than 100), then the program falls through to the next statement (the 'Done . . .' message gets printed out).
3. During the execution of the compound statement, the value of **Count** is written to the screen and then **Count** is incremented by 1.
4. Back to Step 2 to check the condition **again**.

There is a major difference between the **WHILE** and the **FOR** statements. In the **FOR** statement, the **control value, initial value,** and **final value** *must not be changed by the statement section.* In the **WHILE** statement, the value(s) in the condition section *must* be modified in the statement section. Consider the following program fragment:

```
READLN(Number);
WHILE (Number > 0) AND (Number < 10) DO
   BEGIN
      Sum := Sum + 5;
      WRITELN(Sum);
   END;
```

If **Number** isn't between 0 and 10, the compound statement will not be executed because the condition is FALSE. However, let's say the user enters the number 7. Now the condition is TRUE and the compound statement will be executed. But since

85

the value of **Number** is not affected by the compound statement, the condition will *remain* TRUE and the compound statement will execute forever or until the electric company turns off your power or you reset your computer, whichever comes first. This is called an "endless loop" for obvious reasons.

Here is another example:

```
READLN(HalfStep);
WHILE HalfStep > 0.0 DO
```

Listing 7-1.

```
PROGRAM WhileDemo1;

VAR    Count : INTEGER;

BEGIN
  Count := 1;

  WHILE Count <= 100 DO
    Count := Count + 1;

  WRITELN('Done...');
END.  (* WhileDemo1 *)
```

```
BEGIN
  HalfStep := HalfStep + 0.5;
  WRITELN(HalfStep:7:1);
END;
```

In this case, the value of the variable in the condition, the **REAL** variable **HalfStep**, *is* changed in the compound statement. *But*, **HalfStep** has to be

Listing 7-2.

```
PROGRAM WhileDemo2;

VAR    Count : INTEGER;

BEGIN
  Count := 1;

  WHILE Count <= 100 DO
    BEGIN
      WRITELN(Count);
      Count := Count + 1;
    END; (* WHILE *)

  WRITELN('Done...');
END.  (* WhileDemo2 *)
```

greater than zero for the compound statement to execute, and continuously adding 0.5 to **HalfStep** (which is what the compound statement does) will never make it into a negative number. So, if the condition ever evaluates as TRUE, we fall into another endless loop! *Changing the value of the variable isn't enough. You must make sure that the condition will eventually evaluate as FALSE!* It is important, therefore, to mentally run through the logic of your **WHILE** statements to see if it really does what you want it to, and to check for possible endless loops.

Check the logic of your **WHILE** statements for possible endless loops or you may run into "recurring" problems. Uncle Pascal says: *If the dog always knocks over the garbage can, then don't put him out with the garbage!*

REPEAT-UNTIL—LOOKING AT IT FROM THE OTHER DIRECTION

This statement is very similar to the **WHILE** statement. It tells the computer to **REPEAT** a number of statements **UNTIL** a specific condition is TRUE. Here are the two major differences between **WHILE** and **REPEAT-UNTIL**:

WHILE	**REPEAT-UNTIL**
Check to see if condition is TRUE *before* the statement section is executed.	Check to see if condition is TRUE *after* the statement section is executed.
Repeat *while* the condition is TRUE.	Repeat *until* the condition is TRUE.

This means that a **REPEAT-UNTIL** statement will always cycle through the loop *at least once* since the condition isn't checked until the *end* of the cycle. A **WHILE** statement may not cycle through at all.

Here is a format of the **REPEAT-UNTIL** statement:

```
REPEAT statement-1;statement-2; . . .
    statement-n;UNTIL condition;
```

Or, more clearly, with indentation:

```
REPEAT
    statement-1;
    statement-2;
         :
         :
    statement-n;
UNTIL condition;
```

You'll notice that the **REPEAT-UNTIL** statement allows for multiple statements *without* having to use the **BEGIN ... END** format of the compound statement. This is because the words **REPEAT** and **UNTIL** bracket the statements and leave no room for doubt as to what is to be repeated. If you use **BEGIN** and **END** within a **REPEAT-UNTIL** statement, you will *not* get an error:

```
REPEAT
  BEGIN
       :
       :
       :
  END
UNTIL condition;
```

but doing so would be redundant.

Listing 7-3 presents a version of the **While-Demo-2** (Listing 7-2) program to count from 1 to 100 using **REPEAT-UNTIL**.

Listing 7-3.

```
PROGRAM RepeatUntilDemo;

VAR    Count : INTEGER;

BEGIN
  Count := 1;

  REPEAT
    WRITELN(Count);
    Count := Count + 1;
  UNTIL Count > 100;

  WRITELN('Done...');
END.  (* RepeatUntilDemo *)
```

And here are the steps the computer goes through in this program:

1. Initialize **Count** to 1.
2. Output the value of **Count** to the screen.
3. Increment **Count** by 1.
4. Check to see if the condition in the **UNTIL** line is TRUE (**Count** > 100). If so, then fall through and execute the next statement (**WRITELN('Done...');**), otherwise, go back to Step 2).

As with the **WHILE** statement, you must watch out for the endless loop which will occur if the condition can't become **TRUE**.

REVISING THE METRIC PROGRAM

Do you remember our impertinent waitress from the last chapter? We will now replace her with a polite, efficient waitress who can't be fooled. In Listing 7-4 is the revised portion of the Metric Conversion Program. Refer to Listing 6-4 to see the original version.

First, we added a CONSTant called **Conversions** at the top of the program. This global constant is set to the number of different conversions our program will currently do. Also notice that this constant is not a number but a **CHAR**acter. This is so we can compare it with the character (stored in **Select**) which the user will enter in the **Selection** procedure. We moved **Select** from a local variable within **Selection** to a global variable because it will be accessed in the main program section—we want to extend the "domain" in which this variable is defined.

Now look at the Selection procedure. We added a **BOOLEAN** variable, **ErrorClear**, to let us know if the input was free of errors. Let's follow this procedure's logic:

1. Position the cursor at the beginning of the 13th line.
2. Begin the **REPEAT-UNTIL** loop.
3. Print the prompt line and accept a single character input using **READ**.
4. Check to see whether the character entered is outside the acceptable range.
   a. If it is then reposition the cursor at the beginning of the 13th line, print 'Try again. ', and set **ErrorClear** to FALSE.
   b. Otherwise, set **ErrorClear** to TRUE— the character entered is a legal response and we are "clear of errors."
5. Next comes the condition checking part of the **REPEAT-UNTIL** statement.
   a. If the user didn't press a correct letter, the **ErrorClear** variable will have been set to FALSE and the prompt will be repeated (back to Step 3).
   b. Otherwise, **ErrorClear** will be TRUE, the **REPEAT-UNTIL** loop will be terminated, and the following **IF-THEN-ELSE** statement will be executed.

This **Selection** procedure is the first of many examples we will be giving you which illustrate

Listing 7-4.

```
PROGRAM MetricConversion2;

CONST    Conversions = '3';         (* Number of different conversions
                                       this program will currently do. *)
VAR      Select : CHAR;



(*                              :                              *)
(*                              :                              *)
(*          This part of program is the same as before         *)
(*                              :                              *)
(*                              :                              *)



PROCEDURE Selection;
VAR     ErrorClear : BOOLEAN;

BEGIN
  GOTOXY(0,12);
  REPEAT
    WRITE('Your selection, please: ');
    READ(Select);
    IF (Select < '0') OR (Select > Conversion) THEN
      BEGIN
        GOTOXY(0,12);                (* Error Checking routine -      *)
        WRITE('Try again.  ');       (* any key may be pressed here;  *)
        ErrorClear := FALSE;         (* the program won't go on until *)
      END                            (* there is a legal input.       *)
      ELSE ErrorClear := TRUE;
  UNTIL ErrorClear;

  IF Select = '1' THEN InchesToCentimeters
    ELSE IF Select = '2' THEN PoundsToKilograms
      ELSE IF Select = '3' THEN QuartsToLiters;
END; (* Selection *)



BEGIN  (* Main Program *)
  REPEAT                             (* Loop until a 0 is pressed. *)
    MenuDisplay;
    Selection;
  UNTIL Select = '0';

  ClearScreen;
  GOTOXY(13,7);
  WRITELN('Bye for now...');
END. (* MetricConversion2 *)
```

user-oriented, errorproof entry of data. This procedure has a number of important features:

1. It allows the user to press one key for the input. No RETURN is needed.
2. The program will not proceed until a looked-for response is entered (error checking).
3. It has cursor control to avoid having the screen fill up with the same error message.
4. It doesn't invalidate the user for experimenting with unasked for answers. It corrects the user with a polite error message (not 'HEY DUMMY, YOU BLEW IT!')
5. It presents the computer in a very personable, friendly way.

We think computers have had enough bad PR already and plan to do whatever we can to improve their manners.

We also added a **REPEAT-UNTIL** loop in the main program section. The program will now continue to ask you for conversions until you press '0' in the **Selection** procedure.

Unfortunately, the entire program is still not bombproof. Our chef (the conversion procedures) will throw his knife at you if you enter anything but a number, and he will *not* allow you to change your mind (back-space) during entry. We plan to remedy this by hiring a new cook in Chapter 9 who can show your programs how to accept *all* numeric inputs as **STRING**s, check them for correctness, and *then* convert these **STRING**s to numbers.

GOTO WHERE?

By now, you are probably wondering if there is an unconditional branching statement like BASIC's "GOTO linenumber" statement. Yes, there is, but we aren't going to cover it in this book. The GOTO statement is one of structured programming's worst potential enemies. It is all too easy to obscure a program's logic flow by adding a bunch of GOTOs. You will soon discover that in almost all cases, you can write your programs using the flow of control statements we have just introduced to you and not even need GOTO. But be prepared for the infamous symptoms of "GOTO withdrawal" (e.g., the thoughts: "BASIC is so much easier," "Who cares about structured programming anyway?," or "N. Wirth, GOTO ___"). This dreaded disease can be alleviated with two aspirins and a little extra thought applied towards your program.

CASE: AN EASIER WAY TO MAKE MULTIPLE CHOICES

For those of you who think that using a long **IF-THEN-ELSE-IF-THEN-ELSE-IF-THEN-ELSE** ... statement (like the one in the Metric Conversion program, Listings 6-4 and 7-4) is rather unwieldy, we have a present for you. It is the **CASE** statement. **CASE** is used when you want to execute *one* statement out of a list of statements, in some ways similar to BASIC's ON X GOSUB 100, 200, 300. Let's explain **CASE** through an example. Look at the program in Listing 7-5.

Here is a run of this program:

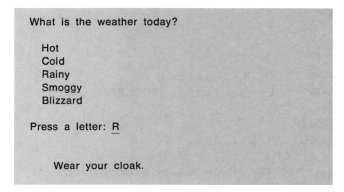

```
What is the weather today?

    Hot
    Cold
    Rainy
    Smoggy
    Blizzard

Press a letter: R


    Wear your cloak.
```

As you can see, pressing the first letter of one of the words on the menu will result in the computer printing out the appropriate "dressing instructions." An equivalent **IF-THEN-ELSE** statement would be:

```
IF Weather = 'H' THEN
   WRITELN('Wear your shorts.')
ELSE IF Weather = 'C' THEN
   WRITELN('Wear your fur coat.')
ELSE IF Weather = 'R' THEN
   WRITELN('Wear your cloak.')
ELSE IF Weather = 'S' THEN
   WRITELN('Wear your gas mask.')
ELSE IF Weather = 'B' THEN
   WRITELN('STAY HOME!!');
```

Most people would much rather play with **CASE** than mess around with the mess above! Using the **CASE** statement makes the logic much easier to follow.

In our example program, the variable **Weather** is called the **case-index** and the characters 'H,' 'C,' 'R,' 'S,' and 'B' are called the **case-constants**. When the **CASE** statement is executed, Pascal looks for a **case-constant** which has the same value as the **case-index** and executes the statement to the right of the matched **case-constant**.

The general format for **CASE** is:

```
CASE case-index OF
    case-constant : statement;
    case-constant : statement;
              :
              :
    case-constant : statement;
END;
```

where the **case-index** can either be an ordinal variable (**CHAR**, **INTEGER**, or **BOOLEAN**), or an expression which reduces to an ordinal variable (e.g., $i + 5$)—it can't be a **STRING** or a **REAL**. As we said, the **case-constants** are the possible *values* that the **case-index** can have. These values can be declared **CONST**ants but they can't be variables. There can be *no duplication* of values among the **case-constants.** Of course, the statement to the right of a **case-constant** can be a compound statement.

An END With No Beginning? Notice that the **CASE** statement is terminated with an **END**. This is one of the only places in Pascal where an **END** is used without a matching **BEGIN**. This means that you will not have an equal number of **BEGIN**s and **END**s in your program if you are using **CASE** statements. You may need to remember this while you are debugging your programs and trying to match the number of **BEGIN**s to the number of **END**s.

Protection Against Crashed CASEs

In UCSD Pascal, if the value of the **case-index** *doesn't* appear in any of the **case-constants**, the statement *following* the **CASE** statement will be executed. However, this condition is "undefined" in standard Pascal. In many versions of Pascal this occurrence will result in a run-time error, a crashed program, or Uncle Pascal knows *what!* Therefore, it is usually a good idea to make sure that the **case-index** will *always* be one of the expected values if you want your program to be transportable to other versions of Pascal.

You'll notice that the program **CaseDemo1** is *not* crashproof for versions of Pascal which require a match of the **case-index** and the **case-constant.** For example, if the user pressed a 'Z,' the program could bomb. Here are a few of the ways this problem can be corrected:

Listing 7-5.

```
PROGRAM CaseDemo1;

VAR    Weather : CHAR;

BEGIN
  PAGE(OUTPUT);            (* Clear the screen *)
  WRITELN('What is the weather today? ');
  WRITELN;
  WRITELN('   Hot');
  WRITELN('   Cold');
  WRITELN('   Rainy');
  WRITELN('   Smoggy');
  WRITELN('   Blizzard');
  WRITELN;
  WRITE('Press a letter: ');
  READ(Weather);
  GOTOXY(5,15);

  CASE Weather OF
    'H' : WRITELN('Wear your shorts.');
    'C' : WRITELN('Wear your fur coat.');
    'R' : WRITELN('Wear your cloak.');
    'S' : WRITELN('Wear your gas mask!');
    'B' : WRITELN('STAY HOME!!');
  END;  (* CASE *)

END.  (* CaseDemo1 *)
```

Listing 7-6.

```
PROGRAM CaseDemo2;
VAR    n : INTEGER;

BEGIN
  REPEAT
    WRITELN;
    WRITELN('Enter an integer between 1 and 9');
    WRITE('   (0 to quit): ');
    READLN(n);
    IF (n < 0) OR (n > 9) THEN n := 10;   (* Make sure n is valid *)

    CASE n OF
      1,3,5,7,9 : WRITELN('That was an odd number.');
      2,4,6,8   : WRITELN('That was an even number.');
      10        : WRITELN('That number was out of range.');
      0         : ; (* Empty statement *)
    END;  (* CASE *)

  UNTIL n = 0;

  WRITELN('BYE...');
END.  (* CaseDemo2 *)
```

1. Use the **REPEAT-UNTIL** solution we offered in the last section to repeatedly ask the question until a proper response to it is given.
2. Use an **IF-THEN** statement to check the values of the **case-index**—if the value is legal then execute the **CASE** statement:

```
IF (Digit > 0) AND (Digit < 9) THEN
    CASE Digit OF
        :
        :
    END;
```

This **CASE** statement will only execute if **Digit** is from 1 to 8.

3. Check the values with an **IF-THEN**. If they don't match any of the **case-constants** then set the **case-index** to a preset error value which *is* one of the **case-constants** (see Case-Demo2, Listing 7-6).
4. Have very complete lists of **case-constants**!

Listing 7-6 shows an example using method three. Here is a run of this program:

```
Enter an integer between 1 and 9
   (0 to quit): 3
That was an odd number.

Enter an integer between 1 and 9
   (0 to quit): 8
That was an even number.

Enter an integer between 1 and 9
```

```
   (0 to quit): —1233                  n is set to 10
That number was out of range.

Enter an integer between 1 and 9
   (0 to quit): 0
BYE . . .
```

The first thing you'll probably notice about this program is that there is more than one **case-constant** on each line (separated by commas). These are called **case-constant-lists** or **ccls** for short. If the **case-index** matches any constant in a **ccl**, the statement to the right is executed. The **IF-THEN** before the **CASE** statement will check if the number entered (**n**) is outside the requested range (between 1 and 9). If it is, **n** is set to 10. Then we include 10 as one of the **case-constants** followed by an error message. There is an answer for any **INTEGER** which can be entered. Notice the use of an "empty statement" to the right of the **case-constant** 0.

CASE AND BOOLEANs

Here is a program which uses a **BOOLEAN** **case-index** and **case-constants**. It also introduces another built-in routine which tells you whether an **INTEGER** is odd or not. Here is the format of the routine:

$$b := ODD(n)$$

where **b** is a **BOOLEAN** variable, and **n** is an **INTEGER**. This routine will return the Boolean

Listing 7-7.

```
PROGRAM CaseDemo3;
VAR   n : INTEGER;
      Boo : BOOLEAN;

BEGIN
  REPEAT
    WRITELN;
    WRITE('Enter an integer (0 to quit): ');
    READLN(n);

    Boo := ODD(n);          (* Function will return a TRUE if
                                n is odd, otherwise a FALSE    *)
    CASE Boo OF
      TRUE  : WRITELN('That was an odd number.');
      FALSE : WRITELN('That was an even number.');
    END;  (* CASE *)

  UNTIL n = 0;
  WRITELN('So long...');
END.  (* CaseDemo3 *)
```

value TRUE if **n** is an odd number. Otherwise, it returns a FALSE. Of course, since there are only two possible values for a **BOOLEAN** variable, we have all the bases covered in the program shown in Listing 7-7.

And a run of this program:

```
Enter an integer (0 to quit): 325
That was an odd number.

Enter an integer (0 to quit): -2146
That was an even number.

Enter an integer (0 to quit): 0
That was an even number.
So long . . .
```

THE METRIC CONVERSION PROGRAM ONCE AGAIN

Finally, in Listing 7-8 is shown another modification of the Metric Conversion program from Chapter 6 (Listings 6-4 and 7-4). We rewrote the **IF-THEN-ELSE** portion of the **Selection** procedure to make use of the **CASE** statement.

The output of this procedure will look exactly the same as it was before we added **CASE**. However, it is easier to follow now, especially if you add more conversion choices to the program. In addition to increased clarity, the **CASE** statement will execute faster (in most cases) than multiple **IF-THEN-ELSE** statements.

QUIZ

True or False

1. A WHILE loop will always cycle through at least once.

2. You must always make sure that the value of WHILE's condition section changes to FALSE during execution of the loop.

3. A REPEAT-UNTIL loop will always cycle through at least once.

4. It is necessary to use a BEGIN and an END within a REPEAT-UNTIL loop.

5. The case-index of a CASE statement can be a STRING.

6. The case-index and the ccls must be of the same type.

7. It is necessary to make sure there is a match between the case-index and one constant in the ccls.

Listing 7-8.

```
CASE Select OF
   '1' :  InchesToCentimeters;
   '2' :  PoundsToKilograms;
   '3' :  QuartsToLiters;
   '0' :  (* Dummy value to exit *);
END;  (* CASE *)
```

chapter 8

Procedures (The Second Time Around) and Functions

In this chapter, we will take a second look at PROCEDUREs and see how to make them even more useful. We will also look at some of Pascal's "intrinsic functions" (functions that are already built into the language) and how to write our own functions.

PROCEDURES ONCE AGAIN . . .

So far, we have only shown one way in which to allow different procedures to "talk" to each other—that is, to pass data to each other. This is by making use of global variables. If a variable is global to two different procedures, both procedures can access the variable, receive the data from the variable, and even change the value of the variable. However, as we said, there is one major problem with using global variables as the communication channels between procedures —the old "modify-a-program-and-get-a-remote-bug" problem. It is all too easy to alter the value of a global variable in such a way as to cause unpredictable results elsewhere in the program —if our global variable has an undelivered message from procedure Beta to procedure Alpha and, in the meantime, procedure Delta makes a change in the variable's value (not knowing it was "busy"), procedure Alpha would get the wrong message, and the poor programmer would have a mess to unravel.

By now you probably guessed that we must be ready to introduce a new tool to help with this problem. Indeed, we are. . . .

Parameters—The Procedure Messengers

There are two types of parameters—**value parameters** and **variable parameters**. The *value parameter** is the Western Union messenger of Pascal. It takes a value (or values) and sends it to a procedure at the time that procedure is called, but it doesn't wait for an answer to take back to the sender. It handles "one-way" communications only.

ParamDemo1 in Listing 8-1 is a sample program using value parameters. And here is a run of the program:

```
Enter a sentence (press RETURN to end)
: Can I have a piece of gum?

Can I have a piece of gum?
Can I have a piece of gum?
Can I have a piece of gum?
Can I have a piece of gum?
Can I have a piece of gum?
Can I have a piece of gum?
Can I have a piece of gum?
Can I have a piece of gum?
Can I have a piece of gum?
Can I have a piece of gum?

Enter a sentence (press RETURN to end)
:
```
———— *RETURN pressed here*

First look at the Main Program section. By initializing the **STRING** variable **Sentence** to one space, the **WHILE** statement will cycle through at least once. Look at how we are calling the procedure **RepeatPhrase**. We are placing the variable **Sentence** inside parentheses. **Sentence** is the *parameter* we are passing to **RepeatPhrase**. This is called the *actual parameter* because it is the value actually passed to the procedure. Now look

———
* Also called "pass-by-value" or "call-by-value" parameters.

Listing 8-1.

```
PROGRAM ParamDemo1;
VAR    Sentence : STRING;

PROCEDURE RepeatPhrase(Line : STRING);
VAR    i : INTEGER;

BEGIN
  IF Line <> ''  THEN              (* Don't print if null string *)
    FOR i := 1 TO 10 DO
      WRITELN(Line);
END;  (* RepeatPhrase *)


BEGIN  (* Main Program *)
  Sentence := ' ';                 (* Initialize to one space    *)
  WHILE Sentence <> '' DO          (* Continue until null string *)
    BEGIN
      WRITELN;
      WRITELN('Enter a sentence (press RETURN to end)');
      WRITE(': ');
      READLN(Sentence);
      WRITELN;
      RepeatPhrase(Sentence);
    END;  (* WHILE *)
END.  (* ParamDemo1 *)
```

at **RepeatPhrase**. To the right of the procedure name is what is called a *parameter list*. It's the list of variables which will "take on" the value(s) of the actual parameters. In this example, the variable **Line** is called the *value parameter*. It receives the value that is in the variable **Sentence** when **RepeatPhrase** is called. The type of the variable is also declared in the parameter list, and it must be of the same type as the actual parameter. The variables in the parameter list are also called *formal parameters*—they will "formally" represent the values sent to them in this procedure.

So, what we have here is the Main Program section sending a string value to the **RepeatPhrase** procedure. This string value is then stored in the local string variable **Line** which is a formal parameter. After this variable is printed 10 times, we return to the Main Program section and repeat the process as long as the user enters strings from the keyboard. When the user enters an "empty string" by pressing just RETURN, the **RepeatPhrase** procedure will not execute the **FOR** loop (because of the **IF-THEN** statement checking for these empty strings), the expression in the **WHILE** loop will be FALSE, and the program will end.

One-Way Communication

We said that the value parameter is used for one-way communication. Let's make a couple of changes in our program and test this (Listing 8-2). In **RepeatPhrase**, we are setting the value of **Line** to 'Done' after the **FOR** loop. Then in the Main Program section, we print out the contents of **Sentence** after **RepeatPhrase** is called. Here is a run of the modified program:

```
Enter a sentence (press RETURN to end)
: Sure, here's a piece for you.

Sure, here's a piece for you.
Sure, here's a piece for you.
Sure, here's a piece for you.
Sure, here's a piece for you.
Sure, here's a piece for you.
Sure, here's a piece for you.
Sure, here's a piece for you.
Sure, here's a piece for you.
Sure, here's a piece for you.
Sure, here's a piece for you.
Again: Sure, here's a piece for you.

Enter a sentence (press RETURN to end)
:                                    ── RETURN pressed
Again:
```

Listing 8-2.

```
PROGRAM ParamDemo2;
VAR     Sentence : STRING;

PROCEDURE RepeatPhrase(Line : STRING);
VAR    i : INTEGER;

BEGIN
   IF Line <> '' THEN              (* Don't print if null string *)
     FOR i := 1 TO 10 DO
        WRITELN(Line);
   Line := 'Done';
END;  (* Print *)


BEGIN  (* Main Program *)
   Sentence := ' ';                (* Initialize to one space    *)
   WHILE Sentence <> '' DO         (* Continue until null string *)
     BEGIN
        WRITELN;
        WRITELN('Enter a sentence (press RETURN to end)');
        WRITE(': ');
        READLN(Sentence);
        WRITELN;
        RepeatPhrase(Sentence);
        WRITELN('Again: ',Sentence);
     END;  (* WHILE *)
END.   (* ParamDemo2 *)
```

Listing 8-3.

```
PROGRAM ParamDemo3;
VAR    Sentence : STRING;
          Number : INTEGER;

PROCEDURE RepeatPhrase(Line : STRING; Number : INTEGER);
VAR    i : INTEGER;

BEGIN
  FOR i := 1 TO Number DO
    WRITELN(i,' ',Line);
END;  (* Print *)


BEGIN   (* Main Program *)
  REPEAT
    WRITELN;
    WRITELN('Enter a sentence');
    WRITE(': ');
    READLN(Sentence);
    WRITELN('How many times do you want it printed?');
    WRITE('(0 to end): ');
    READLN(Number);
    WRITELN;
    RepeatPhrase(Sentence, Number);
  UNTIL Number = 0;
END.  (* ParamDemo3 *)
```

You'll notice that even though we change the value of the formal parameter **Line**, the actual parameter **Sentence** remains *unchanged*. This means we can now send information to a procedure with no fear of tampering with the data of the original variable!

Passing More Than One Parameter

Many more than one parameter can be passed to a procedure. Let's modify **ParamDemo1** in a different way so we can pass two parameters (Listing 8-3). Here's a run of this program:

```
Enter a sentence
: I will not chew gum in class.
How many times do you want it printed?
(0 to end): 500


1 I will not chew gum in class.
2 I will not chew gum in class.
3 I will not chew gum in class.
             :
             :
             :
499 I will not chew gum in class.
500 I will not chew gum in class.

Enter a sentence
:                                    ── RETURN pressed
```

```
How many times do you want it printed?
(0 to end): 0
```

Wouldn't it have been nice if you had one of these computers in school to handle the cruel and unusual punishment of having to write a phrase over and over again? Anyway, notice that we used the same variable name, **Number**, in the Main Program section and as the formal parameter in the **RepeatPhrase** procedure. These are still *two separate variables*. Changing the value of the formal parameter **Number** (actually a local variable in **RepeatPhrase**) will have no effect on the actual parameter **Number** in the Main Program section because of the name precedence rule which states that *the identifier will always refer to the variable with the most limited scope*.

Notice that in **RepeatPhrase**'s parameter list there is a semicolon separating the type declaration of the first parameter from the name of the second parameter. If the parameter list includes more than one variable of the same type, commas are used to separate the names from each other, and semicolons are used to separate the variable type from the following variable name. There is no semicolon at the end of the parameter list (within the parentheses):

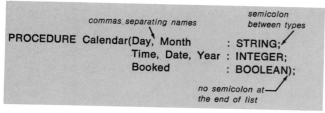

```
             commas separating names          semicolon
                                             between types
PROCEDURE Calendar(Day, Month        : STRING;
                   Time, Date, Year  : INTEGER;
                   Booked            : BOOLEAN);

                                    no semicolon at
                                    the end of list
```

When this procedure is called, the actual parameters must be in the exact order as the formal parameters:

Calendar('Wed', 'Dec', 6, 14, 1983, TRUE);

If they are out of order, you may end up trying to stuff **Month** with a *TRUE!*

Variable Parameters—Two Way Messengers

We've seen how value parameters are used to pass information *to* a procedure. Now we'll see how to get information *out* of a procedure. The type of parameter which can do this is a *variable parameter*. If the value parameter is like a Western Union messenger, the variable parameter is like a telephone line. Program **TwoWayCommunications** in Listing 8-4 gives an example using vari-

able parameters (it's a husband calling his wife at her office). And a run of this program:

From the home to the office:
Could you please bring home a pizza?

From the office to the home:
Sure dear, I'll be right home!

As you can see, the effect of changing the formal parameter in **TheOffice** procedure is very different from our example program **ParamDemo2** (Listing 8-2) which used a value parameter. In this case, changing the formal parameter **Phone-Call** *does* affect the actual parameter **Message**. We have set up "two way communication" between two sections of a program!

Look at the heading line in **TheOffice** procedure. You'll see the reserved word **VAR** in front of the formal parameter **PhoneCall**. This is how you can tell a variable parameter from a value parameter—variable parameters have the word **VAR** before the names of the formal parameters, value parameters don't. The word **VAR** must precede all the formal parameters for each variable type used:

Listing 8-4.

```
PROGRAM TwoWayCommunication;
VAR   Message : STRING;


PROCEDURE TheOffice(VAR  PhoneCall : STRING);

BEGIN
  WRITELN('Message from the home:' );
  WRITELN(PhoneCall );
  PhoneCall := 'Sure dear, I''ll be right home!';
END;  (* TheOffice *)


BEGIN  (* Main Program *)
  PAGE(OUTPUT);
  WRITELN;
  Message := 'Could you please bring home a pizza?'; '
  TheOffice(Message);
  WRITELN;
  WRITELN('Message from the office:' );
  WRITELN(Message);
END.  (* TwoWayCommunication *)
```

```
PROCEDURE (Chug(VAR Wood, Matches : INTEGER;
                TrackNumber       : INTEGER;
                EngineName        : STRING;
                VAR Distance      : REAL);
```

In the above heading, the variables **Wood**, **Matches**, and **Distance** are *variable* parameters. The variables **TrackNumber** and **EngineName** are *value* parameters.

Back to program **TwoWayCommunication**. If you look at where the procedure is called in the Main Program section, you won't be able to tell whether the actual parameter **Message** will end up as a variable parameter or as a value parameter—it is necessary for you to check the heading line of the procedure.

Why bother? You may be wondering, "Why bother with variable parameters when I could use global variables?" Good point! In fact, our **TwoWayCommunication** program could have been written using just the one global variable **Message**. The main advantage gained by using variable parameters is *control*. In a simple program like this one, it probably would be fine to use global variables and not variable parameters. However, in a larger program in which you have procedures calling other procedures, using variable parameters instead of global variables *enables you to exercise specific control over which variables the procedures can affect and which variables they can not affect*. This capability is the cornerstone of program reliability.

The Inner Workings of Parameters

Here's what actually happens with value and variable parameters. With value parameters, where only the value can be sent to a procedure, Pascal creates a *new* variable in a *new* computer memory location which is a *duplicate copy* of the actual parameter being sent. The procedure which receives the value can only access this *copy*, not the original. If the procedure changes the copy, the original is unaffected. However, with a variable parameter, Pascal just assigns a *second name* to the original variable (actual parameter)—the name of the formal parameter used within the procedure which is being called. There is really *only one variable in one memory location*. When the procedure makes a change in the contents of its formal parameter, it changes the contents of this memory location and the *original variable is changed*. No duplicate variables were created.

Sending Empty Boxes

While using variable parameters, it is not necessary to assign the actual parameter a value before the procedure is called. We can "send" a totally unused, empty variable to the procedure. Look at this next program (Listing 8-5).

Here is how this program looks on execution:

```
Enter a number: —14.5

—14.500 cubed is —3048.62
```

Listing 8-5.

```
PROGRAM EmptyBoxes;
VAR    Number, Answer : REAL;


PROCEDURE Cube(Base : REAL; VAR  Result : REAL);

BEGIN
   Result := Base * Base * Base;
END;  (* Cube *)


BEGIN  (* Main Program *)
   PAGE(OUTPUT);
   WRITE('Enter a number: ');
   READLN(Number);
   WRITELN;
   Cube(Number, Answer);
   WRITELN(Number:7:3,' cubed is ',Answer:7:3);
END.  (* EmptyBoxes *)
```

You'll notice that we are passing two parameters to the **Cube** procedure. The second parameter, however, was never assigned a value. When we look at **Cube**, we see that the first parameter, **Base**, is a value parameter and the second parameter, **Result**, is a variable parameter. The variable parameter **Result** is really the actual parameter **Answer** "in disguise." So when we place the value of **Base**^{3} into **Result**, it is also placed in **Answer**. You can think of using variable parameters in this manner as equivalent to sending a self-addressed stamped envelope to a friend. It's empty when you send it to your friend, but it contains a letter (hopefully) when you get it back.

Look again at the heading line of procedure **Cube**. Notice that we placed both parameters on the same line. Many programmers prefer to write the heading this way.

Expressions As Actual Parameters

Since all we are passing to a procedure when using a value parameter is a *value*, we can use values and expressions rather than being restricted just to variables. However, since a variable parameter requires a *variable* as a "return address," only variables can be used as the actual parameter for variable parameters. Let's say we have a procedure with the following heading:

```
PROCEDURE Compute(VAR Result : INTEGER;
                  Number     : INTEGER);
```

Where **Result** is a variable parameter and **Number** is a value parameter. The following calls to **Compute** are correct:

```
Compute(Revits, Malrons);

Compute(Magpies, ORD(n) + 27 * i);

Compute(Broomsticks, Dust * Rooms);

Compute(CherryPies, 1034);
```

The following calls are illegal because the first parameter is a value or an expression and not a variable as it should be:

```
Compute(131, Zorts);

Compute(ORD('z'), Position);

Compute(75 * i, Cucumbers);
```

Intrinsic Procedures

Guess what—you have been working with procedures and parameters since Chapter 2! We mentioned that Pascal was written in Pascal—a number of statements we have used are actually Pascal procedures which were written into the language (predeclared). These are called *intrinsics*. Now that you know the form of a procedure which uses parameters, you can probably think of some yourself. They are **WRITE**, **WRITELN**, **READ**, **READLN**, **GOTOXY**, and **PAGE**. All of these statements have a name, followed by a pair of parentheses, with a variable(s) or value(s) inside.

The scope of these intrinsic or predeclared procedures is considered to be in a block *surrounding* your program. If you invent your *own* procedure and choose to name it **Readln**, then *your* procedure will take precedence over the *intrinsic*

READLN which will no longer be accessible within your program (or the section of your program over which your procedure has scope). This means that if you don't like an intrinsic procedure, you can write your own to replace it!

Once Again

Let's summarize the use of the two parameters. *Value Parameters should be used when:*

1. You want to *send* the value of a variable to a procedure and to *protect* that variable from access or change by that procedure.
2. You want to just *send* a value or expression to a procedure.

Variable Parameters should be used when:

1. You want a procedure to *change* the value of a variable.
2. You want to *receive* a value from a procedure.

In addition, since there is an extra computer processing step when using value parameters (the computer has to make a duplicate copy of the variable), it is sometimes a good idea to use *variable* parameters just for *sending* values to a procedure when speed is a consideration. This is especially true when you are sending many very long strings or large arrays (Chapter 10). When sending ordinal variables, there shouldn't be a problem.

QUIZ—PARAMETERS

1. **Which of the following are value parameters and which are variable parameters?**

```
PROCEDURE ShunkCabbage(Number,
               Address        : INTEGER;
           VAR Bugs           : INTEGER;
           VAR Pounds,
               Mass,
               Height         : REAL;
               City, Block,
               Lawn           : STRING);
```

True or False

2. **Value parameters are used only to send values to procedures.**

3. **Variable parameters are used only to receive values from procedures.**

4. **Using what you now know about parameters, what type of parameters (value or variable) would you guess are *probably* used in Pascal's intrinsic procedures?**

FUNCTIONS—THE COUSIN OF PROCEDURES

Now that you know how to create procedures with parameters, learning about functions will be a snap. A **FUNCTION** is very similar to a procedure. A function is a block with a name above it; it can have its own **CONST**ant and **VAR**iable declarations; it has a **BEGIN** and an **END**; it can receive parameters and return a value. However, there are a few differences between procedures and functions. A procedure is called by using the procedure name as a statement (along with its parameters). It stands by itself as a statement. A function can be used almost any place a variable or constant can be used. It *will not* stand alone as a statement (just like a variable or expression can't stand alone as a statement—i $+$ 5 is not a statement). In other words, *a procedure is a replacement for a statement and a function is a replacement for an expression.* We have already introduced a few Pascal intrinsic functions —functions which are built into Pascal. They are **CHR**, **ORD**, and **ODD**. Each one of these functions returns a value of a different type—**CHR** returns a **CHAR** value, **ORD** returns an **INTE-GER** value, and **ODD** returns a **BOOLEAN** value. These functions can be substituted for a value of like type anywhere within a program. After the function has been called, the value it returns will occupy the *location in the statement* where the function was. In this way it acts like a variable.

The value a function returns must be a "simple type," that is, a variable that has only one value. This means you can't use a function to return a **STRING** value because a **STRING** isn't a simple type—it's actually a *series* of **CHAR**s strung together (a series of *values* strung together). In order to have a function return a **STRING** as a result, you can use variable parameters. However, this returned **STRING** value will not occupy the position of the function name in the statement from which the function was called. For a good example of this see Listing 8-10.

Let's look at the procedure **Power** from the Loan Payment programs again (Listing 8-6). Now let's convert it into a function (Listing 8-7). Let's look at the difference between a procedure and a function. Starting at the top with the head-

Listing 8-6.

```
PROCEDURE Power;
VAR    x    : REAL;
       y, i : INTEGER;
BEGIN
  x := InterestPerPeriod + 1;      (* Routine which will      *)
  y := NumberOfPayments;           (* raise x to the y power, *)
  Temp := 1.0;                     (* that is, x↑y  (x >= 0) *)
  FOR i := 1 TO y DO               (* Answer is in Temp       *)
    Temp := Temp * x;
END; (* Power *)
```

Listing 8-7.

```
FUNCTION Power(x : REAL; y : INTEGER) : REAL;
(* Function which raises x to the y power (x↑y)
           y must be greater than 0            *)

VAR    i    : INTEGER;
       Temp : REAL;

BEGIN
  Temp := 1.0;

  FOR i := 1 to y DO
    Temp := Temp * x;

  Power := Temp;
END;  (* Power *)
```

ing, you'll notice that the keyword **FUNCTION** replaces the keyword **PROCEDURE**. Next, there is the function name. However, the function name has a bigger job to do than just to give the function an identifying label. This name will be the means to return a value to the expression in which the function was called (as we will soon see). Next on the line come the parameters. The syntax for listing these formal parameters is exactly the same as in procedures. And finally, we have the value type which our function **Power** will return. A colon (:) must separate the parameter list from the function's type. Other than the heading, there is one other difference between a procedure and a function. Somewhere in the function we must assign the final value to the function name (**Power := Temp;**). Again you can see that the function name *does* act like a variable.

In the Loan program, we stored the result of x ↑ y in the global variable **Temp**. By using a function, we don't have to bother. Here are some examples of how we can invoke (call) this function and how it will look upon execution:

```
1. WRITELN('5 ↑  6 = ', Power(5, 6));

   5 ↑  6 = 1.56250E4

2. Base := 1.212;
   n := 17;
   WRITELN(Base:5:3,' ↑ ',n,' = ',Power(Base, n):7:3);

   1.212 ↑ 17 = 26.275

3. Num1 := 3.18;
   Num2 := −1.211;
```

```
   Exponent := 7;
   Result := Power(Num1, Exponent) + Power(Num2,
     Exponent − 3);
   WRITELN('The result is ', Result:7:3);

   The result is 3290.59

4. WRITELN(Power(Power(5, 3), 2):7:2);

   15625.0
```

As you can see, the function can be inside a **WRITELN** (Nos. 1, 2, 4) or part of an expression (No. 3). We can pass parameters to a function as values (No. 1), as variables (Nos. 2, 3), as expressions (No. 3), or even as a function (No. 4). Example 4 is executed by calling the inner **Power** first in order to get the parameters for the outer **Power**.

Let's modify this function so it can handle negative exponents as well as positive exponents. You've read that:

$$B^{-n} \text{ is equivalent to } \frac{1}{B^n}$$

If n was equal to 3, we would have:

$$\frac{1}{B^3} = \frac{1}{B} * \frac{1}{B} * \frac{1}{B}$$

AHA! A repetition which could be controlled by a **FOR** loop! We can create a second **FOR** loop in our function which executes only if the exponent is negative. Here in Listing 8-8 is a revised version of **Power**:

The expression **Temp / x** is derived from:

Listing 8-8.

```
FUNCTION Power(x : REAL; y : INTEGER) : REAL;
(* Function which raises x to the y power (x↑y)
        y may be positive or negative          *)

VAR    i    : INTEGER;
       Temp : REAL;

BEGIN
  Temp := 1.0;

  IF y >= 0 THEN
    FOR i := 1 to y DO
      Temp := Temp * x
  ELSE IF x = 0 THEN Temp := 0          (* Check for base of 0 *)
    ELSE
      FOR i := 1 to -y DO
        Temp := Temp / x;

  Power := Temp;
END;  (* Power *)
```

$$\text{Temp} * (1 / x) \rightarrow \text{Temp} / x$$

Since we are dividing by a variable (x), we must protect against the occurrence when x might equal 0. We set **Temp** to 0 and skip the division section if this happens.

Now let's take our **Power** function and plug it into the Loan Payment program from Chapter 5 (Listing 5-7). First, here is the loan formula again:

$$\text{RegularPayment} = \frac{\text{Principal} \times \text{InterestPerPeriod}}{1 - (\text{InterestPerPeriod} + 1)^{-\text{NumberOfPayments}}}$$

By using the **Power** function, we are able to make the **Calculate** procedure resemble the actual formula more closely (Listing 8-9).

Return More Than One Value

Even though a function can return only one value through its name, it is possible to use variable parameters to return additional values, including multivalue types like **STRING**s. Listing 8-10 is an example.

Here is a run of this program:

```
99   I've been to San Jose!   Me too!
```

As you can see, our **SanJose** function was able to pass back a value *and* a couple of strings. When the execution of the **WRITELN** in the Main Program section began, the two variables, **Box1** and **Box2**, were empty. But when the function was called, these two variables were stuffed with messages which could then be immediately printed out.

Pascal Intrinsic Functions

As you may have guessed, in addition to Pascal's intrinsic procedures there are a number of built-in (intrinsic) *functions* which can be used in your programs. We will now cover some of them. (We will skip UCSD Pascal's intrinsic String Functions and Procedures until the next chapter.) We'll list them in alphabetical order:

ABS(x)—This function will return the absolute value of the parameter **x**. The absolute value is determined by making **x** a positive number. If the number is negative, it chops off the minus sign. If the number is positive to begin with, **ABS** leaves it alone. **x** can be either a **REAL** or an **INTEGER** and the type of the result is the same as **x**'s type.

CHR(x)—This one you already know from Chapter 3. It returns the **CHAR** type value which has

the ASCII value (ordinal value) of **x**. **x** must be an **INTEGER**.

ODD(x)—Another old friend. This function will return a **BOOLEAN** TRUE if the **INTEGER** parameter **x** is an odd number, otherwise it will return a FALSE.

ORD(x)—And another familiar function. This one will return the ordinal value of the parameter **x**. **x** may be any ordinal variable (**INTEGER**, **CHAR**, or **BOOLEAN**)—a variable which has an *order* associated with it. **ORD(x)** will return the *position* that **x** holds in its variable type. For **INTEGER**s, it's the integer itself, for **CHAR**s it's the ASCII value, for **BOOLEAN**s it's 0 for FALSE and 1 for TRUE.

PRED(x)—This function will return the *predecessor* of the ordinal parameter **x**. It can be used on the same variable types as **ORD**. **PRED('C')** is the character 'B,' **PRED(TRUE)** is FALSE and **PRED(25)** is 24. If **x** is the lower bound of the range of possible values of **x**'s type, an error will result (e.g., **PRED(FALSE)** does not compute because nothing precedes FALSE).

ROUND(x)—This function will round off a **REAL** number (**x**) to the nearest **INTEGER**. Examples:

```
ROUND(17.48)   →    17
ROUND(3.5)     →    4
ROUND(−0.31)   →    0
ROUND(−5.51)   →   −6
ROUND(−1.499)  →   −1
```

SQR(x)—will return the value of x squared or x^2 or x * x. The result will be of the same type as **x** (either **INTEGER** or **REAL**)

SUCC(x)—This function is opposite of **PRED(x)**. It returns the *successor* of the ordinal value **x**. **SUCC('C')** is the character 'D,' **SUCC(FALSE)** is TRUE and **SUCC(25)** is 26. Again, if **x** is equal to the upper boundary of the range of the variable type, you will get an error.

TRUNC(x)—This function will convert a **REAL** to an **INTEGER** like **ROUND** does. However, this function doesn't do any rounding. It truncates or chops off everything after the decimal point:

```
TRUNC(5.99999)   →    5
TRUNC(−3.99999)  →   −3
```

There is no function to convert from **INTEGER**s to **REAL**s because none is needed. A **REAL** variable can be assigned an **INTEGER** value but an **INTEGER** variable can't be assigned a **REAL** value.

Listing 8-9.

```
(*=================================================*)
(*                                                 *)
(* Program Language: PASCAL                        *)
(* Program Title: Loan Payment - version 3         *)
(* Subtitle:  Introducing the FUNCTION Power which *)
(*            can handle negative exponents.       *)
(*                                                 *)
(* Author:    Mitch Waite / David Fox             *)
(* Program Summary:  Calculates the regular payment*)
(*            on a loan.                            *)
(*                                                 *)
(*=================================================*)


PROGRAM Loan3;

VAR  Principal, AnnualInterest,
     RegularPayment, TotalInterest : REAL;
     PaymentsPerYear, TermInYears  : INTEGER;



PROCEDURE ClearScreen;

BEGIN
  PAGE(OUTPUT);
END; (* ClearScreen *)



FUNCTION Power(x : REAL; y : INTEGER) : REAL;
(* Function which raises x to the y power (x↑y)
         y may be positive or negative          *)

VAR   i   : INTEGER;
      Temp : REAL;


BEGIN
  Temp := 1.0;

  IF y >= 0 THEN
    FOR i := 1 to y DO
      Temp := Temp * x
  ELSE IF x = 0 THEN Temp := 0      (* Check for base of 0 *)
    ELSE
      FOR i := 1 to -y DO
        Temp := Temp / x;

  Power := Temp;
END;  (* Power *)
```

```
PROCEDURE GetData;

BEGIN
  ClearScreen;
  WRITELN('** LOAN PAYMENT **':29);
  WRITELN;
  WRITELN;
  WRITE('Enter amount of loan: ');
  READLN(Principal);
  WRITE('Enter the annual interest: ');
  READLN(AnnualInterest);
  WRITE('Enter payments per year: ');
  READLN(PaymentsPerYear);
  WRITE('Enter term in years: ');
  READLN(TermInYears);
END; (* GetData *)




PROCEDURE Calculate;
VAR    InterestPerPeriod : REAL;
       NumberOfPayments  : INTEGER;

BEGIN (* Calculate *)
  InterestPerPeriod := (AnnualInterest / 100) / PaymentsPerYear;
  NumberOfPayments := PaymentsPerYear * TermInYears;

  RegularPayment :=              Principal * InterestPerPeriod
                                          /
              (1 - Power(InterestPerPeriod + 1, -NumberOfPayments));

  TotalInterest := RegularPayment * NumberOfPayments - Principal;
END; (* Calculate *)




PROCEDURE PrintAnswer;

BEGIN
  WRITELN;
  WRITELN;
  WRITELN('Regular payment = $',RegularPayment:7:2);
  WRITELN;
  WRITELN('Total interest on loan = $',TotalInterest:7:2);
  WRITELN;
  WRITELN;
END; (* PrintAnswer *)
```

```
BEGIN (* Main Program *)
  GetData;
  Calculate;
  PrintAnswer;
  WRITELN('That''s all folks...BYE');
END. (* Loan3 *)
```

```
RealValue := IntValue;  ←——————————This is legal
```

The Transcendental Functions

The following functions are called **TRAN-SCENDENTAL** functions. Explaining these in depth is beyond the scope of this book. If you don't know how to use them, you may check with a trigonometry book. If you are using certain versions of UCSD Pascal (e.g., Apple), these functions are not automatically available for your use. They are stored in a special library of functions and procedures and are available upon request. This saves processing time and memory space by not forcing the compiler to provide these functions unless necessary. If you want to use them, all you have to do is place the line:

```
USES TRANSCEND;
```

immediately after the **PROGRAM Name;** line and before anything else in the program. This instructs the compiler to pull these functions out of the library for use in your program.

Bringing in routines which you don't need just weighs down the computer. Uncle Pascal says: *He who brings his entire wardrobe for a row across the lake ends up being the best dressed fish around!*

In the following functions, all parameters can be either **INTEGER** or **REAL**. All values returned are **REAL** and the **Angle** parameters are in radians:

ARCTAN(x) or **ATAN(x)** (UCSD Pascal)—returns the inverse tangent of **x** in radians.

COS(Angle)—returns the cosine of **Angle**.

EXP(x)—returns the value of the mathematical constant "e" raised to the xth power (e^x).

LN(x)—returns the value of the natural logarithm of **x**. **x** must be greater than 0 or there will be an error.

LOG(x)—returns the value of the logarithm to the base 10 of **x**. This function may not be available in your version of Pascal. It *is* available in UCSD Pascal.

SIN(Angle)—returns the sine of **Angle**.

SQRT(x)—returns the square root of **x**. The value of **x** must be a positive number or there will be an error.

Let's take a couple of these functions and use them in a program. Listing 8-11 shows a **Power** function which uses **EXP** and **LN**. This function is much faster than our old version, but it can only deal with a base **(x)** which is greater than 0.0.

Since the value passed to the function **LN** must be greater than 0 (a very picky eater!), we check

Listing 8-10.

```
PROGRAM Vacation;
VAR   Box1, Box2 : STRING;

FUNCTION SanJose(Number1, Number2      : INTEGER;
                 VAR  Message1, Message2 : STRING) : INTEGER;

BEGIN
  SanJose := Number1 * Number2;
  Message1 := ('  I''ve been to San Jose!');
  Message2 := ('  Me too!');
END;  (* San Jose *)


BEGIN  (* Main Program *)
  WRITELN(SanJose(3, 33, Box1, Box2), Box1, Box2);
END.  (* Vacation *)
```

Listing 8-11.

```
FUNCTION Power(x : REAL; y : INTEGER) : REAL;
(* Function which raises x to the y power (x↑y) using
   TRANSCENDTAL FUNCTIONS - y may be positive or negative,
   x must be greater than 0.0
                                                        *)
BEGIN
  IF x <= 0 THEN WRITELN(' ** Error - Base <= 0.0')
    ELSE Power := EXP(y * LN(x));
END;  (* Power *)
```

the value of **x** before giving it to **LN**. Depending on your application, just noting the error may not be enough. You may need to return some message value (called a flag) indicating an error or let the program abort execution.

FORWARD—NAMING A PROCEDURE OR FUNCTION BEFORE ITS TIME

From time to time, you will find it difficult (or impossible) to avoid calling a procedure or function before it is defined. If you find yourself in this predicament, don't fret! You can use the **FORWARD** reference to tell the compiler to be patient, the procedure (or function) is coming. Here's an example.

```
PROCEDURE WakeUp(Time : INTEGER); FORWARD;

FUNCTION HoursSlept(Minutes : INTEGER) : REAL;
  FORWARD;


PROCEDURE Sleep;
BEGIN
  :
  WRITELN('Zzzzzz');
  :
  IF HoursSlept(GoodSleep) >= WellRested THEN
    WakeUp(Alarm);
END; (* Sleep *)


PROCEDURE WakeUp;   no parameters
BEGIN
```

```
  :
  :
END; (* WakeUp *)


FUNCTION HoursSlept;   no parameters or function type
BEGIN
  :
  :
END; (* HoursSlept *)
```

To use **FORWARD**, all you need to do is separate the heading of the procedure or function from its block (shades of the French Revolution!). Later when the procedure or function is defined, don't include the parameters or the function type.

QUIZ—FUNCTIONS

1. Based on what you now know about functions and procedures, deduce which of the following *underlined* "modules" are functions and which are procedures:
   A. IF *Whistle*(n) THEN *Wait*(50);
   B. *AnimalList*(Zoo, Circus, Wild);
   C. Total := *Sum*(One, Two, Three) + LastChance;
   D. *FireCheck*(3, *HoseDown*(House));

True or False

2. A function may be declared as a *STRING* type.

3. A function may accept as many parameters as you like.

4. A function invocation (call) may stand alone as a statement.

5. A function can use the value of another function as one of its parameters.

chapter 9

Strings and Long Integers

This chapter is all about *STRINGs* and *LONG INTEGERs*. "*STRINGs*", you may say. "But I already know about *STRINGs*". Ah, we have barely scratched the surface on what you can do with *STRINGs*. We will show you how to surgically remove any character in a *STRING*, how to stuff new characters in the middle of a *STRING*, and how to make *STRINGs* into the input/output workhorses of Pascal by using them in conjunction with *LONG INTEGERs*.

We mentioned before that a **STRING** is really a series of **CHARs** strung together. This is literally true. When Pascal was created, **STRINGs** were not a part of the language. Every time someone wanted to store a series of characters together, they had to define a customized variable type which was really an *array of characters*. Think of an array as being like a string of Christmas lights. The elements are the same type (small light bulbs), but they can be different colors (different values). The string of lights is treated as a single unit, but you can access individual bulbs and replace them if you like. (We'll cover arrays in the next chapter.) Fortunately, the creators of UCSD Pascal included a standard variable type called **STRING**, along with a set of powerful intrinsics to manipulate these **STRINGs**. The **STRING** is still an array of **CHARs** but we don't have to worry about screwing in light bulbs, hanging the lights, or plugging them in. All the dirty work has already been handled.

MAXIMUM *STRING* LENGTH

Unless otherwise specified, all **STRINGs** declared in UCSD Pascal can have up to 80 characters in them (their *default* length). This maximum **STRING** size can be adjusted at the time of declaration by square brackets surrounding the **STRING** size (called a "length attribute") :

```
VAR SmallString : STRING[5];
    BigString   : STRING[255];
```

The absolute maximum **STRING** size is 255 characters. If you exceed the declared size of a **STRING** during entry from the keyboard, Pascal will politely ignore all extra letters. But you won't be able to backspace to make a correction if you go over the edge. However, if you try to assign too many letters to a string within the program, you'll get an overflow error :

```
SmallString := 'I am NOT a small string!';
```

This will cause an error because **SmallString's** length can be no longer than five characters.

Accessing the Elements

How do we change the light bulbs of the string? Each character in a **STRING** can be identified by referring to its position in the **STRING**. We indicate this by using the [ ] brackets. For example, the first element (or character) of the **STRING** **Message** would be referred to by **Message**[1], the seventh element by **Message**[7]. Look at this program fragment:

```
Message := 'I think I see two burnt out blubs.';
WRITELN(Message[4]);
```

On execution, an 'h' will be printed out which is the fourth character in the string (don't forget to count the spaces as characters!).

Let's say we want to correct the spelling of the last word in the **STRING** stored in **Message**, 'blubs.' The misplaced letters are in positions 30 and 31.

```
Message[30] := 'u';
Message[31] := 'l';
WRITELN(Message);
```

On execution we would get:

```
I think I see two burnt out bulbs
```

Going in the other direction, we can copy a character into a variable:

```
Ch := Message[16];
WRITELN(Ch);
```

and a 'w' will be printed out. In order for this to work, the variable **Ch** *must be a **CHAR** variable.* This is because the *elements of a **STRING** are* ***CHARs*** and, as we (hopefully) all know, *you can't mix variable types.*

The following program segment will print our string out backwards:

```
FOR i := 33 DOWNTO 1 DO
   WRITE(Message[i]);
```

If this were executed you would get:

```
sblub tuo tnrub owt ees I kniht I
```

That's a pretty neat trick, but it would be very impractical for you to have to count the number of characters in a string in order to perform this feat! Of course, there is another way . . . .

STRING INTRINSICS

This brings us right to the subject of **STRING** intrinsics. We will introduce you to each of the built-in **STRING** functions and procedures of UCSD Pascal.

LENGTH—How Long Is Your STRING?

This function returns the *number of characters in a **STRING*** as an **INTEGER**. Listing 9-1 gives a program based on our earlier backwards printing example.

Here's a run of this program:

```
Enter a sentence (or RETURN to end)
: ANNA SAW OTTO
OTTO WAS ANNA

Enter a sentence (or RETURN to end)
: ←──────────────── Return pressed
```

R. FOX

111

Listing 9-1.

```
PROGRAM BackwardsWrite;
VAR   Sentence : STRING;
         i         : INTEGER;

BEGIN
  PAGE(OUTPUT);

  REPEAT
    WRITELN;
    WRITELN('Enter a sentence (or RETURN to end)');
    WRITE(': ');
    READLN(Sentence);

    FOR i := LENGTH(Sentence) DOWNTO 1 DO
      WRITE(Sentence[i]);
    WRITELN;

  UNTIL LENGTH(Sentence) = 0;
END.   (* BackwardsWrite *)
```

As you can see if RETURN is pressed without entering any characters, the length of **Sentence** will be zero, and the program will end.

Centering Your Lines—Here is a useful tool to make your programs look nice. It's a procedure which will horizontally center a string on your screen (Listing 9-2).

Here's a run of the program:

```
         ** CENTER DEMO **

        This program will make it
        very easy to center text
             on your screen.


                The End
```

We placed a constant at the top of the program that can easily be changed for different screen widths. Planning like this is important if you want your program to be transportable to other computers.

Look at the **Center** procedure. The string to be centered is received through the value parameter **Sentence**. Next, we store the length of **Sentence** in the variable **Len**. In the next line we implement the tabbing technique using formatted printing. We set the **field-length** to equal the length of the string in **Sentence** plus a right margin. The margin is calculated by subtracting the length of the string from the **ScreenWidth** (this yields the total number of empty spaces on the line) and divide this number by two (for equal margins on both sides). This procedure means not having to hand count your strings in order to center them

properly! Also, this allows you to center strings of different lengths which are entered from the keyboard—there is no way to know how long they'll be in advance.

Efficient Code vs. Clear Code—You may have noticed that we have an extra "unnecessary" step in the **Center** procedure. We calculate the length of the string in a separate statement rather than doing so within the **WRITELN** statement. We did this for increased clarity. There were too many parentheses in the **WRITELN** when we did it the other way and it looked rather intimidating. This brings up a good point. Many times the most efficient way to write a routine isn't the best way. *Never sacrifice clarity for brevity!* Stretch out a procedure if it will make it easier to follow.

 What good is it to make your program more efficient if no one (including yourself) can understand it! Uncle Pascal says: *He who scrawls his will on the back of a postage stamp bequeathes nothing but confusion to his heirs.*

Playing With Nothing

We now come to an interesting problem. As you know, you can set a **STRING** to a length of 0:

```
NullString := '';
```

But you can't do the same with a **STRING** element. Doing this:

```
NullString[5] := '';
```

Listing 9-2.

```
PROGRAM CenterDemo;

CONST  ScreenWidth = 40;

VAR  OutString : STRING;


PROCEDURE Center(Sentence : STRING);
(* Procedure to center a string on the screen *)
VAR  Len : INTEGER;

BEGIN
  Len := LENGTH(Sentence);
  WRITELN(Sentence:Len + (ScreenWidth - Len) DIV 2);
END; (* Center *)


BEGIN  (* Main Program *)
  OutString := 'The End';
  PAGE(OUTPUT);

  WRITELN;
  Center(' ** CENTER DEMO **' );
  WRITELN;
  Center('This program will make it' );
  Center('very easy to center text' );
  Center('on the screen.' );
  WRITELN;
  WRITELN;
  Center(OutString);
END. (* CenterDemo *)
```

will yield a compiler error. Remember the rule that **CHAR** variables must have one and only one character in them. Doing the above would break that rule.

Then what happens to the elements of a **STRING** when you set the string to null? That's easy—an empty (null) string *has no elements*. It's empty! This means that if you try to access a nonexistent element of a **STRING**, you will get an error. For example, let's say we place the string 'French' in a **STRING** variable called **Language**.

```
Language := 'French';
WRITELN(Language[7]);
```

If we try to access the seventh element, we will get an error because there *is* no seventh element—the length of the **STRING** is only 6. This means that you have to protect your programs from referencing nonexistent elements of a **STRING** by first checking the **STRING** length!

POS—Finding a *STRING* Within a *STRING*

Let's say you want to search *inside* one **STRING** for a specific pattern of characters. Here is a function which not only lets you know if it found the hidden pattern, but tells you exactly where it is. Here's an example:

```
SourceString :=
   'Can you find where the treasure is hidden?';
Gold := 'treasure';
HidingPlace := POS(Gold, SourceString);
WRITELN('The treasure was hidden at POSition ',
   HidingPlace);
```

On execution we get:

```
The treasure was hidden at POSition 24
```

The function **POS** will return the position in the **SourceString** of the first character in the looked for pattern (the 't' in 'treasure'). The value returned is an **INTEGER**. If there is more than one

113

occurrence of the pattern in the **SourceString**, the first one in line wins the prize. If there are no matches of the pattern in the **SourceString**, the value returned is 0.

One good use of this function is in programs which contain interactive dialogues (the famous program Eliza is a good example of one). The user enters a complete sentence, and the program must scan it for a specific word or words. Listing 9-3 below gives a program fragment to demonstrate this use.

On execution, we get:

```
How are you today? I'm feeling great today, thank you!
So glad to hear it, Rachael.
I feel rather chipper, too!
```

If any one of our "key words" is found in **Sentence**, the sum of the expression will be greater than 0 and the compound statement will be executed. Another way to write this line would be as follows:

```
IF (POS('fine', Sentence) > 0)
   OR (POS('great', Sentence) > 0)
   OR (POS('Ok', Sentence) > 0)
   OR (POS('terrific', Sentence) > 0) THEN
      BEGIN
         :
         :
```

When using **POS**, make sure you place the pattern to be searched for *before* the **SourceString**. To make this easier to remember, you may read the POS function as "I'm looking for the position of a *pattern* in this **SourceString**." Some BASICs have a function that does what POS does. This function is called different things depending on which BASIC is involved. Two that we are aware of are INSTR and SEARCH.

CONCAT—The Pot of Glue for a Ball of *STRING*

This function allows you to "glue" two or more **STRINGs** together to form a *new* **STRING**. This

is known as "CONCATenation." Here's an example:

```
Man := 'Husband';
Woman := 'Wife';
Married := CONCAT('Now you are ', Man, ' and ',
   Woman);
WRITELN(Married);
```

which will print:

```
Now you are Husband and Wife
```

We stuck four **STRINGs** together and placed this new **STRING** in **Married**. You'll notice that two of the strings were contained within the variables **Man** and **Woman**.

It's also possible to do the following:

```
Train := ' ' ; (* Initialize Train to empty string *)
FOR i := 1 TO 5 DO
   Train := CONCAT(Train, '-BoxCar');
Train := CONCAT('Engine', Train, '-Caboose');
WRITELN(Train);
```

This will print:

```
Engine-BoxCar-BoxCar-BoxCar-BoxCar-BoxCar-Caboose
```

After making sure there was nothing in the **STRING Train**, we kept adding on '-BoxCar's to its contents and storing the new **STRING** back into the same variable (**Train**). Of course, the preceding output will not fit on a 40 character screen, but you get the idea. Unfortunately, however, **CONCAT** is horrendously inefficient at execution time—it's slooow!

In BASIC, concatenation is usually carried out in the following manner:

```
C$ = "Hi there" + A$ + "Good bye"
```

using the plus sign to "add" strings together.

COPY—How To Clone a *STRING*

With this function we can copy any section of a **STRING** and do what we please with it. Here is an example:

Listing 9-3.

```
WRITE('How are you today? ');
  READLN(Sentence);
  IF (POS('fine', Sentence) + POS('great', Sentence)
      + POS('Ok', Sentence) + POS('terrific', Sentence)) > 0 THEN
        BEGIN
           WRITELN('So glad to hear it ', Name,'.');
           WRITELN('I feel rather chipper, too!');
        END;
```

```
Payment := 'Here is a ten dollar bill for you.';
Counterfeit := COPY(Payment, 11, 15);
WRITELN(Counterfeit);
```

This will print:

```
ten dollar bill
```

The syntax for **COPY** is:

```
COPY(SourceString, StartPosition, Size)
```

This can be read as "copy from the **SourceString** beginning at the **StartPosition** and take a total of **Size** characters." Remember that the character at **StartPosition** is the first character to be copied. If **StartPosition** or **Size** is outside the range of the **STRING** (e.g., greater than the **STRING** length) then the call to **COPY** returns a null string.

If we only want to copy the eighth character of a **STRING**, we would say:

```
COPY(Flaxmings, 8, 1);
```

You may ask, "Why bother using **COPY** for only one character of a **STRING** when we could directly access the character using **Flaxmings[8]**?" Go ahead and ask . . . . Ah yes, that's an excellent question! The answer is that **COPY** *always* returns a *STRING*, even if it's a STRING of only one character. You'll remember that when you are referencing an element in a **STRING** (**Flaxmings[8]**) will *always* return a *CHAR*. This is an important point to remember since you can't mix variable types. Also, if **Flaxmings** is less than eight characters long, referencing **Flaxmings[8]** will yield an error, while **COPY** **(Flaxmings, 8,1)** will just return a null string.

Sometimes you may want to copy only the last part of a string. Here is an example which will copy from the fifth character to the end of the string:

```
BackEnd :=
     COPY(BackEnd, 5, LENGTH(BackEnd) — 5 + 1);
```

The general formula to copy from a specific position to the end is:

```
COPY(SourceString, StartPos, LENGTH(SourceString)
   — StartPos + 1);
```

BASIC's closest function to **COPY** is called MID$. The main difference is that the third parameter is MID$, the size, is optional. In COPY, it is required.

DELETE—Vacuuming up a STRING

Here is a procedure which has no equivalent in BASIC. We can use **DELETE** to vacuum up and discard a section of a **STRING**. Here is an example:

```
CleanUp :=
     'My, your floor sure looks good and dirty today!';
DELETE(CleanUp, POS('and', CleanUp), 10);
WRITELN(CleanUp);
```

and if this were executed:

```
My, your floor sure looks good today!
```

Here is the general syntax for **DELETE**:

```
DELETE(SourceString, StartPosition, Size);
```

DELETE will remove **Size** characters beginning with the character at **StartPosition**. In our **CleanUp** example, you can see that we were resourceful (lazy?) and used the **POS** function to return the **StartPosition** rather than counting by hand. When using **DELETE** if your parameters are outside the length of the **STRING**, **SourceString** will be left unaffected.

Listing 9-4 shows an example that removes all of the spaces from a STRING. And here is how it looks when run:

```
Enter a sentence (or RETURN to end)
: I think I'll put the garbage into the compactor.
Ithink I'll put the garbage into the compactor.
IthinkI'll put the garbage into the compactor.
IthinkI'llput the garbage into the compactor.
IthinkI'llputthe garbage into the compactor.
IthinkI'llputthegarbage into the compactor.
IthinkI'llputthegarbageinto the compactor.
IthinkI'llputthegarbageintothe compactor.
IthinkI'llputthegarbageintothecompactor.

Enter a sentence (or RETURN to end)
:                                                    — Return pressed
```

The **WHILE** loop will continue to cycle through until there are no more spaces to delete. How else could this program be terminated besides entering a null string (pressing RETURN without typing any characters)? If you said, "Enter some spaces", you were right. If all you entered was a bunch of spaces, they would all be deleted one by one, and you would be left with a null string.

INSERT—Butting into the Conversation

Here is another procedure which has no BASIC equivalent. **INSERT** is the opposite of **DELETE**. Guess what **INSERT** does. Refer to Listing 9-5 on page 117.

Listing 9-4.

```
PROGRAM NoSpace;
(* Program to demonstrate the DELETE intrinsic *)

VAR Space, Sentence : STRING;

BEGIN
  Space := ' ';                      (* Set to one space *)
  PAGE(OUTPUT);
  REPEAT
    WRITELN;
    WRITELN('Enter a sentence (or RETURN to end)');
    WRITE(': ');
    READLN(Sentence);

    WHILE POS(Space, Sentence) > 0 DO
      BEGIN
        DELETE(Sentence, POS(Space, Sentence), 1);
        WRITELN(Sentence);
      END;

  UNTIL LENGTH(Sentence) = 0;
END.  (* NoSpace *)
```

On execution, we get:

> Myrtle 2 cents keeps butting 2 cents in!

As you can see, **INSERT** places a string inside of another string and therefore increases the string's length. Here is the general format of **INSERT**:

INSERT(Source, Destination, Position);

This instrinsic procedure **INSERT**s a **Source** string into a **Destination** string at **Position** in the **Destination** string. Listing 9-6 is another example. And a run:

> Enter a sentence
> : What's happening?
> What's happening ?
> What's happenin g ?
> What's happeni n g ?
> What's happen i n g ?
> What's happe n i n g ?
> What's happ e n i n g ?
> What's hap p e n i n g ?
> What's ha p p e n i n g ?
> What's h a p p e n i n g ?
> What's h a p p e n i n g ?
> What's   h a p p e n i n g ?
> What' s   h a p p e n i n g ?
> What 's   h a p p e n i n g ?
> Wha t 's   h a p p e n i n g ?
> Wh a t 's   h a p p e n i n g ?
> W h a t 's   h a p p e n i n g ?
> W h a t 's   h a p p e n i n g ?

Do you know why we used **DOWNTO** instead of **TO** in the **FOR** loop? We had to start at the end of the **STRING** and work forward for this program to work correctly. If we did it the other way, we would end up with a bunch of spaces at the beginning of the **STRING**—they would be inserted one after the other, pushing the text over to the right. Remember that **INSERT** changes the length of the **STRING**? Every time we inserted a space, the first character in the sentence we entered would move one more space away—like the proverbial carrot held in front of the mule. Try it out for yourself as an experiment (the program, that is, not the carrot).

Overflow—If we try to insert enough characters into a string to cause it to exceed its declared length, the **INSERT** statement will be ignored and the original string will be untouched.

INPUTTING NUMBERS WITH *STRINGS*

This is one of the sections we've been talking about throughout this book. It's all about creating input routines which defy crashes—even a backwards monkey won't be able to cause a program using these routines to crash, even if he walks on the keyboard!

The Problem. When you are entering a numeric value into an **INTEGER** or **REAL** variable, it is all too easy to make a mistake (enter a nonnumeric character) and cause the program to bomb

116

Listing 9-5.

```
Complaint := 'Myrtle keeps butting in!';
Nosey := '2 cents ';
INSERT(Nosey, Complaint, 8);
INSERT(Nosey, Complaint, 30);
WRITELN(Complaint);
```

Listing 9-6.

```
PROGRAM SpaceOut;
(* Program to demonstrate the INSERT intrinsic *)

VAR Space, Sentence : STRING;
    i               : INTEGER;

BEGIN
  Space := ' ';                        (* Set to one space *)
  PAGE(OUTPUT);
  WRITELN('Enter a sentence');
  WRITE(' : ');
  READLN(Sentence);

  FOR i := LENGTH(Sentence) DOWNTO 1 DO
    BEGIN
      INSERT(Space, Sentence, i);
      WRITELN(Sentence);
    END;

END.  (* SpaceOut *)
```

out. Some versions of Pascal will die as soon as you enter an illegal character, some will wait to commit suicide until you press RETURN, some won't allow back spacing to make corrections, and some will assume you've finished entering your number as soon as you press an illegal character. All versions of Pascal are generally unforgiving of the indefensible crime of entering a letter into a numeric variable.

The solution is to use STRINGs for *all* inputs and then use functions or procedures to convert the STRING to the appropriate number type. You may then proceed to do what you will with the number (+ − * or / it). The final result can be printed out as it is, or you may convert it back to a STRING to fancy it up (insert commas, decimals, dollar signs).

Converting STRINGs to INTEGERs

Our first example (Listing 9-7) will allow you to convert a STRING to an INTEGER. Here is the procedure. To use this procedure just write:

```
Val(StringNumber, IntNumber);
```

where **StringNumber** is a STRING which contains a bunch of numbers and **IntNumber** is an INTEGER variable. The conversion is accomplished by using a FOR loop to check the value of each element in **Data**. We start at the left of the string where the "ones" place is. By using the ORD function, we can convert from characters to their ordinal (ASCII) value. By subtracting the ASCII value of the '0' (zero) from the ASCII value of the character we're currently working with, we get the INTEGER value of the number. For example, let's say **Data** contains '7326.' The character we're looking at is a '6' and its ASCII value is 54. The ASCII value of '0' is 48. 54 − 48 is 6 and we get the correct answer. This should work even if your computer uses a numbering scheme other than ASCII—and so the difference between ORD('6') and ORD('0') will still be 6.

After we get our value, we multiply it by the value in **Tens** and add the result to the value in **Number**. At first, **Tens** is set to 1 and **Number** is set to 0 so the value in **Number** becomes 6. Next we multiply **Tens** by 10 to get ready for the character in the "tens" column. In our example, this character is a '2'. We go through the same process

117

and multiply the resultant 2 by the 10 in **Tens** to get 20. This is added to the value in **Number** (6), and we get 26. We again multiply **Tens** by 10 to get 100 in preparation for converting the character in the "hundreds" column. This loop continues until all characters have been converted and the value in **Number** will be 7326. The conversion is complete!

Of course, the creative reader will try out this routine and pretend to be the backwards monkey. The program may not bomb (unless you try to enter a number larger than **MAXINT**—your Pas-

cal's **INTEGER** limit) but it's much too easy to get inaccurate results. This is because we have not added *error checking* and we haven't allowed for negative **INTEGER**s.

Adding Error Checking to Val

One solution would be to return a value of 0 if there are any problems in the conversion. A more practical solution is to have the conversion procedure pass back an additional Boolean value which is **TRUE** when the entry is legal and **FALSE** if it isn't. This value is called an *error flag*. Listing 9-8

Listing 9-7.

```
PROCEDURE Val(Data        : STRING;
              VAR Number : INTEGER);
VAR    Tens, Len, i : INTEGER;

BEGIN
  Tens := 1;
  Number := 0;

  Len := LENGTH(Data);

  FOR i := Len DOWNTO 1 DO          (* Begin conversion to INTEGER *)
    BEGIN
      Number := Number + (ORD(Data[i]) - ORD('0')) * Tens;
      Tens := Tens * 10;            (* Increment decimal place *)
    END;

END; (* Val *)
```

gives an example of a program with a modified **Val** procedure which includes extensive error checking.

Now you can turn your pet monkey loose and you'll see your program survive his attack! Here are a few entries which will be graciously *rejected* by **Val**:

13A25	27.24	Illegal characters
8397680	—32712	Out of range
——314	+—0	Too many signs
null string		

Here are some legal entries:

Listing 9-8.

```
PROGRAM ValDemo;

CONST   MaxEntry = '32767';
        MaxLength = 5;

VAR    IntString : STRING;
       IntNumber : INTEGER;
       Good      : BOOLEAN;



PROCEDURE Val(Data        : STRING;
               VAR Number : INTEGER;
               VAR Ok     : BOOLEAN);

CONST   Plus  = 1;
        Minus = -1;

VAR    Sign, Len, Tens, i : INTEGER;

BEGIN
  Ok := TRUE;                              (* Initialize *)
  Tens := 1;
  Number := 0;
  Sign := 0;

  Len := LENGTH(Data);

  IF Len = 0 THEN Ok := FALSE              (* Check for null string *)
    ELSE IF Data[1] = '+' THEN Sign := Plus (* Check for + or - sign *)
      ELSE IF Data[1] = '-' THEN Sign := Minus;

  IF ABS(Sign) = 1 THEN                    (* If + or - sign is present, *)
    IF Len = 1 THEN Ok := FALSE            (* check if length is greater *)
      ELSE                                 (* than 1.  If so, then delete *)
        BEGIN                              (* the sign from Data.         *)
          DELETE(Data, 1, 1);
          Len := LENGTH(Data);
        END;

  IF (LENGTH(Data) >= MaxLength) AND (Data > MaxEntry) THEN
    Ok := FALSE;                           (* Number is out of range   *)

  IF Ok THEN                               (* Begin conversion to INTEGER *)
    FOR i := Len DOWNTO 1 DO
      IF (Data[i] < '0') OR (Data[i] > '9') THEN Ok := FALSE
        ELSE                               (* Character is valid number *)
          BEGIN
            Number := Number + (ORD(Data[i]) - ORD('0')) * Tens;
            Tens := Tens * 10;             (* Increment decimal place *)
          END;

  IF Sign <> 0 THEN Number := Number * Sign;  (* Adjust sign if negative *)

END; (* Val *)
```

```
BEGIN  (* Main Program *)
  PAGE( OUTPUT );


  REPEAT                                   (* Loop to accept a valid integer *)
     GOTOXY(0,5);
     WRITE('Enter an integer: ');
     READLN( IntString );
     VAL( IntString, IntNumber, Good );
  UNTIL Good;


   WRITELN('Valid integer: ', IntNumber );
END.  (* ValDemo *)
```

+39	−1189	0	457

Let's go through this procedure step by step:

1. Constants and variables initialized.
2. Check for sign in the first **STRING** position. Before we can do this, we must check to see if there *is* a first position—because accessing **Data[1]**, if we are working with a null string, would yield a run time error. If the length of **Data** is 0 we set our error flag **Ok** to **FALSE**. Otherwise, set the variable **Sign** to the value in **Plus** or **Minus** depending on what the sign is. We are using the constants **Plus** and **Minus** for added clarity.
3. Delete the sign from **Data**—if the value now in **Sign** is 1 or −1, we know there is a sign character to be deleted from the string. However, if the length of **Data** is 1, we know that *all there is* in our string is a sign, so we set **Ok** to **FALSE**. Otherwise, we delete the sign and set **Len** to the new string length.
4. Check the range of **Data**. Before doing the actual conversion, we must check to see if the value in **Data** is larger than **MAXINT** to prevent an overflow error. We can accomplish this by making sure no more than 5 characters (the number of characters in **MaxEntry**, a **STRING** representation of **MAXINT**) were entered, and also making sure these 5 characters don't represent a value greater than **MAXINT**. When checking to see if one **STRING** is "greater" than another, the ordinal values are compared on a character by character basis. This means that '99' is considered to be *greater* than

'10000000' because when comparing the first characters of each, the '99' wins. For now, we are setting the value of **MaxEntry** by hand (see the **CONST** section of this program). Again we set **Ok** to **FALSE** if we find that **Data** *is* out of range. We don't have to check for the minimum range (−32767) because we've already chopped off the negative sign from **Data** (if there was one), making it look like a positive number.
5. Begin actual conversion. If **Ok** is still **TRUE** (no errors so far) we now begin our conversion loop. This time, however, we check the validity of each character before converting it to a number. If the character is either less than '0' or greater than '9', it must be a nonnumeric ASCII character so we set **Ok** to **FALSE**. If our character has survived all these rigorous tests, it is ready to graduate to **INTEGER**-hood!
6. Fix the sign. The final step is to give our newly created **INTEGER** the **Sign** of its heritage as a **STRING**. If **Sign** does not contain a 0, we multiply our **Number** by **Sign** and the transformation is complete.

There is no way that an illegal **STRING** can make it through all the tests without being "found out." The value in **Ok** (which is passed as a variable parameter along with **Number**) will give it away. All you have to do is check the value in the actual parameter (**Good** in **ValDemo**) for the stamp of approval—a **TRUE**—before you use the value in **IntNumber**. If **Good** is **FALSE**, have the user re-enter the **STRING** as we do in our example.

Listing 9-9.

```
PROGRAM IntConvert;

VAR    MaxEntry : STRING;

PROCEDURE IntStr(Number       : INTEGER;
                 VAR OutString : STRING);

CONST  Minus = '-';

VAR    Num         : INTEGER;
       Space, Sign : STRING;

BEGIN
  OutString := '';                    (* Set to null *)
  Space     := ' ';                   (* Set to one space *)
  Sign      := '';                    (* Set to null *)

  IF Number < 0 THEN                  (* Check for negative number *)
    BEGIN
      Sign := Minus;
      Number := ABS(Number);          (* Convert to positive number *)
    END;

  REPEAT
    Num := Number - ((Number DIV 10) * 10); (* Isolate last digit *)
    OutString := CONCAT(Space, OutString);  (* Open slot for CHAR *)
    OutString[1] := CHR(Num + ORD('0'));     (* Convert Num to CHAR *)
    Number := Number DIV 10;                  (* Prepare for next digit *)
  UNTIL Number = 0;

  IF Sign = Minus THEN
    INSERT(Minus, OutString, 1);       (* Replace minus sign *)
END; (* IntStr *)


BEGIN  (* Main Program *)
  IntStr(MAXINT, MaxEntry);
  WRITELN(MaxEntry);
END.  (* IntConvert *)
```

Converting *INTEGERs* Into *STRINGs*

We will now go in the other direction. This next program in Listing 9-9, **IntConvert**, has a procedure which will convert an **INTEGER** to a **STRING**.

We are using this procedure to convert the **MAXINT** value to the **STRING** MaxEntry which can then be used in our **Val** procedure. On execution, this program will print out the **MAXINT** value as a **STRING**. For an Apple II it will look like this:

32767

Now for the explanation. First of all, there is no error checking in procedure IntStr. This is because no errors are possible when converting from an **INTEGER** to a **STRING**. Regardless of what value is passed to the actual parameter Number, this procedure will produce an accurate result. Starting at the top:

1. Initialize the variables. Set **OutString** to null, **Space** to one space.
2. Check for minus sign. If **Number** is negative, **Sign** is set to a minus sign, then **Number** is changed to a positive value.
3. Begin the conversion. We again want to start

at the right with the ones' column. The plan is to first isolate the right-most digit and store it in **Num**:

   a. **DIV**ide **Number** by 10 to eliminate the right-most digit. Using the value of **MAXINT** we get:

> 32767 DIV 10 = 3276

   b. Multiply the result by 10 to create a sort of "filter":

> 3276 * 10 = 32760

   c. Subtract this result from **Number** (push the value of **Number** through the filter):

> 32767 − 32760 = 7

4. Initialize **OutString**. Add a space to the left side of **OutString**. Since **OutString** was null before, now it holds one space.
5. Place digit into **OutString**. We calculate the ASCII value of '7' by adding **Num** to the ASCII value of '0':

> 7 + 48 = 55

then convert this ASCII code to the corresponding character using the **CHR** function. We then make this character the first element of **OutString**. Why did we choose this somewhat roundabout method? Since **CHR** produces a **CHAR** type value, we had to match it with the same type on the left side of the expression. The elements of a **STRING** are also **CHAR**s. But before we could do this, we had to create a "slot" to drop the character into. This was done in the previous step (Step 4). If we hadn't carried out Step 4 first, we would have received a run-time error—accessing a nonexistent element of a **STRING**. You may wonder why we couldn't combine steps 4 and 5 into the statement:

> OutString := CONCAT(CHR(Num + ORD('0')), OutString);

We can't do this because *CONCAT only works with STRINGs*, and, as we said before, *CHR returns a CHAR type*.

6. Knock off right digit. Now that we have converted the first digit, we can throw it away by dividing the value of **Number** by 10 and storing the result back in **Number**:

> 32767 DIV 10 = 3276

7. Check to see if finished. If **Number** has been reduced to nothingness (to 0), the conversion is complete. (DIViding a number less than 10 by 10 yields a 0.) Otherwise, go back to step 3.
8. Insert sign. If the original **Number** was negative, we must not deprive **OutString** of carrying on the tradition. So we **INSERT** the minus sign into the first position of **OutString**.

STR—Instant Number String

Now that you fully understand how this procedure works, we have to tell you that UCSD Pascal (as well as some other Pascals) has a built-in procedure to accomplish the same thing. It is called **STR** and it is used with the same syntax as our IntStr procedure:

> STR(Number, IntString);

By creating an existing procedure from scratch, you will now have a better understanding of how the creators of Pascal did it.

For those of you who are wondering whether Pascal also has a built-in function to convert a **STRING** to an **INTEGER** (like BASIC's VAL function), sorry it doesn't.

Uncle Pascal says: *Now that you can convert from STRINGs to INTEGERs and from INTEGERs to STRINGs, how about trying it with lead and gold!*

QUIZ—STRINGS

True or False

1. The maximum length to a *STRING* is 255 characters.
2. Accessing a nonexistent element of a *STRING* will yield a run-time error.
3. Using *LENGTH* on a null string yields a run-time error.
4. The *STRING* intrinsic *POS* returns the value *FALSE* if no match is found.
5. You will get a run-time error if you use parameters for the *STRING* intrinsics which are beyond the size of the *STRING*.

USING *LONG INTEGERS* FOR INCREASED ACCURACY

A number of times throughout this book we have said that all kinds of wonderful things could be accomplished with **LONG INTEGER**s. This is the section of the book where we fulfill all of your expectations.

What Are *LONG INTEGERs*?

LONG INTEGERs are a special data type which is not part of standard Pascal. This type was added to UCSD Pascal (and certain other Pascals) to provide the level of accuracy which is missing in **REAL**s. To declare a **LONG INTEGER**, just place a length attribute after the word **INTEGER**.

```
VAR BigNumber : INTEGER[15];
```

UCSD Pascal treats **LONG INTEGER**s very much like ordinary **INTEGER**s. You can perform the four basic arithmetic operations on them (+ − * DIV) and you can use the relational operators (<, >, =, >=, <=, <>). But **LONG INTEGER**s are special with some special features and restrictions. They can be up to 36 digits in length, the operator MOD can't be used with them, and since they *are* a different type than **INTEGER**s, you must be careful when working with **LONG INTEGER**s and normal **INTEGER**s together. When mixing **INTEGER**s and **LONG INTEGER**s in arithmetic expressions, the result is always a **LONG**. A **LONG** can be assigned an **INTEGER** value:

```
LongValue := IntValue;
```

but to go in the other direction you must use the **TRUNC** function (also used to convert **REAL**s to **INTEGER**s):

```
IntValue := TRUNC(LongValue);
```

However, if the **LONG** in this expression is greater than **MAXINT**, you will get an overflow error.

LONGs can also be converted to **STRING**s using the **STR** procedure:

```
STR(LongNumber, LongString);
```

Even though **LONG**s can be very large numbers, you still must guard against overflow. If a **LONG** becomes larger than its declared length (or greater than 36 digits), you will get a run-time error.

Using *LONGs* in Place of *REALs*

Using **LONG**s merely as very big **INTEGER**s is extremely simple and straightforward—you just do it. But using **LONG**s in place of **REAL**s can become somewhat more complex. This is because you have to keep track of an imaginary decimal point (since you can't *really* insert one

into a **LONG**). We have come up with a few simple rules to help you handle this problem. Consider the following:

$$
\begin{array}{r}
2.25 \\
\times\ 2.25 \\
\hline
1125 \\
450\ \ \\
450\ \ \ \ \\
\hline
50625
\end{array}
$$

The numbers are correct but we haven't inserted the decimal point yet. We were taught in school to count the total number of digits to the right of the decimal point in the two numbers which are multiplied together. Each number has *two* decimal digits so $2 + 2 = 4$. This means that our answer must have 4 decimal places in it:

$$5.0625$$

What if we wanted to cube 2.25 instead of square it? The product of $2.25 * 2.25 * 2.25$ will have 6 decimal places (11.390625). If we continue to multiply the products by 2.25, we could eventually end up with a number with a very large number of digits to the right of the decimal point. 2.25^{15} would have 30 decimal places!

$$2.25^{15} = 191751.0592328840866684913635253906 25$$

What if the numbers we were multiplying together had *8* decimal places!! You can see that even with **LONG INTEGER**s we could rapidly run into an overflow. The solution is to round off the number of decimal places which were added on *after each successive multiplication operation*:

$$
\begin{array}{l}
2.25 * 2.25 = \ \ 5.0625 \text{ round to } \ \ 5.06 \\
5.06 * 2.25 = 11.3850 \text{ round to } 11.39 \\
11.39 * 2.25 = 25.6275 \text{ round to } 25.63 \ldots \text{ etc.}
\end{array}
$$

By following this technique, we can keep the number of decimal places under control and also keep track of where the imaginary decimal point is (always two places from the right). The choice to round to two places is an arbitrary one—we could just as easily have chosen to round to eight decimal places. So much for the background material; here comes a concrete example.

The Loan Payment Program Revisited

What follows is a souped up version of our Loan Payment Program (Listings 5-7, 8-9) which uses error checking, the accuracy of **LONG INTE-GER**s, and fancy output. We will explain the program to you in bite-sized chunks, then print the entire program at the end of this chapter (Listing 9-11). *Don't become overwhelmed by its size—*

it really isn't difficult to understand. Also, don't feel obligated to figure it all out—take the major ideas (error checking and use of **LONG INTEGER**s) and try using them in your programs.

An Overview of the Program—We've categorized the functions of the program into three main parts:

1. Entry of the data and conversion to **LONG**s—we enter all numbers as **STRING**s, and then use a modified **Val** procedure to check for illegal numbers and convert the **STRING**s to **LONG**s or **INTEGER**s (two of each are entered).
2. Calculations—this section is very similar to the calculation section of our earlier version. The only difference is that we are dealing with **LONG**s and have to make sure we don't misplace our imaginary decimal point.
3. Output—the final **LONG** values are rounded off, converted to **STRING**s, and made to look pretty by adding commas.

Before we explain this program further let's use it on a couple of examples. For the first example, we will use the earlier data for purchasing a $100,000.00 home with a 20% downpayment. This means financing $80,000.00 for 30 years at 15%:

```
           ** LOAN PAYMENT **

    Enter the following information
    (You may use commas in your numbers):

    Amount of loan:        80,000.00
    Annual interest (%):   15
    Payments per year      12
    Term in years:         30


            Regular payment =
               $ 1,011.55

         Total interest on loan =
              $ 284,159.73


    Would you like to calculate another? Y
```

You'll notice that we used commas both during entry and output to make reading large numbers easier. We also obtained a much more accurate figure on the total interest on the loan. Let's put our program to a bigger test. As you are well aware, we Americans have to pay taxes to the U.S. Government. In 1979, we paid a total of $370.5 billion! Let's not think of this as throwing away our money, let's think of it as a *Loan* to Uncle Sam (no relation to Uncle Pascal). If it's a loan, we need to get payments back in order for this loan to be paid off. Since we pay taxes every year, the Term of the loan will be one year. And since we're not greedy, we will only charge Uncle Sam what we would get if we could place the money in a standard passbook account at 5.25% interest. One payment per month isn't enough, though, so let's make it one payment per day. Let's see how much we (as taxpaying citizens) should be receiving back from Uncle Sam in the form of services, if not money.

```
           ** LOAN PAYMENT **

    Enter the following information
    (You may use commas in your numbers):

    Amount of loan:        370,500,000,000.00
    Annual interest (%):   5.25
    Payments per year:     365
    Term in years:         1


            Regular payment =
             $ 1,041,978,387.69

         Total interest on loan =
           $ 9,822,111,506.85


    Would you like to calculate another? N

         That's all folks . . . BYE
```

Now let's take the regular payment and divide it by the number of Americans (about 227 million) and we get approximately $4.59 per American per day! Oh, if only it were that simple!!

How It Works

So much for our little diversion, let's see how this program works.

The Constants—We'll start at the top of the program (Listing 9-10A) with the list of constants.

Accuracy is set to the maximum number of digits we will allow to remain to the right of the decimal point. In our previous demonstration in which we multiplied 2.25 times itself, and then rounded back to two places, we could say we had an **Accuracy** of 2. An **Accuracy** of 8 means we will be rounding off to 8 decimal places. Since we are working in dollars and cents, this will give us *more* than enough accuracy since the final answer will be further rounded down to 2 decimal places (cents).

Listing 9-10A.

```
PROGRAM Loan4;

CONST  Accuracy = 8;   (* Number of decimal places used during calculations *)
       ScreenWidth = 40;
       MaxEntry = 20; (* Maximum allowable digits in this program's LONGs   *)
       LongValue = TRUE;
       IntValue = FALSE;

TYPE  LONG = INTEGER[36];          (* Declare new TYPE so LONGs can be used as
                                      parameters.  Up to 36 digits of accuracy *)

VAR  Principal, AnnualInterest,
     RegularPayment, TotalInterest, One    : LONG;
     PaymentsPerYear, TermInYears, VertPos : INTEGER;
     YesNo                                 : CHAR;
```

ScreenWidth is set to the width of your computer's screen. This value is used in the **Center** procedure which we introduced earlier in this chapter.

MaxEntry is the maximum number of digits we will allow the user to enter for a number in this program. With the formulas we use in this program, entering a number of more than 20 digits will invariably lead to overflow errors. Although, the input and conversion routines have been protected from overflows, the calculation section of this program has not. If the user enters unrealistically large numbers for all entries or zeroes for certain entries, the program will bomb when it tries calculating with these numbers. The next two Boolean constants will be used as flags—we will cover them later on.

A New Data Type—After the constant declaration section (Listing 9-10A) there is a line that is unfamiliar to you. Here it is again:

```
TYPE LONG = INTEGER[36];
```

The right side of this line should look familiar—it shows that we will be using 36 digit **LONG INTEGER**s. This line says that we are now creating a new *data type* which, in this case, we will call **LONG**, and it will equal a 36 digit **LONG INTEGER** (we will be covering new data **TYPE**s in the next chapter). We had to do this because of an idiosyncrasy in UCSD Pascal. **TRUNC** and **STR** are the only two routines which will accept **LONG INTEGER**s as parameters. We would get a syntax error if we attempted to declare a **LONG INTEGER** in a parameter list for the procedures of this program. This is because in a parameter list, the identifier (variable name) is *bound* to a *type name* (e.g., **CHAR**, **INTEGER**, **REAL**, etc.). However, declarations such as **INTEGER[36]** or **STRING[40]** are not type *names*, they are type

descriptions. So, to assign a *name* to a type *description* we use the **TYPE** declaration, in this case **LONG**. We can now use this "new" type when we declare variables and parameters throughout the program. An example of this follows in the **VAR** list for the program block (Listing 9-10A). All of the variables which were declared as **REAL**s in the original versions of this program are now declared as **LONG**s.

Stepping Through the Logic

Let's follow this program through a run. Look at the Main Program section (Listing 9-10B).

The Power Procedure—The first thing we do is to initialize the variable **One** to $10^{Accuracy}$ using a modified **Power** procedure (from Listing 8-7). You'll find this procedure in Listing 9-10C and again near the beginning of the complete program listing at the end of this chapter. We had to convert **Power** from a function to a procedure because a function can't return a **LONG** as its result. We also reverted back to the version which only calculated positive exponents—raising an integer to a negative exponent will cause a rapid loss of accuracy. Otherwise, this procedure is very much like our earlier **Power** function. We are just using **LONG**s in place of **REAL**s. The value in **One** (10^8) is what a 1 would look like if the imaginary decimal was in position. Since we are working with 8 decimal places of **Accuracy**, if we were using **REAL**s rather than **LONG**s, the number would be written as:

```
1.00000000
```

Remove the decimal point and we have:

```
100000000 or 10⁸ or 10Accuracy
```

Listing 9-10B.

```
BEGIN (* Main Program *)
  Power(10, Accuracy, One);  (* Compute the number "One" by raising 10
                                to the Accuracy power (10 ↑ Accuracy) *)
  YesNo := ' ';               (* Initialize to one space *)

  REPEAT
    GetData;
    Calculate;
    PrintAnswer;
    GOTOXY(0,19);
    WRITE('Would you like to calculate another? ');
    READ(YesNo);
  UNTIL (YesNo = 'N') OR (YesNo = 'n');

  GOTOXY(0,22);
  Center('That''s all folks...BYE');
END. (* Loan4 *)
```

We use this value *in place of the number 1* when we want to combine a 1 with a **LONG**. If this is what a 1 looks like, a 0.05 would look like:

```
          5000000
```

Converting a number to what we will call an "adjusted **LONG**" can be accomplished by multiplying the number by the variable **One**:

```
   0.05   * One =    5000000

   21.0031 * One = 2100310000
```

Getting the Data—Let's go on. After initializing **YesNo** to one space, the **GetData** procedure is called and we enter the input and conversion portion of this program (Listing 9-10D). Look at **GetData**.

After initializing **VertPos** and setting up the screen (using two recycled procedures, **Clear-Screen** and **Center**) the user is prompted for the amount of the loan. Rather than using **READLNs** to enter numbers, we are using two custom procedures, **ReadLong** to enter **LONGs** and **ReadInt** to enter **INTEGERs**. Look at **ReadLong** (Listing 9-10E) first.

This is the "housekeeping" procedure that positions the cursor (now you see where **VertPos** is used), and accepts a **STRING** from the user. Next comes the conversion to a **LONG** using the **Val** procedure. You'll notice that we are passing an extra parameter to **Val** called **LongValue**. This is a Boolean constant (declared at the beginning of the program) with a value of **TRUE**. Since both **ReadLong** and **ReadInt** call **Val**, we needed a way to let **Val** know whether the **STRING** is to be converted to a **LONG** or an **INTEGER**. This Boolean parameter is the means to do this. The only

Listing 9-10C.

```
PROCEDURE Power(x          : LONG;
                y          : INTEGER;
                VAR Result : LONG);
(* Procedure which raises x to the y power (x↑y) y
   must be greater than 0.  A procedure must be used
   because functions can't produce LONGs as a result. *)

VAR   i : INTEGER;

BEGIN
  Result := 1;
  FOR i := 1 TO y DO
    Result := Result * x;
END; (* Power *)
```

Listing 9-10D.

```
PROCEDURE GetData;

BEGIN                                    (* Set vertical cursor position *)
  VertPos := 6;
  ClearScreen;
  Center('** LOAN PAYMENT **');
  WRITELN;
  WRITELN;
  WRITELN('Enter the following information');
  WRITELN('(You may use commas in your numbers):');
  WRITELN;
  WRITE(' Amount of loan:');
  ReadLong(Principal);                   (* Call routine to accept data *)
  WRITE(' Annual interest (%):');
  ReadLong(AnnualInterest);
  WRITE(' Payments per year:');
  ReadInt(PaymentsPerYear);
  WRITE(' Term in years:');
  ReadInt(TermInYears);
END; (* GetData *)
```

way to exit **ReadLong** is to enter a valid **LONG**, then the value sent back to **Good** will be **TRUE**. If **Good** is **FALSE**, another procedure, **ClrLine** (also in Listing 9-10E), is called to clear the entry and reposition the cursor. When **Good** is **TRUE**, **VertPos** is incremented by one in prepara-

Listing 9-10E.

```
PROCEDURE ClrLine;
(* Erase the contents of line VertPos to the right of
   horizontal position 22, reposition cursor for next try. *)

BEGIN
  GOTOXY(22,VertPos);
  WRITELN(' ':30);
  GOTOXY(22,VertPos);
END; (* ClrLine *)




PROCEDURE ReadLong(VAR LongNumber : LONG);
(* Read a STRING and send it to Val to be converted
   to a LONG until a valid LONG is returned.          *)
VAR  InpString : STRING;
     Good       : BOOLEAN;

BEGIN
  REPEAT
    GOTOXY(22,VertPos);
    READLN(InpString);
    Val(InpString, LongNumber, LongValue, Good);
    IF NOT Good THEN ClrLine;
  UNTIL Good;
  VertPos := VertPos + 1;              (* Increment vertical cursor position *)
END; (* ReadLong *)
```

Listing 9-10F.

```
PROCEDURE ReadInt(VAR IntNumber : INTEGER);
(* Read a STRING and send it to Val to be converted
   to a INTEGER until a valid INTEGER is returned. *)
VAR   InpString  : STRING;
      LongNumber : LONG;
      Good       : BOOLEAN;

BEGIN
  REPEAT
    GOTOXY(22,VertPos);
    READLN(InpString);
    Val(InpString, LongNumber, IntValue, Good);
    IF NOT Good THEN ClrLine;
  UNTIL Good;
  IntNumber := TRUNC(LongNumber);       (* Convert LONG to INTEGER *)
  VertPos := VertPos + 1;        (* Increment vertical cursor position *)
END; (* ReadInt *)
```

tion for the next entry. Now look at **ReadInt** (Listing 9-10F).

It is very similar to **ReadLong**. There are two main differences:

1. It sends the Boolean constant **IntValue** (set to **FALSE**) to **Val**. This lets **Val** know that the entered **STRING** is to be converted to an **INTEGER**.
2. The **LONG** received from **Val** is converted to an **INTEGER** using **TRUNC**.

Converting to Numbers With Val—Now look at procedure **Val** (Listing 9-10G). This is the longest procedure in the program (also the longest single block procedure in this book) and it does the most difficult job—trying to second guess a backwards monkey who's in a hurry isn't easy!

You'll recognize many sections from the version of **Val** which we used to convert from **STRING**s to **INTEGER**s (Listing 9-8). In addition to maintaining most of the previous features, this version also has to watch for decimal points and shift the size of the final number accordingly. Let's follow the steps:

1. Initialize variables. We have two new variables—**DecimalPlaces** will hold the number of decimal places the entered "number" has. **FoundDecimal** is a flag which will be set to **TRUE** when the first decimal point is encountered during the conversion process.
2. Delete commas from entry. To make it easier to enter large numbers, we set the program up so the user could use commas if desired. Therefore, we must check for and delete all commas. We are using a variation of the **NoSpace** program (Listing 9-4) which deleted all of the spaces from a sentence. When our **STRING Data** exits this **WHILE** loop, it will be free of commas.

3. Sign check. In this section we check for the presence of a plus (+) or minus (−) sign in the **STRING**. Before we reference the first element, we check to see if there *is* a first element. You already know what happens if we try to access a nonexistent **STRING** element! If **Data** survives this first test, we check for the sign. This section was taken from the earlier version of **Val**.

4. Delete sign. This section was also from the old **Val**. If there is a sign in the **STRING**, we check to make sure there's something else there too. If the **STRING** length isn't equal to one, we delete the first character (the sign) and reset **Len** to the new length of **Data**.

5. **STRING** set to decimal point. Check to see if all that is left in the **STRING** is the decimal point. If so, set **Ok** to **FALSE**.

6. Check length of **Data**. If the **STRING** length is greater than the value in **Max-Entry** (20) we set **Ok** to **FALSE**. The chances are quite high that a number with more than 20 digits will cause an overflow error during the calculation stage.

7. Convert to number. This is the section which does the actual conversion. The first part is stolen from our old **Val** procedure. What we added was a section that holds the

Listing 9-10G.

```
PROCEDURE Val(Data        : STRING;
              VAR Number  : LONG;
              LongFlag    : BOOLEAN;
              VAR Ok      : BOOLEAN);
CONST   Plus  = 1;
        Minus = -1;
VAR     Sign, Len, i,
        DecimalPlaces : INTEGER;
        Tens, Offset  : LONG;
        FoundDecimal  : BOOLEAN;
BEGIN
  Ok := TRUE;                            (* Initialize *)
  Tens := 1;
  Number := 0;
  Sign := 0;
  DecimalPlaces := 0;
  FoundDecimal := FALSE;

  WHILE POS(',', Data) > 0 DO
    DELETE(Data, POS(',', Data), 1);  (* Delete all commas from Data *)

  Len := LENGTH(Data);
  IF Len = 0 THEN Ok := FALSE              (* Check for null string *)
    ELSE IF Data[1] = '+' THEN Sign := Plus (* Check for + or - sign *)
      ELSE IF Data[1] = '-' THEN Sign := Minus;

  IF ABS(Sign) = 1 THEN                 (* If + or - sign is present,  *)
    IF Len = 1 THEN Ok := FALSE         (* check if length is greater  *)
      ELSE                              (* than 1.  If so, then delete *)
        BEGIN                           (* the sign from Data.         *)
          DELETE(Data, 1, 1);
          Len := LENGTH(Data);
        END;

  IF Data = '.' THEN Ok := FALSE;       (* Another invalid entry     *)

  IF Len > MaxEntry THEN Ok := FALSE;   (* Number is out of range    *)

  IF Ok THEN                            (* Begin conversion to LONG *)
    FOR i := Len DOWNTO 1 DO
      BEGIN
        IF (Data[i] < '0') OR (Data[i] > '9') THEN Ok := FALSE
          ELSE                          (* Character is valid number *)
            BEGIN
              Number := Number + (ORD(Data[i]) - ORD('0')) * Tens;
              Tens := Tens * 10;        (* Increment decimal place *)
            END;
        IF LongFlag AND (Data[i] = '.') AND NOT FoundDecimal THEN
          BEGIN                         (* First decimal found in LONG *)
            DecimalPlaces := Len - i;
            Ok := TRUE;
            FoundDecimal := TRUE;
          END;
      END; (* FOR Loop *)
```

```
IF NOT LongFlag AND (Number > MAXINT) THEN Ok := FALSE;

IF Sign <> 0 THEN Number := Number * Sign;  (* Adjust sign if negative *)

(* If LONG then make it into an "adjusted LONG" by moving the
   imaginary decimal over the right number of spaces to give it
   a total of Acuracy decimal places.                            *)
IF LongFlag THEN
  (* If the number of decimal places exceeds Accuracy then Roundoff *)
  IF DecimalPlaces > Accuracy THEN
    Roundoff(Number, DecimalPlaces - Accuracy)
    ELSE
      BEGIN
        Power(10, Accuracy - DecimalPlaces, Offset);
        Number := Number * Offset;   (* Move decimal over the     *)
      END;                           (* correct number of places *)
END; (* Val *)
```

number of "decimal places" there are in the variable **Data**. Here are the steps:

  a. Check to see if this is a **LONG** (**Long-Flag** will hold the **TRUE** from **Read-Long**) and if the character we're looking at is a decimal point (.) *and* make sure this is the *first* decimal point we have encountered (**FoundDecimal** is still set to **FALSE**). If all these conditions are met, then continue.

  b. The number of decimal places is calculated by subtracting **i** from the length of **Data**. Store this in **DecimalPlaces**.

  c. Set **Ok** back to **TRUE**. It was set to **FALSE** when it was discovered that the current character wasn't a numeric character.

  d. Set the **FoundDecimal** flag to **TRUE**. This flag will protect the program from the dot-happy user who enters more than one decimal point. Only the first one counts.

8. Check value of **INTEGER**. If we are converting an **INTEGER** and not a **LONG**, we need to make sure the value of **Number** isn't greater than **MAXINT**. If it *is* we will get an overflow error later on in **ReadInt** when we try to convert the **LONG** down to an **INTEGER** with **TRUNC**.

9. Put back the sign. We next stick the sign back on the **Number** if it should have one. Of course, if it's a positive number, the sign remains invisible. This step is somewhat ludicrous for this program since it's unlikely anyone will have to pay back a loan with *negative dollars!* But if you want to use this entire procedure in another application, you may need to convert to negative numbers.

10. Create "Adjusted **LONG**." The final step in

Val is necessary for **LONG**s only. We need to make sure that the number of digits to the right of the decimal point in our number is consistent with all other **LONG**s in this program. (We explain why shortly.) As said before, this number is stored in the constant **Accuracy** and its value is 8. There are two possibilities here, either **Number** has 8 or more "decimal places" already (in which case we must chop some off), or it doesn't have enough decimal places (we must add some):

a. To chop off the extra decimal places, we use the **Roundoff** procedure (Listing 9-10H). The second parameter in **Roundoff** is the number of places to remove. We arrive at this number by subtracting **Accuracy** from **DecimalPlaces**. For example, if our number had 11 decimal places and we only want 8 (**Accuracy** = 8) we subtract 8 from 11 and get 3 (11 − 8 = 3) so 3 decimal places are chopped off and we are left with 8. If there are already 8 places, **Roundoff** does nothing with **Number**.

b. If **Number** doesn't have enough decimal places (less than **Accuracy**), all we have to do is add the correct number of zeroes to the end of **Number** to make up the difference. We find how many places we are short (**Accuracy** − **DecimalPlaces**) and use **Power** to return **Offset** (10 raised to the number of places short). Finally, by multiplying **Number** by **Offset**, we get our Adjusted **LONG**.

So when we leave **Val**, we will either have a **LONG** with **Accuracy** decimal places, a value within the **INTEGER** range, or an error flag which says to do it again.

By The Way . . .
Adjusted *LONG*s

Why make all **LONG**s consistent? We want to make all of the **LONG**s consistent with each other because this is easier than trying to keep track of where the

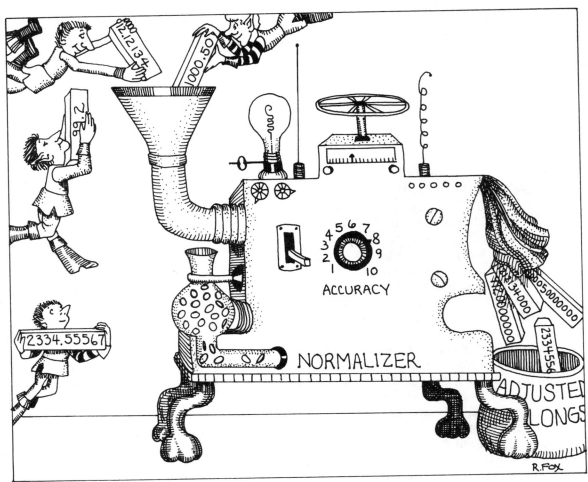

decimal is with each number using additional variables or flags or whatever. When working with **REALs**, all this is unnecessary—if we add 12.12134 to 1000.50, the decimals automatically line up:

$$\begin{array}{r} 12.12134 \\ +1000.50 \\ \hline 1012.62134 \end{array}$$

But what if we erase the decimals? The computer would add them together like this:

$$\begin{array}{r} 1212134 \\ +\ 100050 \\ \hline 1312184 \end{array}$$

and the result would bear no relationship to the truth.

But what if we adjust the numbers so they will all have 8 decimal places:

$$\begin{array}{rcr} 12.12134000 & \rightarrow & 1212134000 \\ 1000.50000000 & \rightarrow & +100050000000 \\ & & \hline \\ & & 101262134000 \end{array}$$

Now let's replace the decimal point 8 places from the right:

$$1012.62134000$$

And our result is accurate! So, we don't have to worry about where the decimal point is for a given **LONG** once the **LONG** has been "adjusted" (sometimes called "normalized") because we know it will always be **Accuracy** places from the right.

Roundoff—Let's delve a little deeper to see how the **Roundoff** procedure (Listing 9-10H) accomplishes its task.

Here are the steps:

1. Initialize **Up** to 0.
2. Create the divisor. **Dv** is created by raising 10 to the **Places** power. **Places** is the value sent by **Val** which indicates how many decimal places to lop off. If **Places** received a 3, **Dv** would be set to 10^3 or 1000.
3. Check for rounding. Isolate the most significant digit which will be lost when the number is rounded. That is, if we wanted to knock off 3 places from 593621 we would get 593. However, by checking the left-most of the digits which are truncated, the 6 in this case, we can tell whether we should round up. To isolate the number we plug our values into the expression:

> LastDigit := (Number DIV (Dv DIV 10)) − ((Number DIV Dv) * 10);

This expression reduces to:

$$5936 - 5930 = 6$$

4. Save rounding factor. If **LastDigit** is greater than or equal to 5, we must round up so **Up** is set to 1. If **LastPlace** is less than or equal to −5, **Up** is set to −1.
5. Adjust **Number**. Finally we **DIV**ide **Number** by **Dv** to adjust it to the consistent size and add **Up** to it for rounding.

Listing 9-10H.

```
PROCEDURE Roundoff(VAR Number : LONG;
                       Places    : INTEGER);

(* Procedure to round off a LONG INTEGER by Places positions *)

VAR   Up            : INTEGER;
      Dv, LastDigit : LONG;

BEGIN
  Up := 0;
  Power(10, Places, Dv);                (* Create Dv := 10 ↑ Places *)

  (* Isolate the imaginary decimal place which
     will be lost when Number is adjusted.      *)
  LastDigit := (Number DIV (Dv DIV 10)) - ((Number DIV Dv) * 10);

  (* Next set Up := 1 if number needs to be rounded up
     or set Up := -1 if number needs to be rounded down *)
  IF LastDigit >= 5 THEN Up := 1
     ELSE IF LastDigit <= -5 THEN Up := -1;
                                 (* Divide number by Dv, add Up *)
  Number := Number DIV Dv + Up;  (* to correctly round Number.  *)
END; (* Roundoff *)
```

Listing 9-10I.

```
PROCEDURE Calculate;
VAR    Numerator, Denominator,
       InterestPerPeriod, Temp : LONG;
       NumberOfPayments        : INTEGER;

BEGIN (* Calculate *)
  GOTOXY(13,19);
  WRITE('Calculating...');

  InterestPerPeriod := (AnnualInterest DIV 100) DIV PaymentsPerYear;
  NumberOfPayments := PaymentsPerYear * TermInYears;

  (* Two "adjusted LONGs" will be multiplied together; we must bring
     the decimal place back in line by rounding off Accuracy places. *)
  Numerator := Principal * InterestPerPeriod;
  Roundoff(Numerator, Accuracy);

  PowerMod(One + InterestPerPeriod, -NumberOfPayments, Temp);
  Denominator := One - Temp;

  (* One "adjusted LONG" will be divided by another so we must allow
     for the cancellation of significant places by multiplying by
     "One" first.  "One" is equal to 10 ↑ Accuracy               *)
  RegularPayment := One * Numerator DIV Denominator;

  TotalInterest := RegularPayment * NumberOfPayments - Principal;
END; (* Calculate *)
```

Phew!! All that just to enter four numbers! Well, the numbers are now stored in their proper variables and we are ready to perform the calculations on them.

The Calculate Procedure—This procedure (Listing 9-10I) is fundamentally the same one that we used in the previous Loan programs. As we saw earlier, adding and subtracting "adjusted **LONGs**" (again, **LONGs** with a uniform number of imaginary decimal places) is straightforward—just do it. But multiplying and dividing leads to a slight complication. Multiplying two adjusted **LONGs** together will cause a *doubling* of the number of imaginary decimal places. So, when multiplying two adjusted **LONGs** together always *round the result back down to **Accuracy** places after every multiplication.*

When dividing two adjusted **LONGs** together, the opposite happens—we *lose* **Accuracy** places. All the extra places we so carefully added cancel each other out:

$$\frac{500000000}{700000000} = \frac{5}{7} = 0$$

We obviously can't have this happen and we can't recover the lost digits by multiplying by $10^{Accuracy}$ *after* the division takes place ($10^{Accuracy} * 0 = 0$)

so we *multiply by* $10^{Accuracy}$ **before** *the division takes place!* This way we retain our **Accuracy** decimal places:

$$100000000 * \frac{500000000}{700000000} = \frac{50000000000000000}{700000000} =$$

$$\frac{500000000}{7} = 71428571$$

When multiplying or dividing an adjusted **LONG** by an **INTEGER**, there is no need for any corrections—decimal places are neither lost nor gained. However, we can't add or subtract **INTEGERs** and adjusted **LONGs** together unless the **INTEGERs** have been adjusted too.

During the calculations of this procedure, the value $10^{Accuracy}$ is stored in the variable **One**. We can multiply **LONGs** which are to be divided by each other by **One** before the division. We also use **One** wherever a 1 is called for in our formula since **One** is really an adjusted **LONG** with the value of 1.

Now that you have the explanation, you will be able to follow our actions. You'll notice that we printed the word 'Calculating...' on the screen when the calculations began—working with **LONGs** is much slower than **INTEGERs** or

Listing 9-10J.

```
PROCEDURE PowerMod(x        : LONG;
                   y        : INTEGER;
                   VAR Result : LONG);
(* Procedure which raises x to the y power (x↑y) and adjusts
   the imaginary decimal by rounding off Accuracy places
   with the Roundoff procedure.  This procedure must be used
   in place of Power when our "adjusted LONGs" are involved. *)

VAR   i : INTEGER;

BEGIN
  Result := One;
  IF y >= 0 THEN
    FOR i := 1 TO y DO
      BEGIN
        Result := Result * x;
        Roundoff(Result, Accuracy);   (* Adjust Result to *)
      END                             (* Accuracy places  *)
    ELSE IF x = 0 THEN Result := 0    (* Check for base of 0 *)
      ELSE
        FOR i := 1 to -y DO
          Result := One * Result DIV x;  (* Increase decimal places prior to
                                            division by multiplying Result by One *)
END; (* PowerMod *)
```

REALs. If the values are very large or the number of payments is high, the user may have to wait minutes rather than seconds. We don't want the user to think the poor computer died! (Perhaps we could interface the computer to a MU-ZAK™ machine and have it melodiously fill the calculating time.)

In order to do the adjustments to the numbers after multiplications, we had to break the formula into sections and use some temporary variables (**Numerator, Denominator, Temp**). Since we are using the technique of successive multiplications when raising a number to a power, we had to create a new power procedure called **PowerMod** (Listing 9-10J) which can handle our adjusted **LONGs**. It also follows the rules above.

Output of the Results—We now are finally ready to output the results. But we must first convert the **LONGs** back to **STRINGs** so we can insert a decimal point. Our old **PrintAnswer** procedure calls an output procedure, **WriteLong**, which does this plus more. Take a look at **WriteLong** (Listing 9-10K).

We'll go through the steps:

1. Round off the **LONG** so that it has only two imaginary decimal places instead of **Accuracy**.

2. Convert the **LONG** to a **STRING** using the intrinsic **STR** procedure.
3. Check for the presence of a minus sign. If it's there, set **Sign** to 1, otherwise set **Sign** to 0.
4. There is a possible rare occurrence which may happen—if the number we are working with is less than .10 (or ten cents) we must manually insert a '0' so the upcoming decimal point insertion routine will function properly. For example, if the **LONG** we are converting was a 4, it will now be a '4', and after the '0' is inserted we will have '04'.
5. Insert the decimal point two places from the right.
6. Insert commas if necessary. Commas are inserted every three places counting from the decimal point and going to the left. Try some values to see how this routine works.
7. Center and print our final **STRING** concatenated with a '$'.

The last step in the Main Program section (Listing 9-10B) is to find out if the user wants to calculate another loan payment. The user must press 'N' or 'n' to exit the program.

Learn by Example—Take your time going over this program (Listing 9-11). Feel free to alter or modify different sections of it to see what will hap-

Listing 9-10K.

```
PROCEDURE WriteLong(OutNumber : LONG);
(* Convert our final LONG to a STRING and print it. *)
VAR    OutString   : STRING;
       i, Sign, Ln : INTEGER;

BEGIN
  Roundoff(OutNumber, Accuracy - 2); (* Round off to two decimal places *)
  STR(OutNumber, OutString);          (* Convert LONG to STRING          *)

  IF OutString[1] = '-' THEN Sign := 1 (* Check for minus sign *)
    ELSE Sign := 0;

  IF LENGTH(OutString) - Sign = 1 THEN         (* If answer is less than *)
    INSERT('0', OutString, LENGTH(OutString)); (* 10 cents, insert a '0' *)

  INSERT('.', OutString, LENGTH(OutString) - 1); (* Insert decimal point *)

  Ln := LENGTH(OutString);
  FOR i := 1 TO (Ln - 4 - Sign) DIV 3 DO       (* Insert commas in answer *)
    INSERT(',', OutString, Ln - (i * 3 + 2));

  Center(CONCAT('$ ',OutString));              (* Add $ to answer and center *)
END; (* WriteLong *)




PROCEDURE PrintAnswer;

BEGIN
  GOTOXY(0,12);
  Center('Regular payment =');
  WriteLong(RegularPayment);
  WRITELN;
  Center('Total interest on loan =');
  WriteLong(TotalInterest);
END; (* PrintAnswer *)
```

pen. One of the best ways to learn a computer language is to first examine how someone else solved a problem and then see if you can do it differently. Can you improve this program so that there is no possible combination of entries which will lead to an overflow condition? How about adding a bell sound if an error is made during entry (printing an ASCII 7 will ring the bell if your computer or terminal has one). Make this program "yours" by tearing it apart and putting it back together!

EXERCISES

Here are a few exercises you may do.*

_____

*The "solutions" to these exercises are not included in this book.

1. Write a procedure to convert all lower case letters to upper case.
2. Write a procedure which will convert REAL numbers to STRINGs and insert commas if necessary.
3. Write a procedure to convert STRINGs to REALs.
4. Write a procedure which checks for a leading space or spaces in a STRING and deletes them.

QUIZ—LONG INTEGERS

True or False

1. All LONGs must be declared to have 36 digits.
2. When multiplying three numbers together, each with 7 decimal places, the product will have 14 decimal places.
3. When multiplying two adjusted LONGs together, you must round off the extra "decimal places."
4. When dividing two adjusted LONGs together, you must add extra decimal places after the division.

Listing 9-11.

```
(*=====================================================*)
(*                                                     *)
(* Program Language: PASCAL                            *)
(* Program Title: Loan Payment - version 4             *)
(* Subtitle:  Introducing STRING entry, LONG           *)
(*            calculations, and STRING output.         *)
(*                                                     *)
(* Author:    David Fox                                *)
(* Program Summary:  Calculates the regular payment    *)
(*            on a loan.                                *)
(*                                                     *)
(*=====================================================*)


PROGRAM Loan4;

CONST  Accuracy = 8;  (* Number of decimal places used during calculations *)
       ScreenWidth = 40;
       MaxEntry = 20; (* Maximum allowable digits in this program's LONGs  *)
       LongValue = TRUE;
       IntValue = FALSE;

TYPE   LONG = INTEGER[36];       (* Declare new TYPE so LONGs can be used as
                                    parameters.  Up to 36 digits of accuracy *)

VAR  Principal, AnnualInterest,
     RegularPayment, TotalInterest, One      : LONG;
     PaymentsPerYear, TermInYears, VertPos : INTEGER;
     YesNo                                   : CHAR;


PROCEDURE ClearScreen;

BEGIN
  PAGE(OUTPUT);
END; (* ClearScreen *)




PROCEDURE Center(Sentence : STRING);
(* Procedure to center a sentence on the screen *)
VAR  Len : INTEGER;

BEGIN
  Len := LENGTH(Sentence);
  WRITELN(Sentence:Len + (ScreenWidth - Len) DIV 2);
END; (* Center *)
```

```
PROCEDURE Power(x        : LONG;
               y         : INTEGER;
               VAR Result : LONG);
(* Procedure which raises x to the y power (x↑y) y
   must be greater than 0.  A procedure must be used
   because functions can't produce LONGs as a result. *)

VAR   i : INTEGER;

BEGIN
  Result := 1;
  FOR i := 1 TO y DO
    Result := Result * x;
END; (* Power *)




PROCEDURE Roundoff(VAR Number : LONG;
                   Places      : INTEGER);

(* Procedure to round off a LONG INTEGER by Places positions *)

VAR  Up             : INTEGER;
     Dv, LastDigit : LONG;

BEGIN
  Up := 0;
  Power(10, Places, Dv);              (* Create Dv := 10 ↑ Places *)

  (* Isolate the imaginary decimal place which
     will be lost when Number is adjusted.    *)
  LastDigit := (Number DIV (Dv DIV 10)) - ((Number DIV Dv) * 10);

  (* Next set Up := 1 if number needs to be rounded up
     or set Up := -1 if number needs to be rounded down *)
  IF LastDigit >= 5 THEN Up := 1
    ELSE IF LastDigit <= -5 THEN Up := -1;
                                        (* Divide number by Dv, add Up *)
  Number := Number DIV Dv + Up;         (* to correctly round Number.  *)
END; (* Roundoff *)




PROCEDURE PowerMod(x        : LONG;
                   y         : INTEGER;
                   VAR Result : LONG);
(* Procedure which raises x to the y power (x↑y) and adjusts
   the imaginary decimal by rounding off Accuracy places
   with the Roundoff procedure.  This procedure must be used
   in place of Power when our "adjusted LONGs" are involved. *)

VAR   i : INTEGER;
```

```
BEGIN
  Result := One;
  IF y >= 0 THEN
    FOR i := 1 TO y DO
      BEGIN
        Result := Result * x;
        Roundoff(Result, Accuracy);   (* Adjust Result to *)
      END                             (* Accuracy places  *)
    ELSE IF x = 0 THEN Result := 0    (* Check for base of 0 *)
      ELSE
        FOR i := 1 to -y DO
          Result := One * Result DIV x;  (* Increase decimal places prior to
                                            division by multiplying Result by One *)
END; (* PowerMod *)




PROCEDURE Val(Data       : STRING;
              VAR Number : LONG;
              LongFlag   : BOOLEAN;
              VAR Ok     : BOOLEAN);
CONST  Plus  = 1;
       Minus = -1;
VAR    Sign, Len, i,
       DecimalPlaces : INTEGER;
       Tens, Offset  : LONG;
       FoundDecimal  : BOOLEAN;
BEGIN
  Ok := TRUE;                                 (* Initialize *)
  Tens := 1;
  Number := 0;
  Sign := 0;
  DecimalPlaces := 0;
  FoundDecimal := FALSE;

  WHILE POS(',', Data) > 0 DO
    DELETE(Data, POS(',', Data), 1);  (* Delete all commas from Data *)

  Len := LENGTH(Data);
  IF Len = 0 THEN Ok := FALSE                 (* Check for null string *)
    ELSE IF Data[1] = '+' THEN Sign := Plus  (* Check for + or - sign *)
      ELSE IF Data[1] = '-' THEN Sign := Minus;

  IF ABS(Sign) = 1 THEN                        (* If + or - sign is present,  *)
    IF Len = 1 THEN Ok := FALSE                (* check if length is greater  *)
      ELSE                                     (* than 1.  If so, then delete *)
        BEGIN                                  (* the sign from Data.         *)
          DELETE(Data, 1, 1);
          Len := LENGTH(Data);
        END;
```

```
   IF Data = '.' THEN Ok := FALSE;        (* Another invalid entry    *)

   IF Len > MaxEntry THEN Ok := FALSE;    (* Number is out of range   *)

   IF Ok THEN                             (* Begin conversion to LONG *)
     FOR i := Len DOWNTO 1 DO
       BEGIN
         IF (Data[i] < '0') OR (Data[i] > '9') THEN Ok := FALSE
           ELSE                           (* Character is valid number *)
             BEGIN
               Number := Number + (ORD(Data[i]) - ORD('0')) * Tens;
               Tens := Tens * 10;         (* Increment decimal place *)
             END;
         IF LongFlag AND (Data[i] = '.') AND NOT FoundDecimal THEN
           BEGIN                          (* First decimal found in LONG *)
             DecimalPlaces := Len - i;
             Ok := TRUE;
             FoundDecimal := TRUE;
           END;
       END; (* FOR Loop *)

   IF NOT LongFlag AND (Number > MAXINT) THEN Ok := FALSE;

   IF Sign <> 0 THEN Number := Number * Sign;  (* Adjust sign if negative *)

   (* If LONG then make it into an "adjusted LONG" by moving the
      imaginary decimal over the right number of spaces to give it
      a total of Acuracy decimal places.                        *)
   IF LongFlag THEN
     (* If the number of decimal places exceeds Accuracy then Roundoff *)
     IF DecimalPlaces > Accuracy THEN
       Roundoff(Number, DecimalPlaces - Accuracy)
       ELSE
         BEGIN
           Power(10, Accuracy - DecimalPlaces, Offset);
           Number := Number * Offset;  (* Move decimal over the  *)
       END;                            (* correct number of places *)
END; (* Val *)




PROCEDURE ClrLine;
(* Erase the contents of line VertPos to the right of
   horizontal position 22, reposition cursor for next try. *)

BEGIN
  GOTOXY(22,VertPos);
  WRITELN(' ':30);
  GOTOXY(22,VertPos);
END; (* ClrLine *)
```

```
PROCEDURE ReadLong(VAR LongNumber : LONG);
(* Read a STRING and send it to Val to be converted
   to a LONG until a valid LONG is returned.        *)
VAR  InpString : STRING;
     Good      : BOOLEAN;

BEGIN
  REPEAT
    GOTOXY(22,VertPos);
    READLN(InpString);
    Val(InpString, LongNumber, LongValue, Good);
    IF NOT Good THEN ClrLine;
  UNTIL Good;
  VertPos := VertPos + 1;          (* Increment vertical cursor position *)
END; (* ReadLong *)




PROCEDURE ReadInt(VAR IntNumber : INTEGER);
(* Read a STRING and send it to Val to be converted
   to a INTEGER until a valid INTEGER is returned. *)
VAR  InpString  : STRING;
     LongNumber : LONG;
     Good       : BOOLEAN;

BEGIN
  REPEAT
    GOTOXY(22,VertPos);
    READLN(InpString);
    Val(InpString, LongNumber, IntValue, Good);
    IF NOT Good THEN ClrLine;
  UNTIL Good;
  IntNumber := TRUNC(LongNumber);            (* Convert LONG to INTEGER *)
  VertPos := VertPos + 1;          (* Increment vertical cursor position *)
END; (* ReadInt *)




PROCEDURE WriteLong(OutNumber : LONG);
(* Convert our final LONG to a STRING and print it. *)
VAR   OutString   : STRING;
      i, Sign, Ln : INTEGER;

BEGIN
  Roundoff(OutNumber, Accuracy - 2); (* Round off to two decimal places *)
  STR(OutNumber, OutString);              (* Convert LONG to STRING       *)

  IF OutString[1] = '-' THEN Sign := 1  (* Check for minus sign *)
    ELSE Sign := 0;

  IF LENGTH(OutString) - Sign = 1 THEN           (* If answer is less than *)
    INSERT('0', OutString, LENGTH(OutString)); (* 10 cents, insert a '0' *)
```

```
      INSERT('.', OutString, LENGTH(OutString) - 1); (* Insert decimal point *)

    Ln := LENGTH(OutString);
    FOR i := 1 TO (Ln - 4 - Sign) DIV 3 DO        (* Insert commas in answer *)
      INSERT(',', OutString, Ln - (i * 3 + 2));

    Center(CONCAT('$ ',OutString));            (* Add $ to answer and center *)
END; (* WriteLong *)




PROCEDURE GetData;

BEGIN                                      (* Set vertical cursor position *)
    VertPos := 6;
    ClearScreen;
    Center('** LOAN PAYMENT **');
    WRITELN;
    WRITELN;
    WRITELN('Enter the following information');
    WRITELN('(You may use commas in your numbers):');
    WRITELN;
    WRITE(' Amount of loan:');
    ReadLong(Principal);                       (* Call routine to accept data *)
    WRITE(' Annual interest (%):');
    ReadLong(AnnualInterest);
    WRITE(' Payments per year:');
    ReadInt(PaymentsPerYear);
    WRITE(' Term in years:');
    ReadInt(TermInYears);
  END; (* GetData *)




PROCEDURE Calculate;
VAR    Numerator, Denominator,
       InterestPerPeriod, Temp : LONG;
       NumberOfPayments        : INTEGER;

  BEGIN (* Calculate *)
    GOTOXY(13,19);
    WRITE('Calculating...');

    InterestPerPeriod := (AnnualInterest DIV 100) DIV PaymentsPerYear;
    NumberOfPayments := PaymentsPerYear * TermInYears;

    (* Two "adjusted LONGs" will be multiplied together; we must bring
       the decimal place back in line by rounding off Accuracy places. *)
    Numerator := Principal * InterestPerPeriod;
    Roundoff(Numerator, Accuracy);
```

```
      PowerMod(One + InterestPerPeriod, -NumberOfPayments, Temp);
      Denominator := One - Temp;

      (* One "adjusted LONG" will be divided by another so we must allow
         for the cancellation of significant places by multiplying by
         "One" first.  "One" is equal to 10 ↑ Accuracy               *)
      RegularPayment := One * Numerator DIV Denominator;

      TotalInterest := RegularPayment * NumberOfPayments - Principal;
END; (* Calculate *)



PROCEDURE PrintAnswer;

BEGIN
   GOTOXY(0,12);
   Center('Regular payment =' );
   WriteLong(RegularPayment);
   WRITELN;
   Center('Total interest on loan =' );
   WriteLong(TotalInterest);
END; (* PrintAnswer *)



BEGIN (* Main Program *)
   Power(10, Accuracy, One); (* Compute the number "One" by raising 10
                                to the Accuracy power (10 ↑ Accuracy) *)
   YesNo := ' ';               (* Initialize to one space *)

   REPEAT
     GetData;
     Calculate;
     PrintAnswer;
     GOTOXY(0,19);
     WRITE('Would you like to calculate another? ' );
     READ(YesNo);
   UNTIL (YesNo = 'N') OR (YesNo = 'n');

   GOTOXY(0,22);
   Center('That''s all folks...BYE' );
END. (* Loan4 *)
```

chapter 10

More Data Types

Now that you have become good friends with all the different variable types that are built into "standard" Pascal (*INTEGER, REAL, CHAR, BOOLEAN*) plus the two additional types provided by UCSD Pascal (*STRING* and *LONG INTEGER*), we are ready to enter the world of Arrays, customized types (User-Defined), Subrange Types, and Sets.

All of the variable types we've worked with so far (with the exception of **STRINGs** and **LONG INTEGERs**) are said to be simple or *scalar data types*. They all have two main things in common:

1. *They are ordered.* This means that within a specific type, one value will either be greater than, less than, or equal to another value of that same type. (Note that "ordinal data types" have this same characteristic. Ordinal types are a *subset* of scalar types—a type can be scalar but not ordinal, i.e., **REALs**, but all ordinal types are scalar.)
2. You can't break a scalar value into elements (as you can with **STRINGs**)—it already *is* an individual element.

Scalar data types can be divided into two categories—Standard scalar data types (those types standard to Pascal) and User-Defined scalar data types (which we will be covering later in this chapter).

By using scalar data types as building blocks, we can create another major category of data types—*structured data types*. This type is created by putting together the scalar types (both standard and user-defined) in new ways. The first of the structured data types we will look at is the *Array.*

ARRAYS—LINKING SCALARS TOGETHER

An array is a bunch of scalar data types linked together. To help illustrate arrays, we will use the problems of a certain freight train company. One day, this company, we'll call it P-Express (after Uncle Pascal), decided to do an inventory of one of its trains. This train had 10 freight cars, each of which was either a boxcar, a flatcar, a tank car, or a cattle car. The company wanted to find out how many of each type car there were in the train. Since counting the cars by hand was much too difficult for P-Express, they came to us and asked for help. First we tried letting each car be represented by one of ten **INTEGER** variables named **Car1, Car2, Car3,... Car10**. Then we checked the contents of each variable to see what kind of car it was. We used **CONST**ants to make our program clearer:

```
CONST  Boxcar   = 1;
       Flatcar  = 2;
       Tankcar  = 3;
       Cattlecar = 4;
```

Here is a procedure which counts the different car types:

```
PROCEDURE CheckCar(FreightCar : INTEGER);
BEGIN
  CASE FreightCar OF
    Boxcar    : BoxSum := BoxSum + 1;
    Flatcar   : FlatSum := FlatSum + 1;
    Tankcar   : TankSum := TankSum + 1;
    Cattlecar : CattleSum := CattleSum + 1;
  END; (* CASE *)
END; (* CheckCar *)
```

So far, we had no problems. However, sending each of the 10 variables to the **CheckCar** procedure was rather awkward:

```
CheckCar(Car1);
CheckCar(Car2);
CheckCar(Car3);
CheckCar(Car4);
CheckCar(Car5);
CheckCar(Car6);
CheckCar(Car7);
CheckCar(Car8);
CheckCar(Car9);
CheckCar(Car10);
```

Awkward, but not unbearable. But what if P-Express all of a sudden discovered they had *100* cars on their train (maybe someone had forgotten to write the last zero on the number)!! Using the above method *would* be unbearable and very impractical. However, since the same operation needed to be carried out on each car, we found we could do the counting much more easily by using an *array*. Each car could be thought of as an *element* in the array. If the name of the array was still **Car**, then each freight car could be accessed by **Car[n]** where **n** was an **INTEGER** from 1 to 10 (the number of freight cars in the train). This number within the square brackets is called a *subscript*. The first car can be referred to by **Car[1]**, the last car by **Car[10]**. Equipped with an array, we sent the parameters to **CheckCar** much more easily:

```
Number := 10;
FOR ThisCar := 1 TO Number DO
   CheckCar(Car[ThisCar]);
```

Ten times more easily, to be exact! If their train had 100 cars we would just have to change the value in **Number** to 100 (**Number := 100**).

To declare the freight train array, we wrote the following line:

```
VAR   Car : ARRAY[1..10] OF INTEGER;
```

The numbers within the brackets show the lower and upper boundaries to this array. In this case they are **INTEGER** constants, but they could be *any ordinal values*. The general declaration is:

```
VAR   Name : ARRAY[LowerBound..UpperBound] OF TYPE;
```

TYPE can be *any data type* that is defined at this point in the program. Notice the two periods* between the LowerBound and the UpperBound.

---
* In some versions of Pascal, these are called "lazy colons" because they look like a colon lying down on the job.

By now, you may have noticed a similarity between how we access an element in our freight train array and how we access elements in a **STRING**. There's no coincidence in this similarity because a **STRING** is essentially an *array of CHARs*. If Pascal didn't come equipped with **STRING**s, they could be declared in the following manner:

```
VAR   NewString : ARRAY[1..80] OF CHAR;
```

The **UpperBound** (80) is the maximum length of this string of characters.

Multidimensional Arrays

The arrays we have presented so far are called "one-dimensional arrays" because they can be thought of as having elements in only one direction. A string is a good example of this—it is a series of elements strung together in a row. Here in Fig. 10-1 is a representation of a one-dimensional array with ten elements (like our train).

1	2	3	4	5	6	7	8	9	10

Fig. 10-1. Representation of one-dimensional array with ten elements.

Two-Dimensional Arrays—After we did the inventory for P-Express, they presented us with a new problem. It seems this freight train had been out of commission for quite a while and had picked up a few unwanted pests (mice, flies, and fleas). P-Express wanted to bring in an exterminator who charged $.50 per mouse, $.10 per fly and $.05 per flea (we thought this was rather absurd—charging per pest, but that's the way P-Express liked doing business). We knew how many of each pest there were in each car (providing expert pest counters was part of the extermination package) but we didn't know the totals for the entire train. We stored this important information in our **Car** array by making it into a "two-dimensional" array. Here is how we declared it:

```
VAR   Car: ARRAY[1..10] OF (* Which freight car *)
              ARRAY[1..3] OF (* Pest type *) INTEGER;
```

This declaration says that each of the original elements now has three *additional* elements of its own. Every car can contain a specific number of each of the three different pests. To find out how many flies that the fifth car has, we can access **Car[5,2]***. The second number (2) refers to the

---
* Another way to access element 5,2 is **Car[5][2]**. However, in this book we will use the other method (**Car[5,2]**).

flies (not the *number* of flies, but the *element* in which the number of flies is stored). In the representation of this two-dimensional array (Fig. 10-2), we placed the number 12 in element 5,2. This means there are 12 flies buzzing around in freight car number 5:

	1	2	3	4	5	6	7	8	9	10
1 (Mice)										
2 (Flies)					12					
3 (Fleas)										

Fig. 10-2. Representation of two-dimensional array.

Each square represents an element in the array. There are a total of 10 * 3 or 30 elements here.

Following is a fragment of the program we used to estimate the exterminator's bill (the variable **Cost** is a **REAL** variable):

```
Cost := 0.0;

FOR ThisCar := 1 to 10 DO
  BEGIN
    Cost := Cost + 0.50 * Car[ThisCar,1];
    Cost := Cost + 0.10 * Car[ThisCar,2];
    Cost := Cost + 0.05 * Car[ThisCar,3];
  END;
```

By storing the costs per pest type in another array, we can make this even more efficient (Listing 10-1).

Notice that we used **CONST**ants in the variable declaration section to make this program clearer. We also used two nested **FOR** loops, the outer loop (**i**) moves the program through each of the 10 freight cars and the inner loop (**j**) moves the program through each of the three different pests.

Three-Dimensional Arrays — The company which owned this pest-ridden train was *not* doing well *at all* (with all the "undesirables" on board it's no wonder!). They had four *more* trains in exactly the same condition. We solved their new problem with a *three-dimensional* array. Here is how we declared it:

```
VAR   Car : ARRAY[1..5] OF (* Which train *)
               ARRAY[1..10] OF (* Which freight car *)
                  ARRAY[1..3] OF (* Pest type *) INTEGER;
```

By using **CONST**ants, we can make this declaration look clearer:

```
CONST   Trains      =   5;
        FreightCars =  10;
        Mice        =   1;
        Flies       =   2;
        Fleas       =   3;

VAR   Car : ARRAY[1..Trains] OF (* Which train *)
               ARRAY[1..FreightCars] OF
                              (* Which freight car *)
                  ARRAY[Mice..Fleas] OF
                              (* Pest type *) INTEGER;
```

Note: Although you can use constants for the lower or upper bounds declaration in an array, you *cannot* use *variables*. This means that the size of the array must be established at the time the program is written so the compiler can set aside the right amount of space. There is no "dynamic space allocation" in Pascal. That is, the size of arrays can't be adjusted *during* the run of the program.

Now that we had a three-dimensional array set up, all we had to do was add one more level to our nested **FOR** loop to do our calculations:

Listing 10-1.

```
PROGRAM ExterminatorCosts;
(* Program to calculate extermination costs for P-Express *)

CONST    FreightCars = 10;        (* Number of cars in the train *)
         Mice        = 1;
         Flies       = 2;
         Fleas       = 3;

VAR   Car         : ARRAY[1..10] OF (* Which freight car *)
                         ARRAY[Mice..Fleas] OF (* Pest type *) INTEGER;
      PestPrice : ARRAY[Mice..Fleas] OF REAL;
      Cost        : REAL;


PROCEDURE Calculate;
VAR    i, j : INTEGER;

BEGIN
   PestPrice[Mice]  := 0.50;      (* Price per pest in dollars *)
   PestPrice[Flies] := 0.10;
   PestPrice[Fleas] := 0.05;

   Cost := 0.0;

   FOR i := 1 to FreightCars DO   (* Loop through freight cars *)
      FOR j := Mice to Fleas DO   (* Loop through pest type    *)
         Cost := Cost + PestPrice[j] * Car[i,j];
END; (* Calculate *)
```

```
FOR k := 1 to Trains DO
   FOR i := 1 TO FreightCars DO
      FOR j := Mice TO Fleas DO
         Cost := Cost + PestPrice[j] * Car[k, i, j];
```

Fig. 10-3 is a representation of this three-dimensional array.

Arrays and Memory—We're sorry to say that P-Express is no longer with us—the spray which the exterminator used rusted out the metal parts in all five of their trains and caused them to fall apart. (Not to worry, though, the insurance money they collected enabled the same folks to resurface as "Wonder Wheels, Inc," manufacturers of solar powered skateboards.)

While we can't do business with P-Express anymore, we can, however, continue adding dimensions to arrays. A four-dimensional array with an upper bound of 6 would have Fig. 10-3 as its first element, and a total of six of these three-dimensional arrays as elements. The only limit to the number of dimensions is memory—multidimensional arrays eat up memory rapidly. For example, our 6 by 5 by 10 by 3 array takes up 6 * 5 * 10 * 3 = 900 memory calls—or more if it takes more than one cell to store an element. A three-dimensional array with only 40 elements in each dimension could feasibly take up 40 * 40 * 40 = 64000 cells or possibly all of the memory in your microcomputer!

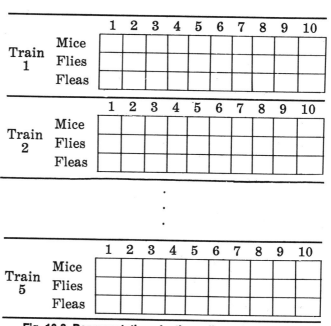

Fig. 10-3. Representation of a three-dimensional array.

So it's a good idea to keep array sizes as small as possible or they'll eat you out of bit and byte! Uncle Pascal says: *He who keeps a tyranosaurus rex for a pet had better own a cattle farm or an elephant herd for its snacks!*

String Arrays

Using arrays of **STRING**s is slightly different than arrays of scalar types. This is because a string is already a one-dimensional array (it is a structured data type, not a scalar type). Using strings in one-dimensional arrays is fairly straightforward. If we have the following declaration:

```
VAR  TestString : ARRAY[1..5] OF STRING;
```

we can access any one of the five string elements with **TestString[n]** where **n** can be an **INTEGER** from 1 to 5. However, as you'll remember, this looks exactly like accessing the individual **CHAR** elements of a single string. Using **STRING** arrays doesn't block you from accessing the **CHAR** elements—just consider a string to be a *two*-dimensional array of **CHAR**. The first subscript addresses the string we are referring to; the second subscript references a specific **CHAR**acter in that string. Thus, **TestString[2,7]** refers to the seventh character of the second string in the array. *However*, we must again warn you about accessing nonexistent **STRING** elements. If **TestString[2]** was only six characters long, the program would crash instantly. So only access the **CHAR** elements of a string array if you know exactly how long it is!

Listing 10-2 gives an example based on the Chapter 9 **BackwardsWrite** program (Listing 9-1).

Here is a run of this program:

```
Enter five strings:
1. This is an example of what
2. happens if you stand on
3. your head too long,
4. not to mention walking backwards!
5. !retteb hcum ,hA

Here they are again, backwards:
5. Ah, much better!
4. !sdrawkcab gniklaw noitnem ot ton
3. ,gnol oot daeh ruoy
2. no dnats uoy fi sneppah
1. tahw fo elpmaxe na si sihT
```

In this program, we use a **FOR** loop to help enter the five strings. Then these strings are printed out in reverse order (the last string entered is printed first), and each string is written backwards (last character in the string is printed first). You'll no-

Listing 10-2.

```
PROGRAM StringArrays;
VAR  TestString : ARRAY[1..5] OF STRING;
     i, j          : INTEGER;

BEGIN
  PAGE(OUTPUT);
  WRITELN('Enter five strings:');
  FOR i := 1 TO 5 DO
    BEGIN
      WRITE(i,'. ');
      READLN(TestString[i]);
    END;

  WRITELN;
  WRITELN('Here they are again, backwards:');
  FOR i := 5 DOWNTO 1 DO              (* Write strings in reverse order *)
    BEGIN
      WRITE(i,'. ');
      FOR j := LENGTH(TestString[i]) DOWNTO 1 DO
        WRITE(TestString[i,j]);  (* Write each string out backwards *)
      WRITELN;
    END;
END.  (* StringArrays *)
```

tice the inner loop (**j**) references the individual character of each string.

Since a one-dimensional string array can *optionally* be considered to be a two-dimensional **CHAR** array, we can *optionally* access the individual character elements (not forgetting the instantaneous crash!). *In all other array types, you must reference all dimensions every time the array name is used.* If **ZooFeed** is a two-dimensional **INTEGER** array, then every time **ZooFeed** is written, you must include both dimensions:

ZooFeed[Chimps, Days];	*Ok*
ZooFeed[Elephants];	*Not Ok—2nd subscript missing*

Miscellaneous Extras

Here are a few more things you should know about arrays, even if you never have to use them.

Noninteger Subscripts—We said that the lower and upper bounds in an array can be *any ordinal data type*. This means the following declarations are legal:

```
VAR   Letter : ARRAY['A'..'Z'] OF INTEGER;
```

This defines a 26 element **INTEGER** array which uses **CHAR**s for subscripts:

```
Letter['M'] := 325;
```

This is not mixing data types. The *values* of the elements in the array **Letter** are **INTEGER**s. However, the subscript which *points* to each of **Letter**'s elements is a **CHAR** type.

```
VAR   Booly : ARRAY[FALSE..TRUE] OF REAL;*
```

This defines a 2 element **REAL** array which can use either **FALSE** or **TRUE** as subscripts:

```
Booly[FALSE] := 12.435;
VAR   LightSwitch : ARRAY[−7..7] OF BOOLEAN;
```

This defines a 15 element array (don't forget to count 0) of type **BOOLEAN**. Each of the 15 elements can only have one of two values—**TRUE** or **FALSE**:

```
LightSwitch[−5] := ODD(n);
```

A Short Cut—There is a faster way of declaring multidimensional arrays. This declaration:

```
VAR   BigOne : ARRAY['A'..'F'] OF
                 ARRAY[1..20] OF
                   ARRAY[−20..0] OF REAL;
```

---

* In some earlier versions of UCSD Pascal, this won't work because of an elusive bug.

could be written like this:

```
VAR   BigOne : ARRAY['A'..'F', 1..20, −20..0] OF REAL;
```

Commas can be used to separate the range for each of the dimensions.

Expressions as Subscripts—The subscript in an array can also be an *expression* which reduces to the ordinal type indicated by the lower and upper bounds in the declaration statement:

Letter[CHR(n + 50)] := Yolu;	subscript of type **CHAR**
Booly[i > 35] := 1.12E6;	subscript of type **BOOLEAN**
LightSwitch[(21 − i) DIV 2] := Xoot;	subscript of type **INTEGER**

Care must be taken so that these expressions evaluate to a value within the range of the declared lower and upper bounds.

We'll say more about arrays at the end of this chapter with the Tic-Tac-Toe program.

QUIZ—ARRAYS

True or False

1. A data type can be scalar but not ordinal.
2. A scalar data type can be broken into elements (like *STRING*s).
3. The elements in an array must be of the same type.
4. The two-dimensional *STRING* array *MyString* can be also thought of as a three-dimensional *CHAR* array.
5. You can use any scalar data type as the subscript in an array.

CUSTOMIZED TYPES— "ENUMERATED" USER-DEFINED TYPES

In the last section, you'll remember that we wanted to make our array example clearer by assigning constant names to some of the integer values (Flatcar, Mice, Flies, etc.). There is a better way—we can *invent* our own data types (called user-defined data types) and define exactly what the possible *values* for each type are.

Our First New Type

Here's an example of a user-defined type. We can create a new type called **Pests** and list all possible values this type can have:

```
TYPE   Pests = (Mice, Flies, Fleas);
```

We now have a new variable type called **Pests**. The values **Mice**, **Flies**, and **Fleas** are the *constants* that a variable of **TYPE Pests** can have. This user-defined type is called an "enumerated"

type because we list its values. We can now declare a variable to be a **Pests** variable:

```
VAR   Varmint : Pests;
```

The only possible values that can be assigned to this **Pests** type variable are **Mice, Flies,** and **Fleas.** Trying to assign any other value of any other data type to a variable of type **Pests** will cause an error:

```
Varmint := Flies;      Ok

Varmint := 'Fleas';    Not Ok—Assigning a STRING
                                to a Pests variable

Varmint := 3;          Not Ok—Assigning an INTEGER
                                to a Pests variable
```

This new data type is still a scalar type—the order of its values is determined *by their order in the above declaration list*. Therefore, **Mice** < **Flies** and **Fleas** > **Flies.** We are *not* assigning any of the "constants" (the values **Mice, Flies, Fleas**) of type **Pests** a numeric value. If we say **WRITELN(Mice);** we'll get the same kind of error as the one that occurs when trying to **WRITELN** a **BOOLEAN** value—user-defined data types can't be written to the screen or read from the keyboard. They are for logic flow only. Let's invent some other data types:

```
TYPE  Televisions  = (BlackAndWhite, Color, Projection);

      Dogs         = (Poodle, GermanShepherd, Collie,
                      Terrier, StBernard, Mutt);

      Months       = (January, February, March, April,
                      May, June, July, August,
                      September, October, November,
                      December)

      SpaceDrives  = (Chemical, Nuclear, Ion, Impulse,
                      AntiMatter, HyperDrive);

      Flavors      = (Vanilla, Chocolate, Carob, Peach,
                      Strawberry, Blueberry, MintChip,
                      MochaChip, MarbleFudge);
```

One of the *values* a variable of **TYPE Months** can use is **August.** One of the *values* a variable of **TYPE SpaceDrives** can use is **AntiMatter.** We are really introducing a new way of thinking here. **HyperDrive** *is* a **SpaceDrive** value, just as **34** is an **INTEGER** value.

Why Define New Types?—You may ask, "Why bother with *new* types when I could make my programs just as clear by using names made of strings or by assigning constant names to integer values?" There are three major reasons why user-defined types are better:

1. They are better than using **STRING** names

150

because they take up less memory space and execute faster.

2. It's more convenient to declare new data types than list a bunch of **CONST**ants along with their appropriate values (which is somewhat awkward).

3. By creating new types, Pascal will automatically make sure that you are not mixing these new types with any other types (just as it does when you try to mix **REAL**s with **CHAR**s). As you must know by now, mixing types will yield an error! This is a *fantastic* debugging tool!!!

Oh great! Another way to have a Pascal program crash! Why is Pascal so unforgiving about mixing variable types? Let's say you choose the method of assigning a plethora of constant names to a series of integer or string values. The larger your program, the more difficult it is to remember when to use which constant name, and the more likely you are to make a mistake involving assigning the wrong constant to a variable. *By declaring new data types, you can use Pascal's pickiness as a tool to help uncover any errors you made mixing data types or assigning an "illegal" value (within the context of your program) to a variable.* Think of Pascal as your friendly detective —tirelessly hunting down mismatched types for your benefit!

This brings us to one of the most important features of Pascal—once you conceive of a solution to a problem and implement it in Pascal, Pascal is designed to "enforce" your conceptualization of the solution. If you decide that a variable of a certain type only needs 6 possible values, Pascal will make sure you don't unwittingly throw in a 7th.

 Uncle Pascal says: *Pascal will make sure you don't try to mix Nuclear SpaceDrives with Peach flavored ice cream, even though your space ship may be painted the color of a peach. Your pet Poodle may have been born in March, but Pascal will protect you from making the mistake of assigning a Months type value to a Dogs type variable (unless your pet happens to be a March Hare)!*

Using the New Types

The **TYPE** declaration appears at the beginning of a block just after the **CONST** declaration and before the **VAR** declaration (if you have any). As with **CONST**ants and **VAR**iables, these new **TYPE**s can be local to one block or global to many blocks (or the entire program).

Now that we have created some user-defined data types, we can declare variables using these new types:

```
VAR   Scoop          : Flavor;
      WinterMonth     : ARRAY[1..3] OF Month;
      CheckMonth      : Month;
      WatchDog,
      YapDog          : Dogs;
```

And in the program itself we can have statements such as:

```
i := ORD(Blueberry);          (* value of i is 5 *)
Scoop := PRED(Chocolate);     (* value of Scoop is Vanilla *)

WinterMonth[1] := December;
WinterMonth[2] := January;
WinterMonth[3] := February;
                         (* will cycle 12 times *)
FOR CheckMonth := January TO December DO
  (* If CheckMonth is a WinterMonth, then get the shovel *)
  FOR i := 1 TO 3 DO
    IF WinterMonth[i] = CheckMonth THEN ShovelSnow;

WatchDog := GermanShepherd;
YapDog := Poodle;
IF WatchDog > YapDog THEN Bark; (* WatchDog IS greater
                                  than YapDog be-
                                  cause GermanShep-
                                  herd > Poodle in or-
                                  iginal type declara-
                                  tion *)
```

You'll notice that the intrinsic function **ORD** can be used with these new scalar types. The first constant of a type has the ordinal value of 0. Since **Blueberry** is the 6th constant listed as a **Flavors** type, its ordinal value is 5 (**Vanilla** is 0). Because the three intrinsic functions which relate to the *order* of a value (**ORD, PRED, SUCC**) can be used with our new types, we must make sure that each constant belongs to only one type:

```
TYPE   Measurements =   (Inches, Feet, Yards,
                         Centimeters, Meters);
       BodyParts    =   (Ears, Hands, Feet, Toes);
                              └ error will occur here
```

How would Pascal know whether the **ORD**inal value of **Feet** was 1 (in **Measurements**) or 2 (in **BodyParts**)? The above type declaration would receive a compiler error! However, if a constant of a user-defined type appears in two **TYPE** declarations, one in an inner block and one in an outer block, there won't be any error unless the inner block tries to access the outer block's type.

Using the Relational Operators With User-Defined Types—The relational operators (=, <, >, <=, >=, <>) can be used on user-defined types (WatchDog > YapDog) but not arithmetic operators (what could **Poodle** + **StBernard** or **Mint-Chip** / **Carob** mean?).

PRED and SUCC — You may have wondered what to do with the intrinsic functions **PRED** and **SUCC**. Now we can demonstrate a good use for them. With numeric types we could do the following:

```
i := 1;
WHILE i <= 10 DO
  BEGIN
    WRITELN(i);
    i := i + 1;        (* Increment i *)
  END;
```

Since you can't use the mathematical operators + or − on a user-defined data type, how could you increment (or decrement) a variable of type **Months**, for example? With **SUCC** or **PRED**! In the next example, **m** is a **Month** type variable:

```
m := January;
WHILE m < December DO
  BEGIN
    WRITELN(ORD(m));
    m := SUCC(m);      (* Increment month (m) *)
  END;
```

On execution, we would see the numbers from 0 to 10 printed on the screen.

QUIZ—ENUMERATED USER-DEFINED DATA TYPES

True or False

1. All user-defined data types have ordinal values starting at 0.
2. User-defined data types can be written to the screen or read from the keyboard.
3. It's all right to have the same constant appear in two or more *TYPE* declaration statements at the same block level.
4. To increment a variable of a user-defined data type, you can use the intrinsic function *PRED*.

SUBRANGE DATA TYPES

Besides the enumerated user-defined types we have just covered, there is another user-defined type called *subrange* data types. Many times it is not necessary to create a completely new data type —a *portion* of an existing scalar type may be what you really want. For example, if the values your **INTEGER** variable will assume are from 0 to 100 (like the score on a driving test), you can specify that range in a subrange type:

```
TYPE  Score = 0..100;        (* Create subrange type *)

VAR   TestResult : Score;    (* Declare variable *)
```

This type statement says that the subrange type **Score** can use any **INTEGER** value from 0 to 100. Why bother when you can use a plain **INTEGER** type? To add clarity to the program and guard against errors, that's why. By stating that the only values **TestResult** can have are from 0 to 100, this variable's purpose takes on additional meaning. And if there is a logic error in your program that allows **TestResult** to exceed 100 or fall below 0, Pascal will let you know!

Besides **INTEGER**s, we can make subrange types using any scalar type except for **REAL**s. Here are some **CHAR** subrange types:

```
Type  CapLetter   = 'A'..'Z';
      SmallLetter = 'a'..'z';
      Digit       = '0'..'9';
```

We can also use user-defined types. Recall our **Flavors** type:

```
Flavors    = (Vanilla, Chocolate, Carob, Peach,
              Strawberry, Blueberry, MintChip,
              MochaChip, MarbleFudge);
FruitFlavor = Peach..Blueberry;
```

FruitFlavor is a subrange of **Flavors**.

The general format for subrange types is:

```
TYPE   Name = LowerBound..UpperBound;
```

This new type can have any value from **Lower-Bound** to **UpperBound**. Also, **LowerBound** must be *less than or equal* to **UpperBound**. The following example:

```
TYPE   SomeInt = 25..−25;
```

is incorrect because the **LowerBound** is *greater* than the **UpperBound**.

It is all right to mix different subranges of the same type in expressions. If we have the following types:

```
TYPE   PosDigit = 0..9;
       NegDigit = −9..−1;
```

and then declare the following variables:

```
VAR    HighNumber : PosDigit;
       LowNumber  : NegDigit;
       Number     : INTEGER;
```

then the following are legal:

```
HighNumber := 5;
LowNumber := −1 * HighNumber;
Number := LowNumber * HighNumber;
```

All of these variables are based on **INTEGER** types so mixing them together is fine. However, we must watch for range errors:

```
HighNumber := 5 + Number;
```

This statement will yield an error if **Number** is greater than 4 or less than −5 because then we'd be assigning **HighNumber** a value beyond the declared range of **PosDigit**.

It's also acceptable to have overlaps or a duplication of values when using subranges:

```
TYPE   Degrees     = 0..360;
       Digit       = 0..9;
       Temperature = 32..212;
```

All these types are subrange types based on **INTE-GER**s. Another example, using user-defined types:

```
TYPE   Days = (Monday, Tuesday, Wednesday, Thursday,
               Friday, Saturday, Sunday);
       Weekend         = Saturday..Sunday;
       ExtendedWeekend = Friday..Sunday;
```

The overlap is legal because the ordinal value had already been established when the type was first declared. We don't change the ordinal value of the type by choosing to include different portions of that type in a subrange type—the compiler never gets confused.

The Shorthand Method May Not Be the Best—
An alternate way to declare new types (both enumerated and subrange) is to skip the **TYPE** declaration and do it in the **VAR** declaration section:

```
VAR   HighNumber : 0..9;
      Scoop      : (Vanilla, Chocolate, Carob, Peach,
                   Strawberry, Blueberry, MintChip,
                   MochaChip, MarbleFudge);
```

However, we feel that it is clearer to declare new types in the **TYPE** declaration section and keep this step separate from **VAR** declarations. This is especially true if you plan to pass these variables as parameters to procedures or functions. As we mentioned in Chapter 9, a parameter *must* be paired with a type name. The variables **High-Number** and **Scoop** have type *descriptions* to their right. If we wanted to pass **Scoop** as a parameter to a procedure called **MakeSundae**, we would have no way of indicating its type in the actual parameter:

```
PROCEDURE MakeSundae(IceCreamFlavor :  ?  );
BEGIN
   :
END; (* MakeSundae *)
```

```
BEGIN (* Main Program *)
   MakeSundae(Scoop);
      :
      :
```

Again, the solution is to create a type *name* in the TYPE declaration section (as we did earlier in this chapter with type **Flavors**), then use this name with parameter lists. We will incorporate subrange types in the Tic-Tac-Toe program at the end of this chapter.

What About *LONG INTEGERs*?

You may have been wondering why we haven't classified **LONG INTEGER**s yet—are they scalars or structured data types? **LONG**s were created as a solution to UCSD Pascal's limitations on accuracy for **REAL**s. They are really unclassified because they have features of simple (scalar) types as well as complex (structured) types. **LONG**s are:

1. Like scalar types—you can use mathematical operators on them.
2. Like structured types — you can't return a **LONG** with a function because they are non-scalar (unless you use variable parameters).
3. Unlike scalar types—see reason No. 2; scalars *can* be returned by a function.
4. Unlike structured types—you can't access individual elements using [subscripts] (or any other direct way).

Because of all this, we won't attempt to figure out what category **LONG**s really fall in, we'll just use them and keep quiet.

QUIZ—SUBRANGE TYPES

True or False

1. Subrange types can be based on any scalar type except for *REAL*s.
2. It's all right for the first boundary in a subrange type to be greater than the second boundary.
3. It's all right to mix different subranges of the same type in expressions.
4. User-defined types can be declared in the *VAR* declaration section instead of the *TYPE* section.

SETS

Have you ever owned a set of chess pieces, a set of silverware, or a set of teeth (natural or false)? A set is a collection of objects which are all of the same type. You won't find a Monopoly marker in your chess set nor a wooden fork mixed in with the silverware. The same holds true for sets in Pascal. A set is a structured data type which can be based on any scalar type. When using sets, we work with the entire set as a whole, rather than worrying about the specific values of an element as we do with arrays.

Using Sets

In the following example, we want the user to enter either a 'Y' for yes or an 'N' for no. We also want to allow for UPPER or lower case letters. Here is how we might write this:

```
REPEAT
  GOTOXY(0,5);
  WRITE('Do you want to play again? ');
  READ(Ch);
UNTIL (Ch = 'Y') OR (Ch = 'y')
  OR (Ch = 'N') OR (Ch = 'n');
```

The last statement is rather awkward. By using sets, we can replace it with the following statement and simplify it:

```
UNTIL Ch IN ['Y', 'y', 'N', 'n'];
```

The characters within the square brackets are *members* in the *set* of acceptable answers for our Yes/No question. **IN** is a reserved keyword. What we are checking is whether or not the value of **Ch** is a *member* of our set. If so, then the expression:

```
Ch IN ['Y', 'y', 'N', 'n']
```

will be TRUE, otherwise the **REPEAT** loop isn't exited.

We can also create set types and set variables:

```
TYPE   CharacterSet = SET OF CHAR;

VAR   Answer : CharacterSet;
```

Here we are creating a new type which can have a set of any **CHAR**s as its value. Next, we declare **Answer** to be a **CharacterSet** type variable. To assign **Answer** a value we do this:

```
Answer := ['Y', 'y', 'N', 'n'];
```

Now our **UNTIL** statement looks like this:

```
UNTIL Ch IN Answer;
```

The general format for declaring a set type is:

```
TYPE   SetName = SET OF BaseType;
```

Where **BaseType** can be any defined scalar type (standard or user-defined) except for **REAL**. When making sets out of user-defined types, the type should be declared before creating the set:

```
TYPE   Fruit   = (Lemon, Orange, Tangerine, Grapefruit,
                  Lime, Pineapple, Banana, Grape, Plum,
                  Apple, Avocado, Tomato, Pear);
       FruitSet = SET OF Fruit;
```

Now we can declare some set variables:

```
VAR   FruitSalad, CitrusFruit,
      SandwichFruit, SourFruit,
      FruitBowl, LeaveOut, SweetCitrus : FruitSet;
```

Next we can assign some values to these variables:

```
CitrusFruit     := [Lemon, Orange, Tangerine,
                    Grapefruit, Lime];
SourFruit       := [Lemon, Lime];
SandwichFruit   := [Avocado, Tomato];
```

If the members of a set are consecutive values in the **BaseType** (as with the **CitrusFruit** set) we can take a short-cut:

```
CitrusFruit := [Lemon..Lime];
```

Or we can combine methods:

```
FruitBowl := [Lemon..Apple, Pear];
```

Set Operators

There are a number of operators that can be used with sets:

+ *Set Union:*

```
LeaveOut := SourFruit + SandwichFruit;
```

LeaveOut will be the set **[Lemon, Lime, Avocado, Tomato]**. Union combines the two sets into a new set—all the members of the two sets will end up in the final set. Duplications will be ignored. For example, the union of **SourFruit** and **CitrusFruit** would have the same members as **CitrusFruit**. This is because **SourFruit** is a "subset" of **CitrusFruit**, that is, all the members in **SourFruit** are already in **CitrusFruit**.

— *Set Difference:*

```
FruitSalad := FruitBowl — LeaveOut;
```

FruitSalad will be the set **[Orange, Tangerine, Grapefruit, Pineapple, Banana, Grape, Plum, Apple, Pear]**. The difference of two sets is created by eliminating all members from the first set which are also found in the second set.

∗ *Set Intersection:*

```
SweetCitrus := CitrusFruit ∗ FruitSalad;
```

SweetCitrus will be the set **[Orange, Tangerine, Grapefruit]**. The intersection of two sets contains only the members which are *common* to both sets.

There are also four relational operators you can use to *compare* sets in Boolean expressions:

= *Set Equality:*

SourFruit = CitrusFruit	→ *FALSE*
[Tomato, Lemon] = [Lemon, Tomato]	→ *TRUE*

Set equality means both sets contain exactly the same members. The order of the members is not important.

<> *Set Inequality:*

FruitBowl <> FruitSalad	→ *TRUE*
CitrusFruit <> [Lemon..Grapefruit]	→ *TRUE*

The members in the two sets *don't* match exactly.

<= *"Is Contained In":*

FruitSalad <= FruitBowl	→ *TRUE*
[Avocado, Tomato] <= SandwichFruit	→ *TRUE*
CitrusFruit <= SourFruit	→ *FALSE*

One set "is contained in" another set if every member in the *first* set is also in the *second* set.

>= *"Contains":*

CitrusFruit >= SourFruit	→ *TRUE*

One set "contains" another set if every member in the *second* set is also in the *first* set.

Other Structured Data Types

In addition to the Array and Set, there are two more structured data types which we won't be covering in this book. They are the Record, that allows you to work with data structures which have elements of *different* types, and the File, that allows you to store data on an external device, like a floppy disk.

QUIZ—SETS

True or False
1. The expression *Ch IN Answer* returns a Boolean value.
2. The *BaseType* of a set can be any scalar type.
3. When sets are combined in set union (+), every member of both sets appears once in the resulting set.

PUTTING IT ALL TOGETHER— THE TIC-TAC-TOE PROGRAM

Arrays, as you now know, are most useful for accessing information which is ordered in a special way. One area in which this is especially true is in the creation of computer games, particularly those employing a board with men or markers that move from position to position. In fact, computer games have quickly become one of the most popu-

lar uses for microcomputers today, offering the opportunity for a battle of wits between man and machine.

In this section, you will learn how the game of Tic-Tac-Toe can be represented in Pascal. This program is a culmination of everything we taught you. We include this program so you can review all the elements in this book, not to teach you game theory or illustrate the best example of a Tic-Tac-Toe playing computer.

In addition to playing against you, the computer will take care of everything—displaying the game board, allowing you to input your move, moving the markers, and checking for ties or a winner. A special "move formula" (algorithm) which allows the computer to decide what move to make will be developed. Before we get into the program, let's review the rules of the game, then we will translate these rules into a program.

Remember the Rules?

For review, there are two players in the game of Tic-Tac-Toe. One player uses an "X" marker and the other player (in this case the computer) uses an "O" marker. The playing board consists of a square divided into nine smaller squares, and the goal of the player is to get three of his/her own markers in a straight line by filling a row, column, or diagonal. Plays are made on the board in alternate moves. If no player gets a line and all squares are filled, the game is a tie or "cat's game." (Uncle Pascal tells us that it's called this because when two tabbies play Tic-Tac-Toe together, there's usually no winner!)

The moves of a typical game may go like this:

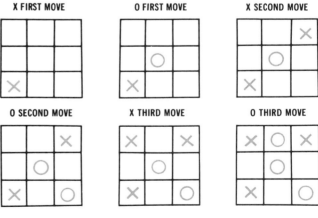

X IS THE WINNER

There are a few simple strategies you can employ to make your chances of winning more likely. Rather than giving them away, enter this program and use your computer as an untiring teacher!

Representing the Board

Our first problem is to represent the board in a manner which makes it easy for the computer to keep track of moves and play a strong game and *also* makes it easy for a human to play. Rather than compromising the play of either player by trying to create one solution for both, we will use two solutions. For the human, we will number each square from 1 to 9 and use cursor control to fill in the markers. For the computer, we will use an array. Since the board has three rows and three columns, we will use a two-dimensional array with three elements in each dimension. We will call this array **Square**. The computer will reference the array like this:

Square[1,1]	Square[1,2]	Square[1,3]
Square[2,1]	Square[2,2]	Square[2,3]
Square[3,1]	Square[3,2]	Square[3,3]

The first subscript represents the row and the second the column.

Representing the Markers

We need some way to represent internally the two players' markers, the X and the O. On the screen, we will use an **X** and an **O** (how original!). The method we chose allows the computer to make decisions rapidly. We will use the integer value -1 to stand for the X and we will store it in the constant **Computer**. The value $+1$ (or just 1) will represent the human and it is stored in the constant **Human**. The value of any element indicates who is in any particular square. (An empty square will be represented by the value 0 which is stored in the constant **Empty**.) So it follows that if **Square[2,2]** contained the value **Computer** (i.e., -1) then the computer has a marker on the center square. If **Square[3,3]** contained the value **Human** (i.e., 1), then the human has a marker on the lower right corner of the board.

Overall Flow of the Game

There are five main sections in this program:

1. Startup—Initialize the variables and the array, get the player's name, find out who gets to go first, and display the initial board.
2. Computer Move Logic — This section will make the decision of how the computer is to move.

3. Display Move—After a move by *either* player the board (screen) must be updated. This section will place the appropriate marker on the screen.
4. Human Input — This section will accept a move from the human and check for its legality.
5. Check for the End of Game—The game is over when either the computer has won, the human has won, or there is a tie game (no moves left and one more for the cat's team).

We will go over each of these major sections and show you the portion of the program as we discuss it. Then you can also look at the entire program reprinted at the end of the chapter (Listing 10-5).

Initialize the Game

First let's examine the beginning of the program (Listing 10-3A). Immediately after the title you see a message to the compiler (**USES APPLE-STUFF**) to bring in some routines from the library. The function we use is the random number generator which is covered in the Computer Move section. (Don't worry, if you aren't using an Apple, we have an equivalent function for you. Since one of our goals was to make this program as transportable as possible, we try to accommodate everyone.)

Next, we set up the global constants, types, and variables. We've already discussed the first three constants, and we'll get to the others when we come to them in the program.

The User-Defined Types—The first three types are all subrange types. **Player** refers to the value a square can have, either **Computer**, **Empty**, or **Human**. **Outcome** refers to the stage of play in the game, either the **Computer** has won, **No-Winner** yet, the **Human** has won, or it's a **Tie**. **Index** refers to the three possible elements of each dimension of our array—the range is from 1 to 3. Finally, **SetOfChar** will be used to make it easier to check the human's responses.

The only global variable declaration we want to look at now is **Square**. Here's something we haven't mentioned before. We're using the subrange type **Index** in place of the **LowerBound** and **UpperBound**. Since **Index**'s boundaries are 1..3, so are the boundaries of the array.

Take a look at Listing 10-3B, the Main Program section. We will refer to the procedures as they are listed in this section.

Initialize—The **Initialize** procedure (Listing 10-3C) is executed only once when the game is first started. The player has the option to play the game

Listing 10-3A.

```
PROGRAM TicTacToe;
USES APPLESTUFF;              (* For random number generator *)

CONST   Computer = -1;
        Empty    = 0;
        Human    = 1;
        Tie      = 2;
        NoWinner = 0;
        Moved    = TRUE;
        NoMove   = FALSE;
        ScreenWidth = 40;

TYPE    Player     = Computer..Human;  (* Computer, Empty, Human *)
        Outcome    = Computer..Tie;    (* Computer, NoWinner, Human, Tie *)
        Index      = 1..3;
        SetOfChar  = SET OF CHAR;

VAR     PlayerOneFlag : Player;
        WinnerFlag    : Outcome;
        Tab1, Tab2    : INTEGER;
        Ch            : CHAR;
        PlayerName    : STRING;
        Square        : ARRAY[Index] OF
                             ARRAY[Index] OF Player;

        FirstMove,
        MoveComplete,
        GameOver      : BOOLEAN;
```

again without having to re-execute the program. We used **Tab1** to center the playing board on the screen and **Tab2** to place the markers on the board. Both variables are affected by the constant **Screen-Width**. If this constant is changed for a different screen width, the display will still have a symmetrical appearance.

GameOver indicates whether or not the player wants to play another game.

Get the Player's Name — Procedure **GetName** (Listing 10-3D) accepts the name from the player. This procedure is also executed only once at the beginning of the program. We fancied it up to prepare for a few possibilities. The player's name is printed on the screen during the play of the game to prompt him/her for a move. We want to make sure that the name plus the messages will fit on the screen. Since 32 spaces are reserved for prompt messages, that leaves **ScreenWidth** − 32 spaces for the name. On a 40 character screen, that's only 8 spaces for a name. The maximum name length is stored in **MaxName**.

After receiving the player's name, we make a few checks on it. The first step is to delete any leading spaces. Next we check for a name with less than 2 characters in it. Since we don't know

of any names like that, we assume the player wants to remain anonymous. We oblige by dubbing him/her 'No Name.' Next we check to see if the name exceeds **MaxName**. If it does, we ask for a shorter name.

Game Preparation—By referring to the Main Program section (Listing 10-3B), you'll notice that **GamePrep**, the next procedure executed (as well as the rest of this section), is within a **RE-PEAT-UNTIL** loop. This loop will allow the player to have another go at the game after it's over. Look at **GamePrep** (Listing 10-3E). This procedure sets all of the elements of **Square** to **Empty**. If this isn't done each time the game's played, you won't get very far! We also set two status variables to their initial values.

Who Goes First? — Next, the human player chooses who will go first (Listing 10-3F). This procedure calls **InputYN** (Listing 10-3G) to get either a 'Y' or an 'N.' The value parameter (11 in this case) specifies on which line an error message should be printed. **Answer** is a variable parameter which will return the response.

After an appropriate message is printed out, the variable **PlayerOneFlag** will be set to the first player to move.

Listing 10-3B.

```
BEGIN (* Main Program *)
  Initialize;
  GetName;

  REPEAT    (* Repeat loop until player doesn't want to play again *)
    GamePrep;
    WhoGoesFirst;
    InitDisplay;

    IF PlayerOneFlag = Computer THEN
      BEGIN
        FirstCompMove;
        Display(Computer);
      END;

    REPEAT          (* Main game loop - repeat until end of game *)

      HumanMove;        (* Get human's move,        *)
      Display(Human);   (*    display it, and       *)
      EndCheck;         (*    check for end of game *)

      IF WinnerFlag = NoWinner THEN
        BEGIN           (* Game's not over yet, computer's turn *)
          IF NOT FirstMove (* Check if this is the computer's first move *)
            THEN
              FirstCompMove          (* Computer's first move *)
            ELSE
              CompMove;              (* Computer's subsequent moves *)

          Display(Computer);   (* Display the move and *)
          EndCheck;            (* check for end of game *)
        END;

    UNTIL WinnerFlag <> NoWinner;  (* End of main game loop *)

    EndGame;

  UNTIL GameOver;
END.  (* TicTacToe *)
```

Now look at **InputYN**. First, the two sets are initialized. We are initializing these sets here rather than within the **Initialize** procedure to keep them as local as possible. The extra processing time to initialize them every time this procedure is called is negligible in this application. Next,

Listing 10-3C.

```
PROCEDURE Initialize;

BEGIN
  Tab1 := 11 + (ScreenWidth - 11) DIV 2; (* Used to center grid on screen *)
  Tab2 := 1 + (ScreenWidth - 11) DIV 2;  (* Used to make moves on grid *)

  GameOver := FALSE;  (* Initialize end of game flag *)
END; (* Initialize *)
```

Listing 10-3D.

```
PROCEDURE GetName;
(* Accept the player's name.  Make sure it will not overflow
   the screen space set aside for it in the program, check for
   leading spaces and eliminate them.                          *)
VAR   MaxName, Len : INTEGER;

BEGIN
  MaxName := ScreenWidth - 32; (* Maximum name length = leftover space *)
  ClearScreen;

  Center(0,'Welcome To The Game Of TIC-TAC-TOE!' );

  REPEAT
    GOTOXY(0,5);
    WRITE('What''s your name? ' );
    READLN(PlayerName );

    WHILE POS(' ',PlayerName) = 1 DO
      DELETE(PlayerName,1,1);                (* Delete leading spaces *)

    Len := LENGTH(PlayerName );

    IF Len < 2 THEN                          (* Check for no entry *)
      PlayerName := 'No Name';

    IF Len > MaxName THEN                    (* Make sure name will *)
      BEGIN                                  (* fit on the screen   *)
        GOTOXY(0,4);
        WRITELN('I can''t remember names that long...' );
        ClearLine(5);
      END;
  UNTIL Len <= MaxName;
END; (* GetName *)
```

this procedure continues to request an input until the value in **YesNo** is contained in the set **YesNoSet**. If the player entered a legal entry in lower case (if it's **IN LowerCase**), it is converted to UPPER case by subtracting the ordinal (ASCII) value of 'a' from the ordinal value of **YesNo** and

then adding the ordinal value of 'A.' This new value is then converted back to a character. This method will work even if the host computer doesn't use an ASCII numbering system. Try plugging in your own values of **YesNo** to see how this works.

Initialize the Display — The last initialization

Listing 10-3E.

```
PROCEDURE GamePrep;
(* Initialize array and flags *)
VAR   i, j : Index;

BEGIN
  FOR i := 1 TO 3 DO
    FOR j := 1 TO 3 DO
      Square[i,j] := Empty;                (* Clear array *)

  WinnerFlag := NoWinner;
  FirstMove  := NoMove;
END; (* GamePrep *)
```

Listing 10-3F.

```
PROCEDURE WhoGoesFirst;
(* Find out who gets to go first *)
VAR    Answer : CHAR;

BEGIN
  GOTOXY(0,8);
  WRITELN('Well, ',PlayerName,',');
  WRITE('  will you let me go first? ');
  InputYN(11, Answer);
  WRITELN;

  IF Answer = 'Y' THEN
    BEGIN
      WRITELN('Why thank you, ',PlayerName,', I''ll');
      WRITELN('remember you in my dreams!');
      PlayerOneFlag := Computer;           (* Set first player flag *)
    END

    ELSE
      BEGIN
        WRITELN('You aren''t giving me much of a chance!');
        PlayerOneFlag := Human;            (* Set first player flag *)
      END;

  Continue;
END; (* WhoGoesFirst *)
```

Listing 10-3G.

```
PROCEDURE InputYN(Vert        : INTEGER;
                  VAR YesNo : CHAR);
(* Procedure to accept a 'Y' or 'N' before exiting, if
   lower case 'y' or 'n' is entered, convert to UPPER case *)

VAR    YesNoSet, LowerCase : SetOfChar;

BEGIN
  YesNoSet  := ['Y', 'y', 'N', 'n'];      (* Initialize sets *)
  LowerCase := ['a'..'z'];

  READ(YesNo);

  WHILE NOT (YesNo IN YesNoSet) DO
    BEGIN
      GOTOXY(4,Vert);
      WRITE('Please type either "Y" or "N": ');
      READ(YesNo);
    END;

  IF YesNo IN LowerCase THEN   (* Convert lower case letter to UPPER case *)
    YesNo := CHR(ORD(YesNo) - ORD('a') + ORD('A'));
  WRITELN;
END; (* InputYN *)
```

Listing 10-3H.

```
PROCEDURE InitDisplay;
(* Display the game squares *)

BEGIN
  Center(0,' ** TIC-TAC-TOE **' );

  Center(2,CONCAT(PlayerName,' has X''s     I have O''s' ));

  GOTOXY(0,5);
  WRITELN('   !   !   ':Tab1);
  WRITELN(' 1 ! 2 ! 3 ':Tab1);
  WRITELN('   !   !   ':Tab1);
  WRITELN(' ---+---+---':Tab1);
  WRITELN('   !   !   ':Tab1);
  WRITELN(' 4 ! 5 ! 6 ':Tab1);
  WRITELN('   !   !   ':Tab1);
  WRITELN(' ---+---+---':Tab1);
  WRITELN('   !   !   ':Tab1);
  WRITELN(' 7 ! 8 ! 9 ':Tab1);
  WRITELN('   !   !   ':Tab1);
END; (* InitDisplay *)
```

step before the game actually starts is to display the board on the screen. This is done with procedure **InitDisplay** (Listing 10-3H). We are using the same **Center** procedure introduced in Chapter 9 to center the headings. Next **Tab1** is used to center the board on the screen regardless of the screen width.

The Computer Makes a Move

Let's say the player is feeling magnanimous and allows the computer to make the first move. **PlayerOneFlag** will be set to **Computer** and **First-CompMove** is carried out (Listing 10-3I).

The Computer's First Move and Random Numbers—FirstCompMove is always executed the first time the computer gets to move (even if the human goes first). Throughout this program we are using what are called "flags." These are variables which we use to store a "game condition." **Move-Complete** is the flag we use to let the computer know whether or not a successful computer move has been made.

We want to give the computer a tactical advantage for its first move. The first choice is the center square. The procedure **FillSquare** is passed the coordinates of this middle square (2,2). **Fill-Square** checks to see if this square is **Empty**, if so it:

1. Fills the square with the **Computer** marker.
2. Sets the **MoveComplete** flag to **Moved**.
3. Calls the nested function **Convert** which converts the [row, column] coordinates passed

to **FillSquare** to a **CHAR** with the '1'..'9' number value of the square (as indicated in **InitDisplay**, Listing 10-3H).
4. Calls a time wasting procedure, **Wait** (Listing 10-3J), that executes a **FOR** loop for 8 "moments." This pause creates the illusion of the computer actually taking the time to "think" before choosing its move. It can be somewhat disconcerting to have the computer announce its move "immediately" after you enter *your* move. People prefer playing with a computer that appears to have "human-like" qualities rather than one which can do things better than they can.
5. Displays the message saying where the computer will move.
6. Calls **Wait** again so the computer doesn't seem to think of a move and place its marker at approximately the same instant.

When **FillSquare** is finished with the center square, **FirstCompMove** checks the **MoveComplete** flag. If the center square wasn't filled (this will happen if the human chose to go first and also chose the center square) the computer's second choice will be one of the corner squares. Rather than choosing the same square each time, we are using a "random number generator" to choose a random corner. Apple Pascal has a function called **RANDOM** which we can use if we say **USES APPLESTUFF** at the beginning of the program. This function returns an **INTEGER** value between 0 and 32767 inclusive. The values **RAN-**

Listing 10-3l.

```
PROCEDURE FillSquare(r, c : Index);
(* Check if computer's move can be completed,
       if so then fill the "square"  *)

  FUNCTION Convert : CHAR;
  (* Convert from r,c coordinates to CHAR to be used in Display *)
  VAR  Temp : INTEGER;
  BEGIN
    Temp := (r - 1) * 3 + c;
    Convert := CHR(Temp + ORD('0'));
  END; (* Convert *)

BEGIN
  IF Square[r,c] = Empty THEN  (* If chosen square is empty, *)
    BEGIN                       (* then fill it with Computer *)
      Square[r,c] := Computer;
      MoveComplete := Moved;    (* Set flag to indicate move made *)
      Ch := Convert;
      Wait(8);      (* Make it look like the computer is thinking *)
      GOTOXY(ScreenWidth - 16,17);
      WRITE('I will move to ',Ch);
      Wait(5);
    END;
END; (* FillSquare *)




PROCEDURE FirstCompMove;
(* Special procedure for computer's first move *)
VAR  RandomRow, RandomColumn : Index;

BEGIN
  MoveComplete := NoMove;

  FillSquare(2,2);             (* Try center square first *)

  IF NOT MoveComplete THEN (* If center square is filled, *)
    BEGIN                    (* try a random corner next.   *)
      RandomRow    := (RANDOM MOD 2) * 2 + 1;
      RandomColumn := (RANDOM MOD 2) * 2 + 1;
      FillSquare(RandomRow, RandomColumn);
    END;

  FirstMove := Moved;   (* First move is complete *)
END; (* FirstCompMove *)
```

DOM produces appear to be random (called pseudo-random) because they are uniformly distributed and the sequence of numbers doesn't repeat for a *very* long time if at all (however, the same sequence will be generated whenever this program is run*). To get a random number from 1 to n, use the following formula:

```
RandomNumber := (RANDOM MOD n) + 1;
```

To get a random number from a to b use this formula:

---

* There is an Apple procedure called **RANDOMIZE** for starting the random number generator in a "random" place (Apple Pascal Reference Manual, p 181).

Listing 10-3J.

```
PROCEDURE Wait(Time : INTEGER);
(* Procedure to create a pause *)
CONST  Delay = 200;

VAR    i : INTEGER;

BEGIN
  FOR i := 1 TO Time * Delay DO;
END; (* Wait *)
END; (* Wait *)
```

```
RandomNumber := (a + RANDOM MOD (b - a + 1));
```

In our program we want either a 1 or a 3 (not a 2) so we generate a number from 0 to 1, multiply this by 2 (now we have 0 or 2) and add 1 (now we have 1 or 3). The values passed to **FillSquare** will be either (1,1), (1,3), (3,1) or (3,3)—the four corners of the board.

If your Pascal doesn't have a random number generator, you may use the function* in Listing 10-4 on page 171.

This function will return a value between 0 and one less than the parameter **Range**—if **Range** is 100 the values will be from 0 to 99. The global variable **Seed** should be initialized to 1.23456 in the **Initialize** procedure. Use a parameter of 2 when calling this function in our program:

---
* This function is based on a function by Kenneth Bowles, *Microcomputer Problem Solving Using Pascal*, page 257.

```
RandomRow := Random(2) * 2 + 1;
```

There are better methods for generating random numbers, however, this one is fine for this application.

When the computer chooses a corner square we know it will be a valid move—there is no way that any of these corners can be occupied:

1. If the computer goes first, it takes the center square.
2. If the human goes first and doesn't take the center square, the computer takes the center square.
3. If the human goes first and takes the center square, the rest of the board will be open, so any computer move has to be valid.

The last thing **FirstCompMove** does is to set the **FirstMove** flag to **Moved** so this procedure won't be executed again in the current game.

Update the Board

Once the computer has moved, we need to update the board. The next procedure called in the Main Program section (Listing 10-3B) is **Display** (Listing 10-3K). A value is passed to the procedure indicating whether to place a computer marker or a human marker on the board.

The global variable Ch will contain the "number" of the square to move to. We use this variable as the **case-selector** in a CASE statement to position the cursor at the approximate screen coordi-

Listing 10-3K.

```
PROCEDURE Display(Move : Player);
(* Procedure to place "marker" on appropriate square.
   Selector is the CHAR entered by human or computer. *)

BEGIN

  CASE Ch OF
    '1' : GOTOXY(Tab2,     6);     (* Tab2 is offset calculated *)
    '2' : GOTOXY(Tab2 + 4,6);     (* in procedure Initialize    *)
    '3' : GOTOXY(Tab2 + 8,6);     (* based on ScreenWidth.       *)
    '4' : GOTOXY(Tab2,     10);
    '5' : GOTOXY(Tab2 + 4,10);
    '6' : GOTOXY(Tab2 + 8,10);
    '7' : GOTOXY(Tab2,     14);
    '8' : GOTOXY(Tab2 + 4,14);
    '9' : GOTOXY(Tab2 + 8,14);
  END; (* CASE *)

  IF Move = Human THEN WRITE('X')          (* Place marker at x,y *)
    ELSE WRITE('O');
END; (* Display *)
```

nates. **Tab2** contains the horizontal offset based on the current **ScreenWidth**. Once the cursor is positioned, the actual parameter **Move** is checked to see whether to write an 'X' or an 'O'.

The Human Moves

Referring back to the Main Program section (Listing 10-3B) you'll see that we now enter into the "main game loop." We will continue in this loop until one of the players has won or there is a tie. It's now the human's turn to move. Look at procedure **HumanMove** (Listing 10-3L).

Here are the steps for this procedure:

1. Clear the line reserved for error messages using the **ClearLine** procedure (also in Listing 10-3L). This procedure just writes **Screen-Width** spaces at the line indicated.
2. Display prompt and read a character.
3. Trap bad input—if the character entered is a legal digit (**IN NumberSet**) then go to the next step, otherwise go back to Step 2.
4. Clear the prompt message from the screen.
5. Convert the character entered from a **CHAR** digit ('1'..'9') to row and column coordinates (i,j).
6. Trap bad move (see if the human's cheating)

—if **Square[i,j]** is **Empty** then fill it with the **Human** marker and set the local **Good-Move** flag to **Moved**, otherwise print an error message and go back to Step 2.
7. Don't exit the loop until a **GoodMove** has been made.

Next we update the screen (Main Program section) using the same **Display** procedure, only this time we tell it to place the human's marker.

Check for the End of Game

The next step is to call procedure **EndCheck** (Listing 10-3M) to see if we have a winner or if anyone can move again.

This procedure contains two nested procedures —one to check for a win and one to check for a tie. **WinCheck** is executed first. Since we are using the value −1 for the computer's markers and 1 for the human's markers, we can locate a win if any of the possible "three-in-a-row" lines add up to either a −3 (computer win) or 3 (human win). The local variables **Diag1** and **Diag2** hold the sum of the two diagonal lines, **Row** stores the sum of the three rows, and **Column** stores the sum of the three columns. A nested **FOR** loop is used to check each of the three rows and columns.

Listing 10-3L.

```
PROCEDURE ClearLine(Vert : INTEGER);

BEGIN
   GOTOXY(0,Vert);
   WRITELN(' ':ScreenWidth);     (* Fill line with spaces - clear line *)
END; (* ClearLine *)




PROCEDURE HumanMove;
(* Human's turn to make a move *)
VAR  i, j       : Index;
     Temp       : INTEGER;
     NumberSet  : SetOfChar;
     GoodMove   : BOOLEAN;

BEGIN
   NumberSet := ['1'..'9'];
   GoodMove := NoMove;
   ClearLine(19);

   REPEAT
     GOTOXY(0,17);WRITE('Your move, ',PlayerName,': ');
     READ(Ch);

     IF Ch IN NumberSet THEN      (* Check for legal character *)
       BEGIN
         ClearLine(17);

         Temp := ORD(Ch) - ORD('0');    (* Convert character to      *)
         i := ((Temp - 1) DIV 3) + 1;   (* row and column coordinates *)
         IF Temp MOD 3 = 0
           THEN
             j := 3
           ELSE
             j := Temp MOD 3;

         IF Square[i,j] = Empty THEN    (* If chosen square is empty, *)
           BEGIN                        (* then fill it, set move flag *)
             Square[i,j] := Human;
             GoodMove := Moved;
           END

         ELSE
           BEGIN
             GOTOXY(0,19);
             WRITELN('Sorry, that square is already filled.');
           END;
       END;
   UNTIL GoodMove;        (* Don't exit until valid move is made *)
END; (* HumanMove *)
```

Listing 10-3M.

```
PROCEDURE EndCheck;
(* Check for a win or a tie *)
VAR  i, j : Index;

  PROCEDURE WinCheck;
  (* Check for win *)
  VAR  Diag1, Diag2, Row, Column : INTEGER;
  BEGIN
    Diag1 := 0; Diag2 := 0;

    FOR i := 1 TO 3 DO
      BEGIN
        Diag1 := Square[i,i] + Diag1;        (* Add diagonals *)
        Diag2 := Square[i,4 - i] + Diag2;

        Row := 0; Column := 0;

        FOR j := 1 TO 3 DO
          BEGIN
            Row := Square[j,i] + Row;         (* Add rows and columns *)
            Column := Square[i,j] + Column;
          END; (* FOR j *)

        IF (Diag1 = -3) OR (Diag2 = -3) OR (Row = -3) OR (Column = -3) THEN
          BEGIN
            WinnerFlag := Computer;   (* If any "lines" total to -3, *)
            EXIT(EndCheck);           (* the computer is the winner. *)
          END;

        IF (Diag1 = 3) OR (Diag2 = 3) OR (Row = 3) OR (Column = 3) THEN
          BEGIN
            WinnerFlag := Human;      (* If any "lines" total to +3, *)
            EXIT(EndCheck);           (* the human is the winner.    *)
          END;

      END; (* FOR i *)
  END; (* WinCheck *)

  PROCEDURE TieCheck;
  (* If any square is empty, then the game is not over yet *)
  BEGIN
    FOR i := 1 TO 3 DO

      FOR j := 1 TO 3 DO
        IF Square[i,j] = Empty THEN EXIT(EndCheck);

    WinnerFlag := Tie;  (* No empty squares, cat's game *)
  END; (* TieCheck *)

BEGIN (* EndCheck *)
  WinCheck;       (* If no winner yet, then check for a tie *)
  TieCheck;
END; (* EndCheck *)
```

The **EXIT** *Procedure*—After each row and column is added up, we check for a win. If we find one, we set the **WinnerFlag** to the appropriate value and execute a special UCSD intrinsic procedure called **EXIT** (not found in standard Pascal). This procedure allows us to prematurely exit from any procedure by naming it as the parameter. By using **EndCheck** as the parameter, we exit both **WinCheck** *and* **EndCheck** and return to the Main Program section. By using **WinCheck** as the parameter, we would exit only one level to the main section of **EndCheck**. When using **EXIT**, make sure you use the name of a valid and activated procedure. It's possible to use **EXIT** to force a program to terminate by using the program name as the parameter, or the word **PROGRAM** **(EXIT(PROGRAM);)**. However, we don't recommend this technique (it's sloppy!). Instead, find a way to let your program terminate "naturally." If you can write your program without using **EXIT** then do so—it's easy to become lazy and use this command when other methods would do just as well. Many versions of Pascal don't have an **EXIT**, so if you want your programs to be transportable, don't use it.

If no wins are found, the **TieCheck** procedure is executed. As soon as **TieCheck** discovers an **Empty** square, it exits **EndCheck**. If it finds each square filled, **WinnerFlag** is set to **Tie**.

If your version of Pascal doesn't have the equivalent of **EXIT** you can rewrite this section of the program and omit the **EXIT**s. Change the line calling **TieCheck** to:

```
IF WinnerFlag = NoWinner THEN TieCheck;
```

You could use a **FoundEmpty** flag in **TieCheck** if an empty square was discovered.

The Computer's Move Again

Back in the Main Program section we check the status of **WinnerFlag** (a winner is highly unlikely after only two moves). If there's **NoWinner** then the computer moves. If the computer has not yet made a move **(IF NOT FirstMove)** then **First-CompMove** is executed, otherwise, **CompMove** is executed.

The Computer's Strategy—In order for the computer to make an intelligent move, it must be able to analyze the current board array and decide the best move to make at the time. The computer program must imitate the way a human would decide where to move. If you examine your thought process carefully while playing Tic-Tac-Toe, you can discover that a certain series of steps, almost

like a formula, is followed. This formula is called an "algorithm." Let's identify the specific mental steps you might take to make a good Tic-Tac-Toe move by coming up with all possibilities and then prioritizing them. If the conditions aren't met in one of the steps indicated below, proceed to the following step:

1. Is there any line (row, column, or diagonal) that has two of your markers in it and the third square empty? If so, then fill it to win.
2. Is there any line which has two of the opponent's markers in it and an empty square in the line? If so, fill it to block the opponent from winning. If there is more than one line like this, take either one because you can't win unless your opponent is daydreaming.
3. Is there any line with one of your markers and two empty squares? If so, fill one of the squares to develop a potential winning line.
4. Is there any line with one of the opponent's markers in it and two empty squares? If yes, fill one of the squares to block.
5. If you've come this far, then find an empty square and fill it with your marker.

Now to implement these steps in Pascal we must find a way to determine each of these five conditions and, based on what we find, fill the respective empty square. Our solution is to find the unique mathematical sum which represents each of our five steps. For example, let's say we have a line meeting the conditions of Step 1 for the computer, that is, the computer has two markers in a line and there is one open square. If we add the value of these two markers we get -2. The only way we can get the sum of the elements in a line to add up to -2 (assuming the computer's markers have the value of -1 and the human's markers the value 1) is for two squares to contain -1 (**Computer**) and one square to contain 0 (**Empty**). Thus we can loop through all the lines on the board (three rows, three columns, and two diagonals) and if the computer finds any line equal to -2, we can have it fill the empty square in that line.

Look at Step 2. It's identical to Step 1 except that we are looking for a sum of 2 so the computer can block a potential loss. The only way we can get a line to add up to 2 is if two squares are 1 (**Human**) and one square is 0 (**Empty**).

The third step involves searching for a sum of -1. This condition could occur if two squares were empty and one square was a -1, or it could happen if two squares were -1 and one square was $+1$. We can still use the same process, except we

Listing 10-3N.

```
PROCEDURE CompMove;
(* Select computer's move *)
VAR  Loop, LineSum : INTEGER;
     i, j          : Index;

  PROCEDURE RowCheck;
  (* Check the rows, if LineSum found then try to fill a square *)
  BEGIN
       :                 (* See listing 10-3o *)
  END; (* RowCheck *)

  PROCEDURE ColumnCheck;
  (* Check the columns, if LineSum found then try to fill a square *)
  BEGIN
       :                 (* See complete listing, 10-3 *)
  END; (* ColumnCheck *)

  PROCEDURE DiagCheck;
  (* Check the diagonals, if LineSum found then try to fill a square *)
  BEGIN
       :                 (* See complete listing, 10-3 *)
  END; (* DiagCheck *)

BEGIN (* CompMove *)
  Loop := 1;
  MoveComplete := NoMove;

  REPEAT

    CASE Loop OF          (* Check possible conditions by priority  *)
      1:  LineSum := -2;  (* Two computer markers in a line - a win *)
      2:  LineSum :=  2;  (* Two human makers in a line - block win *)
      3:  LineSum := -1;  (* Possible one computer marker in a line *)
      4:  LineSum :=  1;  (* Possible one human marker in a line    *)
      5:  LineSum :=  0;  (* Possible open line                     *)
    END; (* CASE *)

    RowCheck; (* Check for LineSum in Rows, Columns, then Diagonals *)
    ColumnCheck;
    DiagCheck;

    Loop := Loop + 1;

  UNTIL Loop = 6;
END; (* CompMove *)
```

must continue searching if the computer can't find an empty square to fill.

The fourth and fifth steps follow the same logic process as Step 3. Add the values and then check for an empty square.

In summary, we want a routine that allows us to check sequentially through each of the five steps of the algorithm, looking for each of the conditions (a sum in a line of −2, +2, −1, +1, or 0) and make a move based on the first one satisfied. We wrote three separate procedures—one each to check the rows, the columns, and the two diagonals. We call each of these procedures from within a loop which cycles as many as five times,

Listing 10-3O.

```
PROCEDURE RowCheck;
  (* Check the rows, if LineSum found then try to fill a square *)
  VAR  Row : INTEGER;

    PROCEDURE RowOpen;
    BEGIN
      FOR i := 1 TO 3 DO
        BEGIN
          FillSquare(i,j);
          IF MoveComplete THEN EXIT(CompMove);
        END;
    END; (* RowOpen *)

  BEGIN (* RowCheck *)
    FOR j := 1 TO 3 DO
      BEGIN
        Row := 0;

        FOR i := 1 TO 3 DO
          Row := Square[i,j] + Row;

        IF Row = LineSum THEN RowOpen;
      END; (* FOR j *)
  END; (* RowCheck *)
```

each time looking for a different **LineSum** value. Here is the basic structure of procedure **Comp-Move** (Listing 10-3N). Look at the main section at the end of this procedure.

First we initialize the **Loop** counter and the **MoveComplete** flag. We next begin cycling through the loop, setting **LineSum** to a different value each time. Once **LineSum** is set, we execute in order **RowCheck**, **ColumnCheck**, and **Diag-Check**. If the value in **LineSum** is discovered within any of these procedures and an open square is found, then CompMove is exited. Here is procedure **RowCheck** (Listing 10-3O).

This procedure increments through each row and checks if the sum of the squares in that row adds up to **LineSum**. If they do, then the procedure nested within **RowCheck** is executed. This procedure, **RowOpen**, checks if there is an open square in the row now being checked by calling **Fill-Square** (up to three times) and passing it the co-ordinates of each square in that row. If **FillSquare** was successful in making a move, then **MoveComplete** has been set to **Moved** (TRUE) and **Comp-Check** is excited. Procedures **ColumnCheck** and **DiagCheck** are essentially the same as **RowCheck**.

As before, the screen is updated with the computer's move (**Display(Computer);**), and **End-Check** checks for a win or a tie.

If the game is not yet over (**WinnerFlag <>**

NoWinner is FALSE) then the main game loop continues. When the game *is* over, the procedure **EndGame** (Listing 10-3P) is executed. This procedure will blink a win or tie message on the screen using the nested procedure **Flash**. Then it will ask if the player wants to play again with **InputYN**. If so, the main loop cycles again (**Game-Over** is still set to FALSE) and **GamePrep** is called to reinitialize the array and flags. Otherwise, the program **GameOver** is set to TRUE and the program ends.

Here is how the game looks on the screen after the computer moves first:

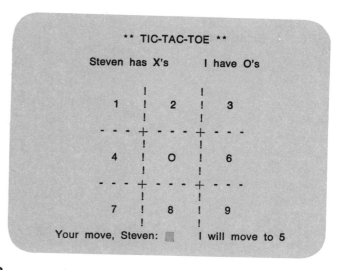

169

Listing 10-3P.

```
PROCEDURE EndGame;
(* End of game wrap up *)
VAR    Again : CHAR;

  PROCEDURE Flash(Message : STRING);
  (* Procedure to flash message on and off *)
  CONST   Times = 4;
          Line  = 19;
  VAR    i : INTEGER;
  BEGIN
    FOR i := 1 TO Times DO
      BEGIN
        ClearLine(Line);
        Wait(4);
        Center(Line, Message);
        Wait(4);
      END; (* FOR i *)
  END; (* Flash *)

BEGIN (* EndGame *)
  ClearLine(19);

  CASE WinnerFlag OF
    Computer : Flash('** I WON **');
    Human    : Flash('** YOU''RE THE WINNER!! **');
    Tie      : Flash('- TIE GAME -');
  END; (* CASE *)

  WRITELN;
  WRITE('Would you like to play again? ');
  InputYN(22, Again);
  ClearScreen;

  IF Again = 'N' THEN    (* Exit the program if player *)
    BEGIN                (* doesn't want to play again *)
      GameOver := TRUE; (* Set end of game flag *)
      Center(5,'Bye for now...');
    END;
END; (* EndGame *)
```

Here is what the screen looks like after the last move of a tie game:

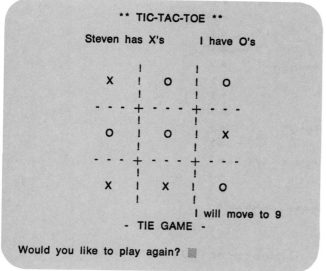

```
              ** TIC-TAC-TOE **

         Steven has X's      I have O's

                 !      !
           X     !  O   !  O
                 !      !
         - - - + - - - + - - -
                 !      !
           O     !  O   !  X
                 !      !
         - - - + - - - + - - -
                 !      !
           X     !  X   !  O
                 !      !
                              I will move to 9
              - TIE GAME -

      Would you like to play again? ▓
```

It is not too difficult to beat the computer if you go first, but the best we could do when we let the computer go first is a tie! Maybe you can do better.

Listing 10-5 contains the complete TicTacToe program, which was introduced in sections in Listings 10-3A through 10-3P.

Listing 10-4.

```
FUNCTION Random(Range : INTEGER): INTEGER;
(* Function to generate a pseudo-random number between 0 and Range *)

BEGIN
  Seed := Seed * 27.1828 + 31.4159;
  Seed := Seed - TRUNC(Seed);
  Random := TRUNC(Seed * Range);
END; (* Random *)
```

Listing 10-5.

```
(*=================================================*)
(*                                                 *)
(* Program Language: PASCAL                        *)
(* Program Title: Tic-Tac-Toe                      *)
(* Subtitle:   Using Arrays, Sets, and sub-range   *)
(*             types in a "practical" example.     *)
(*                                                 *)
(* AUTHOR:     David Fox                           *)
(*             Based on program by Mitch Waite     *)
(*                                                 *)
(* Program Summary:  Have fun trying to outwit the *)
(*             computer in a game.                 *)
(*                                                 *)
(*=================================================*)

PROGRAM TicTacToe;
USES APPLESTUFF;          (* For random number generator *)

CONST   Computer = -1;
        Empty    =  0;
        Human    =  1;
        Tie      =  2;
        NoWinner =  0;
        Moved    =  TRUE;
        NoMove   =  FALSE;
        ScreenWidth = 40;

TYPE    Player    = Computer..Human;  (* Computer, Empty, Human *)
        Outcome   = Computer..Tie;    (* Computer, NoWinner, Human, Tie *)
        Index     = 1..3;
        SetOfChar = SET OF CHAR;

VAR   PlayerOneFlag : Player;
      WinnerFlag    : Outcome;
      Tab1, Tab2    : INTEGER;
      Ch            : CHAR;
      PlayerName    : STRING;
      Square        : ARRAY[Index] OF
                          ARRAY[Index] OF Player;
      FirstMove,
      MoveComplete,
      GameOver      : BOOLEAN;




PROCEDURE ClearScreen;

BEGIN
  PAGE(OUTPUT);
END; (* ClearScreen *)
```

```
PROCEDURE Continue;

BEGIN
  GOTOXY(0,22); WRITE('Press RETURN to continue:  ');
  READLN;            (* Note that READLN can be used without a parameter *)
  ClearScreen;
END; (* Continue *)



PROCEDURE Center(VertPos  : INTEGER;
                 Sentence : STRING);
(* Procedure to center a string at line VertPos *)
VAR   Len : INTEGER;

BEGIN
  Len := LENGTH(Sentence);
  GOTOXY(0,VertPos);
  WRITELN(Sentence:Len + (ScreenWidth - Len) DIV 2);
END; (* Center *)



PROCEDURE ClearLine(Vert : INTEGER);

BEGIN
  GOTOXY(0,Vert);
  WRITELN(' ':ScreenWidth);    (* Fill line with spaces - clear line *)
END; (* ClearLine *)



PROCEDURE Wait(Time : INTEGER);
(* Procedure to create a pause *)
CONST  Delay = 200;

VAR   i : INTEGER;

BEGIN
  FOR i := 1 TO Time * Delay DO;
END; (* Wait *)



PROCEDURE Initialize;

BEGIN
  Tab1 := 11 + (ScreenWidth - 11) DIV 2; (* Used to center grid on screen *)
  Tab2 := 1 + (ScreenWidth - 11) DIV 2;  (* Used to make moves on grid *)

  GameOver := FALSE;  (* Initialize end of game flag *)
END; (* Initialize *)
```

```
PROCEDURE GetName;
(* Accept the player's name.  Make sure it will not overflow
   the screen space set aside for it in the program, check for
                                                               *)
   leading spaces and eliminate them.
VAR    MaxName, Len : INTEGER;

BEGIN
  MaxName := ScreenWidth - 32; (* Maximum name length = leftover space *)
  ClearScreen;

  Center(0,'Welcome To The Game Of TIC-TAC-TOE!');

  REPEAT
    GOTOXY(0,5);
    WRITE('What''s your name? ');
    READLN(PlayerName);

    WHILE POS(' ',PlayerName) = 1 DO
      DELETE(PlayerName,1,1);                (* Delete leading spaces *)

    Len := LENGTH(PlayerName);

    IF Len < 2 THEN                          (* Check for no entry *)
      PlayerName := 'No Name';

    IF Len > MaxName THEN                     (* Make sure name will *)
      BEGIN                                   (* fit on the screen   *)
        GOTOXY(0,4);
        WRITELN('I can''t remember names that long...');
        ClearLine(5);
      END;
  UNTIL Len <= MaxName;
END; (* GetName *)




PROCEDURE GamePrep;
(* Initialize array and flags *)
VAR   i, j : Index;

BEGIN
  FOR i := 1 TO 3 DO
    FOR j := 1 TO 3 DO
      Square[i,j] := Empty;                (* Clear array *)

  WinnerFlag := NoWinner;
  FirstMove  := NoMove;
END; (* GamePrep *)
```

```
PROCEDURE InputYN(Vert        : INTEGER;
                  VAR YesNo : CHAR);
(* Procedure to accept a 'Y' or 'N' before exiting, if
   lower case 'y' or 'n' is entered, convert to UPPER case *)

VAR   YesNoSet, LowerCase : SetOfChar;
  BEGIN
    YesNoSet  := ['Y', 'y', 'N', 'n'];        (* Initialize sets *)
    LowerCase := ['a'..'z'];

    READ(YesNo);

    WHILE NOT (YesNo IN YesNoSet) DO
      BEGIN
        GOTOXY(4,Vert);
        WRITE('Please type either "Y" or "N": ');
        READ(YesNo);
      END;

    IF YesNo IN LowerCase THEN   (* Convert lower case letter to UPPER case *)
      YesNo := CHR(ORD(YesNo) - ORD('a') + ORD('A'));
    WRITELN;
END; (* InputYN *)




PROCEDURE WhoGoesFirst;
(* Find out who gets to go first *)
VAR   Answer : CHAR;

BEGIN
  GOTOXY(0,8);
  WRITELN('Well, ',PlayerName,',');
  WRITE('  will you let me go first? ');
  InputYN(11, Answer);
  WRITELN;

  IF Answer = 'Y'  THEN
    BEGIN
      WRITELN('Why thank you, ',PlayerName,', I''ll');
      WRITELN('remember you in my dreams!');
      PlayerOneFlag := Computer;          (* Set first player flag *)
    END

    ELSE
      BEGIN
        WRITELN('You aren''t giving me much of a chance!');
        PlayerOneFlag := Human;          (* Set first player flag *)
      END;

  Continue;
END; (* WhoGoesFirst *)
```

```
PROCEDURE InitDisplay;
(* Display the game squares *)

BEGIN
   Center(0,' ** TIC-TAC-TOE **');

   Center(2,CONCAT(PlayerName,' has X''s       I have O''s'));

   GOTOXY(0,5);
   WRITELN('    !   !   ':Tab1);
   WRITELN(' 1 ! 2 ! 3 ':Tab1);
   WRITELN('    !   !   ':Tab1);
   WRITELN('---+---+---':Tab1);
   WRITELN('    !   !   ':Tab1);
   WRITELN(' 4 ! 5 ! 6 ':Tab1);
   WRITELN('    !   !   ':Tab1);
   WRITELN('---+---+---':Tab1);
   WRITELN('    !   !   ':Tab1);
   WRITELN(' 7 ! 8 ! 9 ':Tab1);
   WRITELN('    !   !   ':Tab1);
END; (* InitDisplay *)




PROCEDURE Display(Move : Player);
(* Procedure to place "marker" on appropriate square.
   Selector is the CHAR entered by human or computer. *)

BEGIN

   CASE Ch OF
      '1': GOTOXY(Tab2,    6);        (* Tab2 is offset calculated *)
      '2': GOTOXY(Tab2 + 4,6);        (* in procedure Initialize   *)
      '3': GOTOXY(Tab2 + 8,6);        (* based on ScreenWidth.     *)
      '4': GOTOXY(Tab2,    10);
      '5': GOTOXY(Tab2 + 4,10);
      '6': GOTOXY(Tab2 + 8,10);
      '7': GOTOXY(Tab2,    14);
      '8': GOTOXY(Tab2 + 4,14);
      '9': GOTOXY(Tab2 + 8,14);
   END; (* CASE *)

   IF Move = Human THEN WRITE('X')        (* Place marker at x,y *)
      ELSE WRITE('O');
END; (* Display *)
```

```
PROCEDURE FillSquare(r, c : Index);
(* Check if computer's move can be completed,
         if so then fill the "square" *)

  FUNCTION Convert : CHAR;
  (* Convert from r,c coordinates to CHAR to be used in Display *)
  VAR  Temp : INTEGER;
  BEGIN
    Temp := (r - 1) * 3 + c;
    Convert := CHR(Temp + ORD('0'));
  END; (* Convert *)

BEGIN
  IF Square[r,c] = Empty THEN   (* If chosen square is empty, *)
    BEGIN                       (* then fill it with Computer *)
      Square[r,c] := Computer;
      MoveComplete := Moved;    (* Set flag to indicate move made *)
      Ch := Convert;
      Wait(8);      (* Make it look like the computer is thinking *)
      GOTOXY(ScreenWidth - 16,17);
      WRITE('I will move to ',Ch);
      Wait(5);
    END;
END; (* FillSquare *)




PROCEDURE FirstCompMove;
(* Special procedure for computer's first move *)
VAR   RandomRow, RandomColumn : Index;

BEGIN
  MoveComplete := NoMove;

  FillSquare(2,2);               (* Try center square first *)

  IF NOT MoveComplete THEN  (* If center square is filled, *)
    BEGIN                        (* try a random corner next.  *)
      RandomRow    := (RANDOM MOD 2) * 2 + 1;
      RandomColumn := (RANDOM MOD 2) * 2 + 1;
      FillSquare(RandomRow, RandomColumn);
    END;

  FirstMove := Moved;    (* First move is complete *)
END; (* FirstCompMove *)




PROCEDURE CompMove;
(* Select computer's move *)
VAR  Loop, LineSum : INTEGER;
     i, j          : Index;
```

```
PROCEDURE RowCheck;
(* Check the rows, if LineSum found then try to fill a square *)
VAR   Row : INTEGER;

  PROCEDURE RowOpen;
  BEGIN
    FOR i := 1 TO 3 DO
      BEGIN
        FillSquare(i,j);
        IF MoveComplete THEN EXIT(CompMove);
      END;
  END; (* RowOpen *)

BEGIN (* RowCheck *)
  FOR j := 1 TO 3 DO
    BEGIN
      Row := 0;

      FOR i := 1 TO 3 DO
        Row := Square[i,j] + Row;

      IF Row = LineSum THEN RowOpen;
    END; (* FOR j *)
END; (* RowCheck *)

PROCEDURE ColumnCheck;
(* Check the columns, if LineSum found then try to fill a square *)
VAR   Column : INTEGER;

  PROCEDURE ColumnOpen;
  BEGIN
    FOR j := 1 TO 3 DO
      BEGIN
        FillSquare(i,j);
        IF MoveComplete THEN EXIT(CompMove);
      END;
  END; (* ColumnOpen *)

BEGIN (* ColumnCheck *)
  FOR i := 1 TO 3 DO
    BEGIN
      Column := 0;

      FOR j := 1 TO 3 DO
        Column := Square[i,j] + Column;

      IF Column = LineSum THEN ColumnOpen;
    END; (* FOR i *)
END; (* ColumnCheck *)
```

```
PROCEDURE DiagCheck;
(* Check the diagonals, if LineSum found then try to fill a square *)
VAR   Diag1, Diag2 : INTEGER;

  PROCEDURE Diag1Open;
  BEGIN
    FOR i := 1 TO 3 DO
      BEGIN
        FillSquare(i,i);
        IF MoveComplete THEN EXIT(CompMove);
      END; (* FOR i *)
  END; (* Diag1Open *)

  PROCEDURE Diag2Open;
  BEGIN
    FOR i := 1 TO 3 DO
      BEGIN
        FillSquare(i, 4 - i);
        IF MoveComplete THEN EXIT(CompMove);
      END; (* FOR i *)
  END; (* Diag2Open *)

BEGIN (* DiagCheck *)
  Diag1 := 0; Diag2 := 0;

  FOR i := 1 TO 3 DO
    BEGIN
      Diag1 := Square[i, i] + Diag1;
      Diag2 := Square[i, 4 - i] + Diag2;
    END; (* FOR i *)

  IF Diag1 = LineSum THEN Diag1Open;

  IF Diag2 = LineSum THEN Diag2Open;
END; (* DiagCheck *)

BEGIN (* CompMove *)
  Loop := 1;
  MoveComplete := NoMove;

  REPEAT

    CASE Loop OF          (* Check possible conditions by priority  *)
      1:  LineSum := -2;  (* Two computer markers in a line - a win  *)
      2:  LineSum :=  2;  (* Two human makers in a line - block win  *)
      3:  LineSum := -1;  (* Possible one computer marker in a line  *)
      4:  LineSum :=  1;  (* Possible one human marker in a line     *)
      5:  LineSum :=  0;  (* Possible open line                      *)
    END; (* CASE *)
```

```
      RowCheck; (* Check for LineSum in Rows, Columns, then Diagonals *)
      ColumnCheck;
      DiagCheck;

      Loop := Loop + 1;

  UNTIL Loop = 6;
END; (* CompMove *)




PROCEDURE HumanMove;
(* Human's turn to make a move *)
VAR  i, j      : Index;
     Temp      : INTEGER;
     NumberSet : SetOfChar;
     GoodMove  : BOOLEAN;

BEGIN
   NumberSet := ['1'..'9'];
   GoodMove := NoMove;
   ClearLine(19);

   REPEAT
     GOTOXY(0,17);WRITE('Your move, ',PlayerName,': ');
     READ(Ch);

     IF Ch IN NumberSet THEN        (* Check for legal character *)
       BEGIN
         ClearLine(17);

         Temp := ORD(Ch) - ORD('0');    (* Convert character to        *)
         i := ((Temp - 1) DIV 3) + 1;   (* row and column coordinates *)
         IF Temp MOD 3 = 0
           THEN
             j := 3
           ELSE
             j := Temp MOD 3;

         IF Square[i,j] = Empty THEN   (* If chosen square is empty,  *)
           BEGIN                       (* then fill it, set move flag *)
             Square[i,j] := Human;
             GoodMove := Moved;
           END

         ELSE
           BEGIN
             GOTOXY(0,19);
             WRITELN('Sorry, that square is already filled.');
           END;
       END;
   UNTIL GoodMove;        (* Don't exit until valid move is made *)
END; (* HumanMove *)
```

```
PROCEDURE EndCheck;
(* Check for a win or a tie *)
VAR  i, j : Index;

   PROCEDURE WinCheck;
   (* Check for win *)
   VAR  Diag1, Diag2, Row, Column : INTEGER;
   BEGIN
     Diag1 := 0; Diag2 := 0;

     FOR i := 1 TO 3 DO
       BEGIN
         Diag1 := Square[i,i] + Diag1;        (* Add diagonals *)
         Diag2 := Square[i,4 - i] + Diag2;

         Row := 0; Column := 0;

         FOR j := 1 TO 3 DO
           BEGIN
             Row := Square[j,i] + Row;        (* Add rows and columns *)
             Column := Square[i,j] + Column;
           END; (* FOR j *)

         IF (Diag1 = -3) OR (Diag2 = -3) OR (Row = -3) OR (Column = -3) THEN
           BEGIN
             WinnerFlag := Computer;   (* If any "lines" total to -3, *)
             EXIT(EndCheck);           (* the computer is the winner. *)
           END;

         IF (Diag1 = 3) OR (Diag2 = 3) OR (Row = 3) OR (Column = 3) THEN
           BEGIN
             WinnerFlag := Human;      (* If any "lines" total to +3, *)
             EXIT(EndCheck);           (* the human is the winner.    *)
           END;

       END; (* FOR i *)
   END; (* WinCheck *)

   PROCEDURE TieCheck;
   (* If any square is empty, then the game is not over yet *)
   BEGIN
     FOR i := 1 TO 3 DO

       FOR j := 1 TO 3 DO
         IF Square[i,j] = Empty THEN EXIT(EndCheck);

     WinnerFlag := Tie;  (* No empty squares, cat's game *)
   END; (* TieCheck *)

BEGIN (* EndCheck *)
  WinCheck;      (* If no winner yet, then check for a tie *)
  TieCheck;
END; (* EndCheck *)
```

```
PROCEDURE EndGame;
(* End of game wrap up *)
VAR    Again : CHAR;

   PROCEDURE Flash(Message : STRING);
   (* Procedure to flash message on and off *)
   CONST  Times = 4;
          Line  = 19;
   VAR    i : INTEGER;
   BEGIN
     FOR i := 1 TO Times DO
       BEGIN
          ClearLine(Line);
          Wait(4);
          Center(Line, Message);
          Wait(4);
       END; (* FOR i *)
   END; (* Flash *)

BEGIN (* EndGame *)
  ClearLine(19);

  CASE WinnerFlag OF
    Computer : Flash('** I WON **');
    Human    : Flash('** YOU''RE THE WINNER!! **');
    Tie      : Flash('- TIE GAME -');
  END; (* CASE *)

  WRITELN;
  WRITE('Would you like to play again? ');
  InputYN(22, Again);
  ClearScreen;

  IF Again = 'N' THEN    (* Exit the program if player *)
    BEGIN                (* doesn't want to play again *)
      GameOver := TRUE; (* Set end of game flag *)
      Center(5,'Bye for now...');
    END;
END; (* EndGame *)



BEGIN (* Main Program *)
  Initialize;
  GetName;

  REPEAT     (* Repeat loop until player doesn't want to play again *)
    GamePrep;
    WhoGoesFirst;
    InitDisplay;
```

```
  IF PlayerOneFlag = Computer THEN
    BEGIN
      FirstCompMove;
      Display(Computer);
    END;

  REPEAT          (* Main game loop - repeat until end of game *)

    HumanMove;        (* Get human's move,        *)
    Display(Human);   (*    display it, and        *)
    EndCheck;         (*    check for end of game *)

    IF WinnerFlag = NoWinner THEN
      BEGIN          (* Game's not over yet, computer's turn *)
        IF NOT FirstMove (* Check if this is the computer's first move *)
          THEN
            FirstCompMove          (* Computer's first move *)
          ELSE
            CompMove;              (* Computer's subsequent moves *)

        Display(Computer);    (* Display the move and  *)
        EndCheck;             (* check for end of game *)
      END;

  UNTIL WinnerFlag <> NoWinner;  (* End of main game loop *)

  EndGame;

  UNTIL GameOver;
END.  (* TicTacToe *)
```

Pascal's Advantages—A Summary

Depending on your orientation and reasons for investigating Pascal, the various features of the language will have individual significance for you. Generally speaking, Pascal offers the following advantages over other languages, including assembly and high-level types:

1. *Easily Understood Programs.* Because Pascal is a "procedure-oriented language" and has a rich variety of control statements, Pascal coded programs are easier to figure out, and are practically self-documenting. Programmer comments that don't use precious space and use of indentation and meaningful variable names make Pascal programs self-explanatory and an excellent choice when creating software is your main focus. Many pundits predict that hybrid versions of Pascal will become the language of the corporate world of the future . . . leaving FORTRAN and COBOL in the dust.
2. *Manageable Maintenance.* Pascal calls for a top to bottom systematic approach to a program—one that is clear, self evident, and consistent. This means future programmers will be able to chart their way through someone else's Pascal project with relative ease. Recall the "rat's nest" analogy.
3. *Easier Control Over Development by Managers.* Pascal is structured so well that managers can easily monitor the progress of a project involving several programmers; the project can more easily be broken into sections and worked on independently than if FORTRAN or BASIC were used. No more "I thought *you* were writing that subroutine" or "What does GOSUB 10001 mean?"
4. *Superior Standardization.* Compared to BASIC and FORTRAN Pascal is more standardized, and "extensions" are provided in a clearer fashion to the end user. An ANSI, IEEE, and ISO proposal exists for Pascal, making it more international than most languages.
5. *Compiled.* This makes for better protection of your software, as only *you* have the source code, while the end user gets object code. (Of course, FORTRAN is compiled too, and compiler BASICs are fairly common.) Compiled code means it's faster than BASIC and uses less memory. P-code compilers are a compromise.
6. *Can Handle Data Structures With Ease.* Wirth went to the cutting edge with Pascal's data structuring. Lists and tables can be manipulated with extreme ease.

Pascal's Bummers

No book on Pascal could be complete without exploring the weaknesses of Pascal . . . after all, Pascal was designed by Wirth to improve upon the weaknesses of an earlier language (ALGOL), so it would seem sensible to enumerate Pascal's limitations. Here are a few.

1. It is more difficult to debug a Pascal program than an interpreter BASIC program. In BASIC, you can stop the program partway through, print out some variables in the "direct mode" and then resume execution. In Pascal, you must insert tracing **WRITELN** statements wherever you think the problem might be and hope that you catch it. (On the other hand, the compiler catches a lot of bugs before you even execute.) You are left to find the real "toughies."

2. Slow executing code if it's a P-machine type Pascal (compared to N-code). Plus memory space and time lost due to run-time package (interpreter) sitting in RAM. P-machine code must run from RAM, and is not easily ROMable.

3. Dynamic bounds on arrays and sets are not possible. (This is a problem only when writing library routines.) In BASIC, you can change the size of an array in the program, expanding it as more elements are needed. In Pascal, the length of arrays is fixed when the program is run.

4. Random Access Files are not specified in Wirth's Pascal. UCSD Pascal implements random access with the **SEEK** intrinsic (not covered in this book), but other Pascals may call this something else.

5. No **EXIT** statement to absolutely terminate

a procedure is included in Wirth's Pascal, but there is one in UCSD Pascal.

6. No SEGMENTING's specified in Wirth's Pascal, but it's available in UCSD. Segmenting was implemented in UCSD Pascal because in most micros the memory capacity is limited to 64K. Segmenting allows you to split a program up into segments—only one segment is in memory at a time. The Pascal compiler provides a good example of a segmented program. The compiler is so large that it can't completely fit in a microcomputer's memory at one time. It is therefore broken into smaller pieces that are placed in RAM as they are needed during the compilation process.

7. Limited i/o. If you're familiar with BASIC's INPUT and PRINT (which are easy to use) you may find Pascal's **READ** and **WRITE** more difficult. All high level languages have problems in defining the area of i/o, because each computer has a different implementation in hardware. Pascal must be extended to handle i/o the way BASIC does, or it must depend on the i/o features of the particular operating system being used.

8. Limited control-type capability. Pascal seems better suited to scientific data processing than to bit manipulation or time dependent processes with interrupts. However, bit twiddling Pascals are beginning to appear.

9. There is a great distance from the language to where actual hardware actions occur. Tracing Pascal from the source statement to its final machine level end product in RAM is difficult. This is especially true in

the P-code versions. Wirth's Pascal (and UCSD's) has no simple equivalent to PEEK or POKE. UCSD does allow assembly programs to be linked through the Pascal library, and parameters can be passed between functions or procedures to the main program in a clean and logical but rather complex manner. Thus the programmer must work with the machine by "remote control"—the automatic features of the compiler get in the way. This may not change because of a "my way" attitude among manufacturers of Pascal. A funny thing about computer languages is that everyone is gung-ho to make them universal, but the bottom line is *sales* (consumption). Universal languages leave little competitive angles for the sellers, thus each seller makes his Pascal sound like the only way to go.

10. Cost. A Pascal computer may be more expensive than one using BASIC. UCSD Pascal, for example, needs at least 48K of RAM for the compiler and two disk drives for optimum operation. There are versions of Pascal for CP/M, but you can't run Pascal on an AIM, KIM or SIM (yet) . . . some kind of disk operating system is needed.

11. Pascal is more verbose than BASIC.

12. Problems that can be solved in 10 lines of BASIC take 40 lines of Pascal.

13. Pascal is not forgiving on input errors or mixed data types.

14. Time required to become productive on simple jobs is much greater than other languages.

Here are a few other things to be aware of when using Pascal:

1. **CASE** Statement. In standard Pascal, bad selector values for a **CASE** statement cause an error. UCSD Pascal just "falls through" to the statement following the **CASE**.

2. Pascal uses "pointers" which you may not want to learn about, but are extremely powerful when handling data bases.

3. **STRINGs** and **LONG INTEGERs**. Wirth's Pascal has no simple string handling facilities (you must create them) and doesn't support large integers. UCSD handles strings well and allows 36 digit integers!

Other Parts of a Pascal System

If you've come this far then you're concerned with more details about Pascal and its system components. Most Pascals offer (in addition to the Compiler, Editor, and Filer) an Assembler, a Library Linker, and sometimes a dynamic debugger.

ASSEMBLER

The assembler is provided to allow you to create assembly language programs using Pascal. The actual assembler is host dependent—on the Apple, it's a 6502 macro-assembler; on Pascal/Z it's a Z80 macro-assembler. (Macro means "more than just an assembler," it allows custom mnemonics to be created.) The way an assembly language program interfaces with Pascal before it's assembled is arbitrary; you'll need to consult your individual manual for that information. The UCSD 6502 interface is covered in Appendix E. For now, understand that it can be an involved process.

LIBRARY LINKER

The linker lets you combine precompiled files (assembly code or Pascal) in a system library, and have your source program call them up as needed. You can evoke the Linker to change or add to a library. UNITs and EXTERNAL routines may be accessed with the Linker. UCSD Pascal on the Apple does the linking of extensions when you insert "USES APPLESTUFF" at the top of your program immediately following the program name.

DYNAMIC DEBUGGER

This is a program for single stepping a compiled Pascal program (not easily implemented with P-code) or for tracing and debugging your code. Many versions of UCSD Pascal do not have this feature implemented.

ASCII Character Codes

Decimal	Character	Decimal	Character	Decimal	Character
000	NUL	036	$	070	F
001	SCH	037	%	071	G
002	STX	038	&	072	H
003	ETX	039	I	073	I
004	EOT	040	(	074	J
005	ENQ	041	)	075	K
006	ACK	042	*	076	L
007	BEL	043	+	077	M
008	BS	044	'(right	078	N
009	HT		apostro-	079	O
010	LF		phe)	080	P
011	VT	045	-	081	Q
012	FF	046	.	082	R
013	CR	047	/	083	S
014	SO	048	0	084	T
015	SI	049	1	085	U
016	DLE	050	2	086	V
017	DC1	051	3	087	W
018	DC2	052	4	088	X
019	DC3	053	5	089	Y
020	DC4	054	6	090	Z
021	NAK	055	7	091	[
022	SYN	056	8	092	\
023	ETB	057	9	093	]
024	CAN	058	:	094	∧ (or ↑)
025	EM	059	;	095	(under-
026	CONTROL	060	<		score)
027	ESCAPE	061	=	096	' (left apos-
028	FS	062	>		trophe)
029	GS	063	?	097	a
030	RS	064	@	098	b
031	US	065	A	099	c
032	SPACE	066	B	100	d
033	!	067	C	101	e
034	''	068	D	102	f
035	#	069	E	103	g

Decimal	Character	Decimal	Character	Decimal	Character
104	h	112	p	120	x
105	i	113	q	121	y
106	j	114	r	122	z
107	k	115	s	123	{
108	l	116	t	124		
109	m	117	u	125	}
110	n	118	v	126	~
111	o	119	w	127	DEL

LF=Line Feed   FF=Form Feed   CR=Carriage Return   DEL=Rubout

CONTROL CHARACTERS					
NUL	Null	**LF**	Line Feed	**SYN**	Synchronous Idle
SOH	Start of Heading	**VT**	Vertical Tabulation	**ETB**	End of Transmission
STX	Start of Text	**FF**	Form Feed		Block
ETX	End of Text	**CR**	Carriage Return	**CAN**	Cancel
EOT	End of Transmission	**SO**	Shift Out	**EM**	End of Medium
ENQ	Enquiry	**SI**	Shift In	**SUB**	Substitute
ACK	Acknowledge	**DLE**	Data Link Escape	**ESC**	Escape
BEL	Bell (audible or atten-	**DC1**	Device Control 1	**FS**	File Separator
	tion signal)	**DC2**	Device Control 2	**GS**	Group Separator
BS	Backspace	**DC3**	Device Control 3	**RS**	Record Separator
HT	Horizontal Tabulation	**DC4**	Device Control 4 (Stop)	**US**	Unit Separator
	(punched card skip)	**NAK**	Negative Acknowledge	**DEL**	Delete

appendix E

Assembly Language Interfacing

> **Note to Readers About This Appendix**
>
> This appendix shows an example of how to interface an assembly language (AL) program to UCSD Pascal. It is intended for more advanced users who have some familiarity with the 6502 microprocessor. It is *not* a comprehensive tutorial of 6502 assembly language programming. But to make things easier for the more learned reader, we have included various materials to help you follow the examples, and these materials are in Appendix F. Table F-1 in Appendix F is a summary of the 6502 instruction names. Fig. F-1 is a diagram of the internal arrangement of the 6502 register set, i.e., the registers that the instructions in Table F-1 operate on. Fig. F-2 is a more detailed breakdown of the 6502 instruction set. Refer to these if you wish to follow the logic flow and operation of the example we give. If you're not concerned with this, then skip it. If you have a different microprocessor than the 6502, Appendix E will still be useful for your understanding of assembly language interfacing to Pascal.

This appendix describes how to squeeze even more power out of your Pascal through the use of assembly language programs. Assembly language, recall, is the most elementary language on the computer, the one the microprocessor itself understands. By using assembly language with your Pascal programs you increase by many fold the power of the language itself. You will be able to access all of the "memory mapped" features of your computer (the Apple has myriads of them). You will also be able to write special routines that are rapidly executed, consume very little memory, and allow critical timing applications. Lastly, you will be able to create your own custom "keywords" that (when used in your Pascal program) will cause a specific assembly language operation to execute.

Understand that this is not meant to be a course on assembly language programming. There are

plenty of books on the subject, and we advise you to read one or more of them before attempting this appendix. More precisely, this appendix is designed to show you how to get Pascal and an assembly language program working together. Although we use the 6502 microprocessor instructions for our examples (because that's the one the Apple uses), the same methodology applies if your processor is Z80, 1802, or 8086. In these cases, all that changes are the actual instruction mnemonics and the registers used to pass things back and forth.

WHY USE ASSEMBLY LANGUAGE WITH PASCAL?

Perhaps the most compelling reason for using assembly language (AL) with Pascal is that it allows you to access (manipulate) bytes and bits in the computer's memory. Standard Pascal (Jensen and Wirth, that is) does not specify keywords to access memory since there is no way of knowing how wide the memory is (8 bits, 16, 32?) or how long it is (64K, 128K, 1M?) on a specific machine. We can't really blame Jensen and Wirth—Pascal *was* designed to be machine independent. (In fact, you should be aware that as you add AL programs to Pascal, your program will not be executable on machines with microprocessor chips different from your own.) Accessing memory bytes and bits is particularly useful if you're writing "control" type programs, i.e., those that allow your computer to regulate electronic appliances or read the state of a machine or device attached to a memory port. Byte and bit access also comes in handy when you wish to use any memory mapped features of your computer. For example, the Apple has a speaker located at a certain memory address. Normal unadulterated Jenson and Wirth

Pascal requires rather strange techniques to access memory, but an AL program can be created that can easily use the speaker and any other memory-mapped devices attached to the computer. Another advantage for AL programs is when a certain operation is too slow in Pascal . . . you can rewrite it in assembly language to be much faster. Further critical bit fiddling and timing can be done with assembly.

Compared to BASIC, UCSD Pascal's AL interface is cleaner and easier to follow. Recall in a Microsoft-like BASIC we say something like CALL 32000 to access an AL program beginning at memory address 32000. This rather simple statement tells us *nothing* about what the AL program does (this is one of BASIC's biggest weaknesses) and therefore we must rely on documentation or comments in the BASIC program to fish out this information. We will see in an upcoming example how the AL program's purpose in Pascal is self-evident. Other problems exist with BASIC's AL structure that Pascal gets around. For example, passing a variable with BASIC requires use of the USR (user) function plus a strange mechanism called the floating point accumulator. Or, if you prefer the CALL, you must use separate POKEs to send data to the AL and PEEKs to recover data. As we said, Pascal's interface is much cleaner and if you're ready to learn about it, then let's begin.

HOW PASCAL HANDLES ASSEMBLY LANGUAGE

Pascal handles assembly language in an almost intimate manner. Instead of keeping the Pascal program separate and isolated from the AL program as we do in BASIC, the AL program gets "linked" or attached to the *compiled* Pascal program. A special program called, not surprisingly, the Linker, performs this complex connecting of the two programs, so we don't have to think about it. (Of course, the assembly language program has been converted (assembled) into the object code of the microprocessor you're using beforehand . . . we will say more about the exact steps later.) The final combined (linked) Pascal and AL program looks, to the micro, like a single compiled program.

The passing of data from the Pascal program to the AL, and vice-versa, is handled in a unique manner. Instead of using separate memory locations for sending and receiving data, Pascal uses the "stack" for communicating. Lets take a small diversion for a moment to explain how the stack works.

Pascal's Stack

The Pascal compiler is called a "stack" machine because it makes extensive use of the micro's stack. A stack is like the spring-loaded push-up tray holder in a cafeteria. The trays are like bytes of data. You can put trays on the stack or take them off. We say putting something *on* the stack is a *PUSH* while taking something *off* the stack is a *PULL*. The 6502 has both a push (PHA) and a PULL (PLA) instruction. So do the 8080 and all other microprocessors although they have their own unique mnemonics. The stack in the micro is a section of memory (=256 bytes, 0100 to 01FF HEX in the 6502). The stack is also the place where the 6502 saves the address of the last instruction before a subroutine instruction (JSR). We call these "return" addresses. The stack in the 6502 is a "last in first out" stack (LIFO) meaning the last item put on the stack is always the first item removed. (There is also a "first in first out," FIFO, type stack.)

In the 6502, the stack builds from the top of memory down, i.e., from 01FF towards 0100. A special "8-bit stack pointer" register, located in the microprocessor, is used to hold the address of the lowest item on the stack . . . but for using the stack we can ignore it . . . it's mainly there for the micro itself.

Why all this hoopla about the stack? Well, Pascal can use the stack to send data to the assembly language (AL) program and vice-versa. For example, Pascal could send an 8-bit data value by pushing it on the stack. The AL can receive the value by doing a pull. (Understand that a *push* transfers the data in the 6502's accumulator register onto the stack while a *pull* takes data off the stack, and sticks it in the accumulator register.) Conversely, the AL program can do the same thing . . . sending data back to Pascal with a push, that Pascal will retrieve with a pull. It turns out that Pascal's part in a push or pull is handled automatically, in response to the way a special procedure or function statement, called an External, is written in the Pascal source.

EXTERNAL PROCEDURES AND FUNCTIONS

If you read the chapter on procedures and functions, then you should be well aware of their power and flexibility. As a reminder, recall that a procedure in Pascal is executed by just typing its name where you want it executed in the program. Usually the procedure has parentheses after it that contain any variables we wish to "send" to the procedure or "receive" from the procedure. A procedure can stand alone as a statement. A function, on the other hand, is used to take a variable(s), do something with it, and return the result. Functions which normally receive a value (the so called argument), manipulate it and return a resulting value.

Procedures and functions are used to define an assembly language program in a manner that is very similar to their use in a regular Pascal program. The difference is we follow the procedure or function definition with the reserved word **EXTERNAL**. This tells the compiler to look for an AL program to obtain the complete definition of this procedure or function. For example, the following statement:

```
PROCEDURE Poke(Memloc, Data : INTEGER);
EXTERNAL;
```

tells the Pascal compiler that the procedure called **Poke** is an external procedure and has an assembly language section to it. **Memloc** and **Data** are two **INTEGER** parameters (value parameters) that are to be passed to the procedure. Nothing is returned to **Poke**. The statement:

```
FUNCTION Peek(Memloc : INTEGER) : INTEGER;
EXTERNAL;
```

tells the compiler that **Peek** is an external assembly language function. The function passes an **INTEGER** value (**Memloc**) to the AL program. The AL program returns an **INTEGER** value to the function. That is the reason for the label **INTEGER** outside the parentheses.

How does the UCSD Pascal compiler know what part of the AL program ties in with the external definition? We include a special "assembly directive" in the AL source code. An assembly directive is a nonexecutable instruction to the Pascal 6502 assembler that tells it something special. In the UCSD assembler, a directive is differentiated from regular instructions by preceding it with a period (.). The directive for indicating a procedure is:

```
.PROC NAME,X
```

where **NAME** is the name used in the Pascal procedure, and **X** is the number of parameters being passed to the AL program. For example:

```
.PROC POKE,2
```

tells the assembler this is a procedure called **POKE** and that 2 words of parameters are ex-

pected. This could be equivalent to two integers or one real. You'll notice that we are using UPPER case for the **NAME** of the procedure (or function). The assembler isn't as smart as Pascal —it doesn't understand lower case.

Similarly, the directive for an assembly function is:

```
.FUNC NAME,X
```

and an example is:

```
.FUNC PEEK,1
```

where **PEEK** must appear in our Pascal source program. That's the simple part. Now we are equipped with enough knowledge to get into the actual steps to creating a successful AL program that works with Pascal.

THE FIVE STEPS

After all this talk about stacks and externals, the actual steps required to end up with an AL program attached to Pascal may seem trivial. Here are the steps you should follow:

1. *Create the Pascal source program.* This should contain your external definitions.
2. *Compile the Pascal source into P-code.* The compilation will not require you to have written the AL part yet. Don't try to execute this compiled program, however. If you do, you will get an error message saying you must Link first.
3. *Create the assembly language source program.* Again you use the Pascal Editor to create the original source code for the AL program. In a while we'll say more about the assembler that comes with UCSD Pascal.
4. *Assemble the AL source code to object code.* We use the Pascal assembler to do this. The object code is saved in a disk file. The origin for the code (i.e., its final start address) is ignored since when we link the code to Pascal, it will be inserted in the correct place for us.
5. *Link the assembled object code to the Pascal P-code.* We use the Pascal Linker to do this. In UCSD Pascal, this linking involves answering a few questions asked by the Linker. The Linker then combines our assembled assembly language object code with the Pascal P-code and saves it in a new executable file.

That's it (and not a moment too soon!). Now that we have a file which contains the compiled

Pascal program with the linked-in assembly language routine(s) (yes, we can link many procedures and functions), you can execute your program using the normal X(ecute command. Later we will see how to put the assembled AL object code into the Pascal System Library, which eliminates the need to go through step 5, the manual linking. The X(ecute command causes an automatic access to this library and any AL routines specified by the Pascal source code in that library are then linked in. A **USES NAME** statement will appear in the Pascal source where **NAME** is a Pascal declaration program that declares our AL program. Both must be in the library.

It is important to understand that the assembly language object code produced by the assembler for UCSD Pascal is in relocatable form unless overridden with the **.ABSOLUTE** directive. This means you don't have to tell Pascal where to finally put your code . . . it figures out the right spot for you.

To more fully understand the power of externals, we present an example that illustrates several concepts we've discussed.

A PRACTICAL ASSEMBLY LANGUAGE EXAMPLE: PEEKPOKE

As an example of how useful and powerful Pascal's assembly language interface can be, we will use it to create our own custom language extensions to our UCSD Pascal. We will create a **Peek** and **Poke** operator using machine language. Recall that PEEK and POKE are found in practically all commercial versions of BASIC. PEEK is a *function* that takes a memory address and returns an 8-bit value equal to the contents of that address. POKE is a *procedure* that stores an 8-bit data value in a memory address. Our Pascal lacks PEEK and POKE, and this makes it awkward to access all the important memory-mapped features of the computer. For example, Apple's speaker is memory-mapped (at C030 hex), so we could use either operation to make it buzz by repeatedly accessing this the speaker's address. First, the high level Pascal code will be introduced. Here it simply demonstrates (proves) that our techniques work. Then we will explain the AL program.

Pascal Source Demo

Listing E-1 shows a Pascal test demo program called **PeekPokeDemo**. First, four variables are declared as **INTEGERs** (16-bit range − 32767 to 32767). Next, we declare the **Poke** procedure and

Peek function as we described earlier, followed by the **EXTERNAL** statement. Then we set **Memloc** to −16336 which is the address of the speaker. **Memloc** could be any valid address in the memory range of the 6502. Since Pascal treats 16-bit **INTEGERs** in 2's complement (last bit, bit 15, is the sign), we must convert addresses greater than 32767 to a negative equivalent value. Use the formula:

$$\text{2's complement address} = -(65536 - \text{address x})$$

where address x is the address in greater than 32767 form. For example, the speaker is located at C030 hex. This is 49200 in decimal and using our formula:

$$\text{2's complement equivalent} = -(65536 - 49200)$$
$$= -16336$$

and we arrive at the number we use in our program.

The first **FOR** loop tests if the **Peek** function can toggle the speaker (it doesn't really check if **Peek** is returning a correct value). The loop cycles the speaker 1000 times—the speaker is clicked once every time the speaker's memory location is accessed. **Dummy** is a necessary but useless variable. The next **FOR** loop does the same thing to the speaker using the **Poke** procedure, which needs no dummy variable, but does need dummy data; here we use 1. In both cases, the expected effect is a brief tone of a moderately high frequency. The last 5 statements simply **Poke** a known **Data** value (51) at a fixed location (7), then **Peeks** this location, and prints out the **Data** value returned. If everything works correctly after the five steps are followed, we will see "I found 51 at memory location 7" printed on the screen upon execution.

Step 1 is to enter this Pascal program, and Step 2 is to compile it.

By the Way . . .
The Last Assembler

The UCSD assembler is derived from an assembler developed at the University of Waterloo, and ironically called TLA, for *The Last Assembler*. The basic concept underlying TLA, and all UCSD assemblers, is the use of a central machine . . . an independent core that is common to all versions of the assembler. This is the same concept behind Pascal: the central core contains machine-dependent core to handle the differences of individual microprocessors. On the Apple, three files exist that allow the TLA to work: SYSTEM.ASSEMBLER, 6500.OPCODES, and 6500. ERRORS.

Listing E-1.

```
PROGRAM PeekPokeDemo;

(* Demonstrates using machine language programs that do
   a Peek function and a Poke procedure (like PEEK and
   POKE in BASIC) so you can use all your computer's
   memory mapped features.  Here are two examples that
   toggle the speaker.                                    *)

VAR  i, Memloc, Data, Dummy : INTEGER;


PROCEDURE Poke(Memloc, Data : INTEGER);
EXTERNAL;

FUNCTION Peek (Memloc : INTEGER) : INTEGER;
EXTERNAL;

BEGIN
   Memloc := -16336;          (* C030 Hex = address of speaker in the Apple *)

   FOR i := 1 TO 1000 DO    (* Demos Peek by "toggling" the speaker        *)
      Dummy := Peek(Memloc);

   FOR i := 1 TO 1000 DO    (* Demos Poke by "toggling" the speaker        *)
      Poke(Memloc,1);

   Data := 51;                (* Sample data to check Poke procedure        *)
   Memloc := 7;
   Poke(Memloc,Data);
   Dummy := Peek(Memloc);
   WRITELN('I found ',Dummy,' at memory location ',Memloc);

END.   (* PeekPokeDemo *)
```

TLA has many features usually found in the more powerful assemblers, including:
- 13 binary operators
- hex or decimal constants
- 8 pseudo ops (ASCII, BYTE, BLOCK, WORD, EQU, ORG, ABSOLUTE, INTERP)
- macros
- conditional directives (IF, ENDC, ELSE)
- Pascal host directives (CONST, PUBLIC, PRIVATE)
- External reference directives (DEF, REF)
- Listing control directives (LIST, NOLIST, MACROLIST, NOMACROLIST, PATCHLIST, NOPATCHLIST, PAGE, TITLE)
- File directive (INCLUDE)

All in all, this is a fine assembler. Your only problem may be the lack of a dynamic debugger for tracing your TLA program.

Assembly Language Source for PEEK and POKE

Our assembly source code is shown in Listings E-2A, E-2B, and E-2C. The code may look strange at first, but it's not that difficult.

MACRO—First, the two pieces of code (Listing E-2A) at the beginning are called .MACRO POP and .MACRO PUSH. The "macro" is a feature of powerful assemblers; it allows you to create your own custom instruction sequences that are triggered on the appearance of the macro's name in the AL program (the macro is to the assembler as the procedure is to a Pascal program). Here the POP macro takes two bytes off the stack and stores them in addresses 00 and 01 in page 0. We will use them to save the Pascal return address so we can get back to Pascal when done. (We need two addresses because it's a 2 byte (16-bit) address.) Later when we see POP x, we know that the POP macro executes and the 2 bytes are stored at x and x + 1.

PEEK—The code for the PEEK function is shown next, in Listing E-2B. The .FUNC directive starts the code. RETURN is given the value 0 via the .EQU equate statement. Now understand

```
;
;
        .MACRO POP              ; Macro pops 16 bit return address
        PLA
        STA %1
        PLA
        STA %1+1
        .ENDM

        .MACRO PUSH             ; Macro pushes 16 bit return address
        LDA %1+1
        PHA
        LDA %1
        PHA
        .ENDM
```

Listing E-2B.

```
        .FUNC PEEK,1            ; One word parameter

; Sample Peek function
; FUNCTION Peek(Memloc : INTEGER) : INTEGER;

RETURN  .EQU 0                  ; Temp variable to hold return address
                                ; Note: 0-35 hex free
        POP RETURN              ; Save Pascal return address
        PLA                     ; Discard 4 bytes stack bias .FUNC only
        PLA
        PLA
        PLA
        PLA                     ; Get LSB Memloc
        STA 2
        PLA                     ; Get MSB Memloc
        STA 3

        LDY #0
        LDA @2,Y                ; Get Data (indirect indexed)
        TAY                     ; Save Data in Y register
        LDA #0
        PHA                     ; Push MSB = 0
        TYA                     ; Get the Peek value back
        PHA                     ; Push LSB

        PUSH RETURN             ; Restore Pascal return address
        RTS                     ; Return to Pascal
```

that when Pascal executes the machine code, it leaves the 16-bit address of its last instruction on the stack. Our program does a **POP RETURN** to remove the two bytes and save them for later use. Next, we do four successive pulls (**PLAs**) off the stack. This removes 4 bytes of stack bias . . . i.e., useless data left on the stack. (This is only necessary for the **.FUNC** function.) Following the stack bias, the memory location **Memloc** is found in the next 2 bytes of the stack. Recall **Memloc** is the address we want to **Peek** at and is the one parameter we are passing to the AL program.

The instructions **PLA, STA 2, PLA, STA 3** take the bytes of **Memloc** off the stack and put the LSB in 2 and the MSB in 3 (the address is stored in LSB-MSB format on the stack). Now we are ready to use this address to do the actual **Peek**. The instruction **LDY #0** puts zero in the Y register, then the instruction **LDA@2,Y** does all the work. It is an "indirect indexed" 6502 instruction that says "load the accumulator (LDA) with the contents of the memory location formed by using the byte at address 2 as the LSB and the byte at address 3 as the MSB plus the value of the Y-register (zero

Listing E-2C.

```
        .PROC POKE,2              ; Two word parameter

; Sample Poke Procedure
; PROCEDURE Poke(Memloc, Data : INTEGER);

RETURN  .EQU 0

        POP RETURN               ; Save Pascal return address
                                 ; Pull parameters, last first
                                 ; (ie, Data then Memloc)
        PLA                      ; Get LSB Data
        STA 6
        PLA                      ; Get MSB Data - discard
        PLA                      ; Get LSB Memloc
        STA 4
        PLA                      ; Get MSB Memloc
        STA 5
        LDY #0
        LDA 6                    ; Get Data back
        STA @4,Y                 ; Store Data at Memloc

        PUSH RETURN              ; Restore Pascal return address
        RTS                      ; Return to Pascal

        .END
```

here)." We don't take advantage of the indexing with the Y-register here. Now the contents of the accumulator is our desired **PEEK** value, and it is time to return it to Pascal. Since UCSD Pascal expects a 2's complement 2 byte result, we push a zero on the stack for the MSB (since our answer is just 8 bits), first saving the **PEEK** value in the Y-register (we don't want to lose it). The code is: **TAY, LDA #0, PHA.** Next we put the LSB of the answer on the stack (after getting it back from the Y-register) with the code: **TYA, PHA.** We push the return address back on the stack via our **PUSH** macro. Finally we do a return from subroutine (**RTS**) to get back into Pascal (a **JSR** from the Pascal calling routine got us here, but we didn't see it, and we don't have to be concerned with it).

That's it! Note addresses 0-35 hex (0-53 decimal) of page zero are available for AL programs . . . but there's no guarantee Pascal won't alter them later.

POKE—The **POKE** procedure is the last section of machine code in Listing E-2C. It starts with the **.PROC** procedure directive. The way the procedure appears in Pascal is illustrated in a comment statement for reference. Next the **POP** macro appears followed by the code to pull the four bytes of the two procedure parameters, LSB

and MSB. (Recall we are sending the AL program both **Memloc** and **Data**.) The code: **PLA, STA 6, PLA, PLA, STA 4, PLA, STA 5** does this, putting the values in page 0 addresses 6, 5, and 4 as follows:

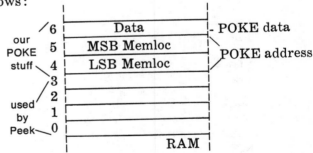

Now we are all set to do the actual **POKE**. The code is like our previous **Peek** example; however, we use an indirect indexed *store* instruction instead of a *load*. The **LDY #0** puts a zero in the Y-register and the **LDA 6** puts the data sent to **POKE** into the 6502 accumulator (recall it's stored in 6).

Next, the **STA @4,Y** stores the data in the accumulator at the address formed by the LSB at 4 and MSB at 5 and the Y-register (here 0).

Since **POKE** has no values to return, we simply restore the Pascal return address with a **PUSH RETURN** and do an **RTS** (return from subroutine) to get back into Pascal. Now we are done with entering both routines so we place an end directive (.END) as the last thing in the program. That's all there is to it.

After entering these AL routines, we follow the remaining steps—assemble, and link—and our job is done; we've added two new extensions to our Pascal: **Peek** and **Poke**. Try inventing your own custom extensions. A useful one would be a **Call** so you could use any monitor routines available in the computer's ROM space. **Call** would be a procedure.

THE PASCAL LIBRARY

There is a problem with the approach we've outlined so far, and that's if we change *anything* in our Pascal source code, we must go back and manually re-link the assembled object code to the new P-code, which is a bother, especially if you're in the debugging stage. UCSD Pascal provides a tidy solution to this problem and it is called the "library." The library, named SYSTEM.LIBRARY, is a collection of programs that contains various intrinsics (e.g., TRANSCENDental functions), graphic routines, external functions, etc., which might be required by your Pascal program. You can put all your assembled programs into this library by using another program called LIBRARY.CODE. To get your Pascal program to automatically link to the assembled program, we use the statement:

USES NAME1;

where **NAME1** is the name of the library routine we installed in the library. The **USES** statement must be located on the line immediately after the Pascal program name. Thus we could say:

USES TRANSCEND, PeekPoke;

to instruct the compiler we intend to use the transcendental functions (**LOG, SIN, LN,** etc.) plus our **PeekPoke** routines. This eliminates the tedious linking step after every compilation. Note in

UCSD Pascal the UNIT cannot be a mixture (linked) of compiled Pascal and assembly code. You must create two modules for the library . . . a Pascal declaration program (just has **PROC, FUNC** and **EXTERNAL** in it) and a separate assembly program. The declaration is called **Peek-Poke,** or whatever.

We can't go into the details of using the Linker as operations vary with each version of Pascal. However, it should be adequately covered in your Pascal manual. Although there are quite a few steps involved in using the library, one can still make excellent use of it with a little practice. Some other interesting applications which could be placed in your library are:

USES SOUNDEFFECTS; — a special set of sound effects, such as TONE, VOLUME, ENVELOPE, DURATION, etc.

USES BIGMATH; — a routine to do double-precision real math, i.e., 12 or more digits.

USES ANIMATION; — routines to allow fantastic moving picture effects.

In the Apple, the library is used to hold the Pascal i/o routines, **LONG INTEGER**s, the transcendental functions, TurtleGraphics, AppleGraphics, paddle routines, and system intrinsics (such as string functions). You can remove any of these you don't want in your library.

QUIZ

True or False

1. A program which uses a customized assembly language routine becomes nontransportable to other types of computers.

2. When used with Pascal, assembly language routines are generally slower executing than built-in Pascal procedures and functions.

3. The only way to mate a Pascal program to an assembly language routine is to use the Linker.

4. The Pascal keyword EXTERNAL alerts the compiler that there is an externally linked assembly language routine.

5. If your AL routines are stored in the library, you no longer have to use the keyword EXTERNAL in your program.

The 6502 Microprocessor

The following is a summary of the 6502 microprocessor instruction names, the 6502 internal register set arrangement, and a detailed instruction operation summary.

Table F-1. 6502 Instruction Names

ADC	Add to Accumulator with Carry
AND	AND Memory with Accumulator
ASL	Accumulator Shift Left
BCC	Branch on Carry Clear
BCS	Branch on Carry Set
BEQ	Branch on Result Equal to Zero
BIT	Test Bits in Memory with Accumulator
BMI	Branch on Result Minus
BNE	Branch on Result Not Equal to Zero
BPL	Branch on Result Plus
BRK	Force Break
BVC	Branch on Overflow Clear
BVS	Branch on Overflow Set
CLC	Clear Carry Flag
CLD	Clear Decimal Mode
CLI	Clear Interrupt Disable Bit
CLV	Clear Overflow Flag
CMP	Compare Memory and Accumulator
CPX	Compare Memory and Index X
CPY	Compare Memory and Index Y
DEC	Decrement Memory by One
DEX	Decrement Index X by One
DEY	Decrement Index Y by One
EOR	Exclusive-OR Memory with Accumulator
INC	Increment Memory by One
INX	Increment Index X by One
INY	Increment Index Y by One
JMP	Jump
JSR	Jump to Subroutine
LDA	Load Accumulator with Memory
LDX	Load Index X with Memory
LDY	Load Index Y with Memory
LSR	Logical Shift Right
NOP	No Operation
ORA	OR Memory with Accumulator
PHA	Push Accumulator on Stack
PHP	Push Processor Status on Stack
PLA	Pull Accumulator from Stack
PLP	Pull Processor from Stack
ROL	Rotate Left
ROR	Rotate Right
RTI	Return from Interrupt
RTS	Return from Subroutine
SBC	Subtract from Accumulator with Carry
SEC	Set Carry Flag
SED	Set Decimal Mode
SEI	Set Interrupt Disable Status
STA	Store Accumulator in Memory
STX	Store Index X in Memory
STY	Store Index Y in Memory
TAX	Transfer Accumulator to Index X
TAY	Transfer Accumulator to Index Y
TSX	Transfer Stack Pointer to Index X
TXA	Transfer Index X to Accumulator
TXS	Transfer Index X to Stack Pointer
TYA	Transfer Index Y to Accumulator

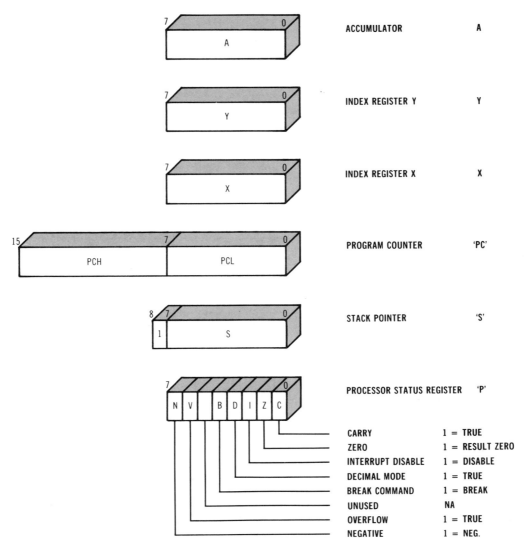

Fig. F-1. 6502 register set arrangement.

199

Fig. F-2. 6502 instruction set summary.

MNEMONIC	OPERATION	IMMEDIATE OP	n	#	ABSOLUTE OP	n	#	ZERO PAGE OP	n	#	ACCUM OP	n	#	IMPLIED OP	n	#	(IND, X) OP	n	#	(IND), Y OP	n	#	Z PAGE, X OP	n	#	ABS, X OP	n	#	ABS, Y OP	n	#	RELATIVE OP	n	#	INDIRECT OP	n	#	Z PAGE, Y OP	n	#	PROC STATUS N V • B D I Z C	MNEMONIC
ADC	A + M + C → A (4)(1)	69	2	2	6D	4	3	65	3	2							61	6	2	71	5	2	75	4	2	7D	4	3	79	4	3										N V · · · · Z C	ADC
AND	A∧M → A (1)	29	2	2	2D	4	3	25	3	2							21	6	2	31	5	2	35	4	2	3D	4	3	39	4	3										N · · · · · Z ·	AND
ASL	C ←[7 0]← 0				0E	6	3	06	5	2	0A	2	1										16	6	2	1E	7	3													N · · · · · Z C	ASL
BCC	BRANCH ON C = 0 (2)																															90	2	2							· · · · · · · ·	BCC
BCS	BRANCH ON C = 1 (2)																															B0	2	2							· · · · · · · ·	BCS
BEQ	BRANCH ON Z = 1 (2)																															F0	2	2							· · ◆ · · · · ·	BEQ
BIT	A∧M				2C	4	3	24	3	2																															M7 M6 · · · Z ·	BIT
BMI	BRANCH ON N = 1 (2)																															30	2	2							· · · · · · · ·	BMI
BNE	BRANCH ON Z = 0 (2)																															D0	2	2							· · · · · · · ·	BNE
BPL	BRANCH ON N = 0 (2)																															10	2	2							· · · · · · · ·	BPL
BRK	BREAK													00	7	1																									· · · · 1 · 1 · ·	BRK
BVC	BRANCH ON V = 0 (2)																															50	2	2							· · · · · · · ·	BVC
BVS	BRANCH ON V = 1 (2)																															70	2	2							· · · · · · · ·	BVS
CLC	0 → C													18	2	1																									· · · · · · · 0	CLC
CLD	0 → D													D8	2	1																									· · · · 0 · · ·	CLD
CLI	0 → I													58	2	1																									· · · · · 0 · ·	CLI
CLV	0 → V													B8	2	1																									· 0 · · · · · ·	CLV
CMP	A - M	C9	2	2	CD	4	3	C5	3	2							C1	6	2	D1	5	2	D5	4	2	DD	4	3	D9	4	3										N · · · · · Z C	CMP
CPX	X - M	E0	2	2	EC	4	3	E4	3	2																															N · · · · · Z C	CPX
CPY	Y - M	C0	2	2	CC	4	3	C4	3	2																															N · · · · · Z C	CPY
DEC	M - 1 → M				CE	6	3	C6	5	2													D6	6	2	DE	7	3													N · · · · · Z ·	DEC
DEX	X - 1 → X													CA	2	1																									N · · · · · Z ·	DEX
DEY	Y - 1 → Y													88	2	1																									N · · · · · Z ·	DEY
EOR	A∀M → A (1)	49	2	2	4D	4	3	45	3	2							41	6	2	51	5	2	55	4	2	5D	4	3	59	4	3										N · · · · · Z ·	EOR
INC	M + 1 → M				EE	6	3	E6	5	2													F6	6	2	FE	7	3													N · · · · · Z ·	INC
INX	X + 1 → X													E8	2	1																									N · · · · · Z ·	INX
INY	Y + 1 → Y													C8	2	1																									N · · · · · Z ·	INY
JMP	JUMP TO NEW LOC				4C	3	3																												6C	5	3				· · · · · · · ·	JMP
JSR	JUMP SUB				20	6	3																																		· · · · · · · ·	JSR
LDA	M → A (1)	A9	2	2	AD	4	3	A5	3	2							A1	6	2	B1	5	2	B5	4	2	BD	4	3	B9	4	3										N · · · · · Z ·	LDA
LDX	M → X (1)	A2	2	2	AE	4	3	A6	3	2																			BE	4	3							B6	4	2	N · · · · · Z ·	LDX
LDY	M → Y (1)	A0	2	2	AC	4	3	A4	3	2													B4	4	2	BC	4	3													N · · · · · Z ·	LDY
LSR	0 →[7 0]→ C				4E	6	3	46	5	2	4A	2	1										56	6	2	5E	7	3													0 · · · · · Z C	LSR
NOP	NO OPERATION													EA	2	1																									· · · · · · · ·	NOP
ORA	A∨M → A	09	2	2	0D	4	3	05	3	2							01	6	2	11	5	2	15	4	2	1D	4	3	19	4	3										N · · · · · Z ·	ORA
PHA	A → Ms S - 1 → S													48	3	1																									· · · · · · · ·	PHA
PHP	P → Ms S - 1 → S													08	3	1																									· · · · · · · ·	PHP
PLA	S + 1 → S Ms → A													68	4	1																									N · · · · · Z ·	PLA
PLP	S + 1 → S Ms → P													28	4	1																									(RESTORED)	PLP
ROL	[7 0 ← C]				2E	6	3	26	5	2	2A	2	1										36	6	2	3E	7	3													N · · · · · Z C	ROL
ROR	[C → 7 0]				6E	6	3	66	5	2	6A	2	1										76	6	2	7E	7	3													N · · · · · Z C	ROR
RTI	RTRN INT													40	6	1																									(RESTORED)	RTI
RTS	RTRN SUB													60	6	1																									· · · · · · · ·	RTS
SBC	A - M - C̄ → A (1)	E9	2	2	ED	4	3	E5	3	2							E1	6	2	F1	5	2	F5	4	2	FD	4	3	F9	4	3										N V · · · · Z C (3)	SBC
SEC	1 → C													38	2	1																									· · · · · · · 1	SEC
SED	1 → D													F8	2	1																									· · · · 1 · · ·	SED
SEI	1 → I													78	2	1																									· · · · · 1 · ·	SEI
STA	A → M				8D	4	3	85	3	2							81	6	2	91	6	2	95	4	2	9D	5	3	99	5	3										· · · · · · · ·	STA
STX	X → M				8E	4	3	86	3	2																												96	4	2	· · · · · · · ·	STX
STY	Y → M				8C	4	3	84	3	2													94	4	2																· · · · · · · ·	STY
TAX	A → X													AA	2	1																									N · · · · · Z ·	TAX
TAY	A → Y													A8	2	1																									N · · · · · Z ·	TAY
TSX	S → X													BA	2	1																									N · · · · · Z ·	TSX
TXA	X → A													8A	2	1																									N · · · · · Z ·	TXA
TXS	X → S													9A	2	1																									· · · · · · · ·	TXS
TYA	Y → A													98	2	1																									N · · · · · Z ·	TYA

(1) ADD 1 to N IF PAGE BOUNDARY IS CROSSED
(2) ADD 1 TO N IF BRANCH OCCURS TO SAME PAGE
    ADD 2 TO N IF BRANCH OCCURS TO DIFFERENT PAGE
(3) CARRY NOT = BORROW
(4) IF IN DECIMAL MODE Z FLAG IS INVALID
    ACCUMULATOR MUST BE CHECKED FOR ZERO RESULT

X	INDEX X	+	ADD	M7	MEMORY BIT 7
Y	INDEX Y	-	SUBTRACT	M6	MEMORY BIT 6
A	ACCUMULATOR	∧	AND	n	NO. CYCLES
M	MEMORY PER EFFECTIVE ADDRESS	∨	OR	#	NO. BYTES
Ms	MEMORY PER STACK POINTER	∀	EXCLUSIVE OR		

Fig. F-2. 6502 instruction set summary.

Inaccuracies of the Amortization
Loan Formula

The textbook formula for calculations with compound interest can lead to some disturbing results when used on a computer (or calculator). This is because there is a loss of accuracy in the answer due to certain values in the equation becoming too small. Recall the loan equation we used was:

$$\text{RegularPayment} = \frac{\text{Principal} \times \text{InterestPerPeriod}}{1 - (\text{InterestPerPeriod} + 1)^{-\text{NumberOfPayments}}}$$

This formula is based on a more basic one that works for compounding interest on a savings account:

$$P = A(1 + I)^N$$

where,

P = present value of account,
A = amount on deposit,
I = interest rate,
N = number of times compounded.

Now a bank that quotes the annual simple interest rate (such as "we give 5.25%") actually compounds your account at the equivalent *daily* rate, not just once a year. Thus, to find the actual daily interest rate to use in our formula, we must divide **I** by **M** where **M** is the number of times the interest is compounded per year (365 times if it's every day). Our daily formula becomes:

$$P = A(1 + I/M)^N$$

Now this is where the trouble begins for a computer. The result of dividing the interest by the number of times the interest is compounded in a year (**I/M**) may be extremely small, yielding a number with several zeroes between the decimal point and the actual significant digits. For example, the daily interest rate for a 5.25% account is:

$$0.0525/365 = 0.00014383562$$

In a computer with 8 digits of accuracy, the term $(1 + I/M)$ would then be rounded to 1.0001438, which would result in an annual interest error of 14 cents on a $10,000 account!

The same thing occurs in our Pascal Loan example:

```
InterestPeriod := (AnnualInterest / 100) / PaymentsPerYr
```

InterestPeriod becomes very small. The way out of this mess is to find a more accurate way to perform the compounding operation. There is a famous expansion formula from Calculus called the binomial expansion:

$$(1 + I)^N = 1 + N * I + \frac{N(N-1)}{2!} * I^2$$
$$+ \frac{N(N-1)(N-2)}{3!} * I^3 + \dots + I^N$$

The formula allows you to calculate the result of $(1 + I)^N$ to any accuracy you wish by simply including as many terms in the calculation as are needed. Each term has less and less of an influence on the final result. In fact, after about five terms, the values become negligibly small. Thus, you can set up a loop in a Pascal program to determine the result. Furthermore, each term may be computed from the previous term. In each pass, the loop would compute a term from the previous one, save the new term for the next round, and add the result to the series total. The result would be compared with the previous total, and if the result was not enough to raise the total within your computer's precision, it would exit the loop. We will leave it as an exercise for you to write the Pascal program for this expansion. A good article on the subject appeared in the April 1980 issue of *Microcomputing*, page 50.

appendix H

Answers to Quizzes

CHAPTER 2

1. B—Contains non letter/number (space)
   D—"Program" is a reserved word
   F—First character is not a letter

2. False—the semicolon is part of the required syntax.

3. False—they are separated with commas.

4. False—all spaces (except within apostrophes) are eliminated when the program is compiled.

5. (1) Space in program name
   (2) No semicolon after program name
   (3) Quotes used in first WRITELN instead of an apostrophe
   (4) No semicolon at the end of the first WRITELN statement
   (5) WRITELN is misspelled.
   (6) One apostrophe is used in the word won't instead of two (won''t).
   (7) No apostrophe after the word *compile*
   (8) No period after the END

6. GOTOXY(11,6)—don't forget to start counting with position 0, line 0.

CHAPTER 3

Variables

1. False—the first 8 characters are significant.

2. False—nothing in the name will tell what the type is. You must look at the declaration section at the beginning of the program.

3. False—it makes no difference how long the variable names are once the program is compiled. Make the names as long as is necessary for *clarity*.

4. False—you must initialize all variables yourself (you should do this even if your version of Pascal does it for you).

5. True— := means "is replaced by," = means "equals."

Inputting

1. False—you must provide your own prompt character (e.g., ? ... : --).

2. False—Pascal will abort the program.

3. False—comments take up absolutely no space during compilation, and programs are only obvious when you are writing them.

4. False—the space between the (and the * changes the Comment symbol into just a couple of characters.

5. True.

6. False—they work in very different ways when you are entering data into CHAR type variables. A READ will accept your single character input and go on *without your having to press RETURN*. READLN always waits for you to press RETURN.

Other Variable Types

1. Legal: A, F, G, H
   Illegal: B—no digit before the decimal point
          C—exponent is not an integer
          D—no digit after the decimal
   Sometimes: E—check your version of Pascal

2. A. 1.2480000E7   C. —1.147E-9
   B. 8.0E1   D. 5.5789E-1

3. A. 80487.9   C. —94800000000
   B. .0021448   D. .000000005148

4. The two values are TRUE and FALSE.

5. False—integers have no decimal point.

6. A. 50 (that was a CHAR, not an INTEGER)
   B. 5 (an INTEGER)
   C. —875
   D. 1
   E. 32
   F. 61

CHAPTER 4

1. False—a procedure should be just long enough to justify its existence—if all it's supposed to do is clear the screen, then only a few lines will suffice.

2. False—it is necessary; the program won't compile if it is too large. However, you should remember the rule that a procedure should not exceed one or two screensful.

3. True.

4. True.

5. False—the procedures must be defined before they are called.

6. False—a variable is *always* "local" within the block in which it was declared. It will also be "global" if there are other blocks *within* its local block.

7. False—the "most local" variable always takes precedence, which means that the outer block variable will be ignored within that inner block.

CHAPTER 5

1. False—no error will occur, but the statement(s) under control of the **FOR** will not execute at all.

2. True.

3. False—there is a better chance that your results are inaccurate. This might be because of the number of significant digits of accuracy your version of Pascal uses, or the bank might be using a different method to calculate the payments.

4. False—if it has six digits of accuracy, then that's all you get.

5. True—but don't use the "places after the decimal point" number unless you are using it with **REAL**s.

CHAPTER 6

1. False—there are only two values possible, a Boolean **TRUE** or **FALSE**.

2. True—as long as the single variable is a Boolean variable.

3. True—unless parentheses are used, in which case the expressions within the innermost parentheses will be evaluated first, then the next innermost, etc.

4. False—by using parentheses, the order can be controlled.

5. False—indenting is only used to make a statement clearer to you—it has no effect on program execution. **ELSE**s always refer to the most recent **IF-THEN**.

CHAPTER 7

1. False—the expression may evaluate to **FALSE** the first time it is checked in which case the loop would not cycle through at all.

2. True—or else you may end up in an endless loop.

3. True—the expression isn't checked until *after* the loop cycles through so it always cycles through at least once.

4. False—it isn't necessary, but it won't bomb the program.

5. False—it can only be an ordinal type, and a **STRING** is *not* an ordinal type.

6. True.

7. True—the condition in which there is no match between the **case-index** and the values of the **ccls** is *undefined* in standard Pascal. However, in UCSD Pascal, this condition *is* defined—the program will drop through to the next statement after the **CASE**, but if you want to make

your programs transportable to other versions of Pascal you should avoid this condition.

CHAPTER 8

Parameters

1. Value: **Number, Address, City, Block, Lawn**
   Variable: **Bugs, Pounds, Mass, Height**

2. True.

3. False—variable parameters can be used to send and receive *or* to just receive.

4. The only two intrinsic procedures which *return a value* in the actual parameter are **READ** and **READLN**, therefore, they *must use* variable parameters. The rest probably use value parameters.

Functions

1. A. Whistle—Boolean function
      Wait—procedure
   B. AnimalList—procedure
   C. Sum—function
   D. FireCheck—procedure
      HoseDown—function

2. False—however, you can use variable parameters to return a **STRING** value.

3. True—of course, you can't exceed the size limit of a block!

4. False—procedures can stand alone, but functions can't stand alone any more than a variable can.

5. True—as long as that parameter is a *value* parameter.

CHAPTER 9

Strings

1. True—however, it defaults to 80 and if you want it to be larger (or smaller) you must say so at the time you declare it.

2. True.

3. False—it will return a 0.

4. False—it will always yield an **INTEGER** value—and 0 if no match is found.

5. False—in UCSD Pascal, the procedure or function will either pretend it didn't hear your error and will leave your **STRING**s alone or it will return a null string (with **COPY**).

Long Integers

1. False—they can be declared to have less than 36 digits but no more than 36 digits.

2. False—21 decimal places $(7 + 7 + 7)$.

3. True.

4. False—you must add the extra decimal places *before* the division.

CHAPTER 10

Arrays

1. True—**REAL**s are an example of this.

2. False—a scaler data type *can't* be broken into elements —it already *is* an individual element. **STRINGs** are a *structured* data type.

3. True—although the *subscripts* may be of different types.

4. True—but be very careful when accessing the **CHAR** elements that one does in fact exist!

5. False—**REALs** can't be used as subscripts.

Enumerated User-Defined Data Types

1. True.

2. False—in this way they are like **BOOLEAN** types.

3. False—a constant may appear only once in a **TYPE** declaration at any level of a block.

4. False—**PRED** can be used to *decrement* an ordinal type, use **SUCC** to increment.

Subrange Types

1. True.

2. False—the **LowerBound** (first boundary) must be *less than* the **UpperBound** (second boundary).

3. True.

4. True—however, we feel it is clearer to use the **TYPE** declaration section to declare new types.

Sets

1. True.

2. False—any but **REAL**.

3. True—if the two sets have identical members, only one is used.

APPENDIX E

1. True—and the limitations are based on whether the routines are processor dependent or computer dependent. A 6502 routine will work on other 6502 systems unless it accesses features in the specific microcomputer (e.g., Apple's speaker).

2. False—assembly language is as fast or faster than Pascal's intrinsics, especially for a P-code Pascal.

3. False—you may install your routines in Pascal's library.

4. True.

5. True—however, you must name the routine with a **USES** statement at the beginning of your program.

Index

TO THE READER

Sams Computer books cover Fundamentals — Programming — Interfacing — Technology written to meet the needs of computer engineers, professionals, scientists, technicians, students, educators, business owners, personal computerists and home hobbyists.

Our Tradition is to meet your needs and in so doing we invite you to tell us what your needs and interests are by completing the following:

1. I need books on the following topics:

_____
_____
_____
_____
_____
_____
_____
_____

2. I have the following Sams titles:

_____
_____
_____
_____
_____
_____
_____
_____

3. My occupation is:

_____ Scientist, Engineer   _____ D P Professional

_____ Personal computerist   _____ Business owner

_____ Technician, Serviceman   _____ Computer store owner

_____ Educator   _____ Home hobbyist

_____ Student   Other _____
                                   _____

Name (print)_____

Address_____

City _____ State _____ Zip _____

Mail to: **Howard W. Sams & Co., Inc.**
Marketing Dept. #CBS1/80
4300 W. 62nd St., P.O. Box 7092
Indianapolis, Indiana 46206

21793

UCSD PASCAL
Quick Reference Card
by
David Fox and Mitch Waite

Declaration/Structure

CONST	STRING
TYPE	USES
VAR	PROGRAM
BEGIN	SET
PROCEDURE	END
FUNCTION	

Ordinal Functions
ORD
PRED
SUCC

Input/Output
PAGE
READ
READLN
WRITE
WRITELN

Flow of Control
CASE
FOR-DO/DOWNTO
IF-THEN
IF-THEN-ELSE
REPEAT-UNTIL
WHILE
GOTO
EXIT

Constant Identifiers
FALSE
TRUE
MAXINT

Misc Functions
CHR
ODD

Numeric Functions

ABS	LOG	
ATAN	ROUND	
ARCTAN	SIN	
COS	SQR	
EXP	SQRT	
LN	TRUNC	

Operators
DIV MOD
AND OR
NOT IN

String Functions and Procedures
CONCAT
COPY
DELETE
INSERT
LENGTH
POS
STR

Types
BOOLEAN
CHAR
INTEGER
LONG INTEGER
REAL

ALGEBRAIC OPERATORS

Symbol	Description	Operand Type*	Result Type*
+	Addition	I or R	I or R
	Set union	Any Set type	Same as operand
–	Subtraction	I or R	I or R
	Set difference	Any SET type	Same as operand
*	Multiplication	I or R	I or R
	Set intersection	Any SET type	Same as operand
/	REAL division	I or R	R
DIV	INTEGER division		
MOD	Modulus (A MOD B yields the remainder when dividing A by B)		
:=	Assigns value to		

* I = INTEGER, R = REAL

RELATIONAL OPERATORS

=	Equal
< >	Not equal
<	Less than
>	Greater than
< =	Less than or equal
> =	Greater than or equal
NOT	Logical "Not"
AND	Logical "And"
OR	Logical "Or"
IN	SET membership

PROGRAM STRUCTURE

PROGRAM ProgName;   *Declares name of program*

[Declarations]

PROCEDURE Proc1Name;   *Declares name of a procedure*

[Declarations]

BEGIN
..
END;

FUNCTION Func1Name;   *Declare name of a function*

[Declarations]

BEGIN
..
END;

BEGIN (* Main Program *)   *Main program section begins*

..
END. (* ProgName *)   *Main program section ends (note period after final END)*

Program or Block Declarations

CONST	Const1Name = constant;
	Const2Name = constant;
	:
	ConstNName = constant;
TYPE	Type1Name = type;
	Type2Name = type;
	:
	TypeNName = type;
VAR	Var1Name, Var2Name : type;
	Var3Name : type;
	:
	VarNName : type;

Procedure Parameter List

PROCEDURE   ProcName(Val1Param, Val2Param : type;
                           : type;
                     VAR Var1Param : type;
                         Val3Param : type);

Function Parameter List

FUNCTION   FuncName(Val1Param,   : type;
                    Val2Param,Val3Param : type; : type;
                    VAR Var1Param : type) : type;

NAMING CONVENTIONS

1. Names start with a letter.
2. Characters that follow must be either letters or numbers.
3. Only first eight characters are guaranteed to be recognized by the computer.
4. Names may *contain* Pascal "reserved words" but *can't be* reserved words.
5. Variations in different versions of Pascal (UPPER and lower case, other characters might be legal).

STANDARD (BUILT-IN) IDENTIFIERS

Constants

FALSE and TRUE	Boolean values
MAXINT	Maximum integer value

Types

The types with an asterisk (*) are available in UCSD Pascal:

BOOLEAN	CHAR	INTEGER
LONG INTEGER*	REAL	STRING*

FUNCTIONS

Numeric Functions

Name	Parameter Type*	Result Type*	Description
ABS(x)	I or R	Same as param	Returns absolute value of x

Ordinal Functions

Name	Parameter Type*	Result Type*	Description
ATAN(x) or ARCTAN(x)	R	R	Returns the inverse tangent of x in radians
COS(Angle)	I or R	R	Returns the cosine of Angle
EXP(x)	I or R	R	Returns e to the xth power (e^x)
LN(x)	I or R	R	Returns the natural logarithm of x (x must be greater than 0)
LOG(x)	I or R	R	Returns the Logarithm to the base 10 of x
ROUND(x)	R	I	Round off x to the nearest integer
SIN(Angle)	I or R	R	Returns the sine of Angle
SQR(x)	I or R	Same as param	Returns x squared (x^2)
SQRT(x)	I or R	R	Returns the square root of x (x must be positive)
TRUNC(x)	R or L	I	Converts x to integer without rounding

* I = INTEGER, R = REAL, L = LONG INTEGER

Ordinal Functions

Name	Parameter Type*	Result Type*	Description
ORD(x)	O	I	Returns the position which x holds in its data type
PRED(x)	O	Same as param	Returns the predecessor of x†
SUCC(x)	O	Same as param	Returns the successor of x†

I = INTEGER, O = Ordinal
† if none exists, there will be an error

Other Functions

Name	Parameter Type*	Result Type	Description
CHR(x)	I	CHR	Returns a character which has the ASCII value x
ODD(x)	I	BOOLEAN	Returns TRUE if x is odd, otherwise returns FALSE

* I = INTEGER

String Functions and Procedures

In the following String intrinsics, the parameters *StartPos*, *Pos* and *Size* are *INTEGERs*. All other parameters are *STRINGS*.

Name	Result Type*	Description
CONCAT(Str1, Str2, ..., StrN)	S,F	Returns a new string which is the concatenation of Str1 through StrN
COPY(SourceStr, StartPos, Size)	S,F	Copies from Source-Str beginning at StartPos taking Size characters
DELETE(SourceStr,StartPos,Size)	P	Removes Size characters from SourceStr beginning at StartPos
INSERT(Source, Dest, Pos)	P	Inserts Source into Dest at Pos
LENGTH(Str)	I,F	Returns the length of Str
POS(Pattern, SourceStr)	I,F	Returns the position of the first occurrence of Pattern in SourceStr
STR(x, DestStr)	P	Converts x (either an I or a LONG INTE-GER) to a STRING. Result is assigned to DestStr

* I = INTEGER, S = STRING, F = Function, P = Procedure

INPUT/OUTPUT INTRINSIC PROCEDURES

	Description
PAGE(OUTPUT);	Causes the screen to clear.
READ(Char1);	If Char1 is a CHAR type variable, READ will accept a single character without having to press RETURN.
READLN(Var1);	Accepts data from keyboard and places in Var1 (requires RETURN keypress).
WRITE(Var1);	Prints parameter on screen and leaves cursor at end of line (no carriage return/linefeed issued)*. (See WRITELN for more examples.)
WRITELN(Var1);	Prints data on screen (with carriage return/linefeed)*.
WRITELN(Var1, Var2, ..., VarN);	Printing multiple variables
WRITELN('Here's a string;', String1);	Printing literals
WRITELN(IntNum : 4, RealNum : 7 : 2);	Using formatted printing

* Var1 – VarN can be of type CHAR, INTEGER, LONG INTEGER, REAL, STRING

FLOW OF CONTROL COMMANDS

Command	Description
CASE	Use when you want to select one of many statements to execute. The statement following the constant which matches the value of the case-index is executed. Constant-list is a list of constants separated by commas. CASE case-index OF constant-list : statement; constant-list : statement; ... END;
EXIT	Use to prematurely leave a procedure or function. EXIT(ProcName);
FOR	Use when you want to repeat a statement(s) a specific number of times. FOR control-value := initial-value TO final-value DO statement; FOR control-value := initial-value DOWNTO final-value DO statement;
IF-THEN	Use when you want to execute a statement(s) only if a specific condition is true. IF condition THEN statement;
IF-THEN-ELSE	Use when you want to execute one of two statements. IF condition THEN statement1 ELSE statement2;
REPEAT-UNTIL	Use when you want to repeat a statement(s) until a specific condition is true. Statement will execute at least once. REPEAT statement1; statement2; ... statementN; UNTIL condition;
WHILE	Use when you want to repeat a statement(s) only while a specific condition is true. Statement(s) may not execute at all if condition starts out false. WHILE condition DO statement;

In the following examples, any statement may be substituted by a Compound Statement.

RESERVED WORDS

The words with an asterisk (*) following them are not covered in this book:

AND	ELSE	MOD	RECORD*
ARRAY	END	NIL*	REPEAT
BEGIN	FILE*	NOT	SET
CASE	FOR	OF	THEN
CONST	FUNCTION	OR	TO
DIV	GOTO*	PACKED*	TYPE
DO	IF	PROCEDURE	UNTIL
DOWNTO	LABEL*	PROGRAM	USES
			VAR
			WHILE
			WITH*

Need Other Books in the
Sams/Waite Primer Series?

Call 1-800-428-3696 for the name of your nearest Sams retailer or distributor (residents in IN, AK, HI call 317-298-5566).

If your retailer or distributor doesn't stock the Sams publication you need, you can order it through him or directly from us. Orders placed directly with us are subject to a $2.00 additional handling charge per order.

PHONE ORDERS

Depending on where you live, call either number listed above and charge your Sams publication to your VISA or MASTERCARD.

MAIL ORDERS

Use the postpaid order form below, or if it's missing, send your order on a plain piece of paper.

(1) Include your name, street or RD address, city, state, and zip.

(2) Tell us the titles of the books you need, the product numbers (see other side of this card) and the quantity of each one you'd like.

(3) Add up the total cost for the books, add your state's sales tax if applicable, and then add $2.00 for handling.

(4) Include your check or money order for the full amount due, or

(5) Charge it to your VISA or MASTERCARD. To charge it to VISA, list your account number and the card expiration date. For MASTERCARD, list the same information and include the 4-digit interbank number near your first name on the face of the card. Shipping charges will be added to credit card orders.

(6) Mail your order to:
Howard W. Sams & Co., Inc.
Dept. No. X0161
4300 West 62nd St., P.O. Box 7092
Indianapolis, Indiana 46206

Prices subject to change without notice. All books available from Sams distributors, bookstores, and computer stores. Offer good in U.S. only. Note: Distributor, computer store and dealer inquiries are welcome.

SAMS/WAITE PRIMER SERIES ORDER FORM

TITLE	PRODUCT NO.	QTY.	PRICE	TOTAL
CP/M® * PRIMER	21791		14.95	
PASCAL PRIMER	21793		16.95	
COMPUTER GRAPHICS PRIMER	21650		14.95	
BASIC PROGRAMMING PRIMER	21586		11.95	
MICROCOMPUTER PRIMER (Second Edition)	21653		14.50	
YOUR OWN COMPUTER (Second Edition)	21860		7.95	

If you phone your order, be sure to give this code number to the Sams operator when she asks for it.

Please Print

CODE X0161

Name _____

Company _____

Position _____

Address _____

City _____

State _____ Zip _____

Telephone _____

_____ Check   _____ Money Order
_____ MASTERCARD•   _____ VISA•
•Minimum credit card order $15.00.
Minimum cash order $10.00

Sub Total _____
Add Sales Tax Where Applicable _____
Add Handling Charges $2.00
Total Amount Enclosed _____

☐ Please Send Sams Book Catalog

Account No. _____

Exp. Date _____

Interbank No. _____
                    (Mastercard Only)

Signature _____

*CP/M is a registered trademark of Digital Research, Inc.